NEW PROCLAMATION

NEW PROCLAMATION YEAR C, 2009–2010

ADVENT THROUGH HOLY WEEK

TIMOTHY J. MULDER
KIM L. BECKMANN
MARGARET AYMER
CHARLES L. RICE

DAVID B. LOTT, EDITOR

FORTRESS PRESS
MINNEAPOLIS

NEW PROCLAMATION
Year B, 2009–2010
Advent through Holy Week

Library of Congress Cataloging-in-Publication Data
The Library of Congress has catalogued this series as follows.
New Proclamation: Year B, 2009–2010 Advent through Holy Week.
    p. cm.
    Includes bibliographical references.
    ISBN 978-0-8006-2077-6
      1. Church year. I. Moloney, Francis J.
    BV30 .N48 2001
    2511.6dc21 2001023746

13   12   11   10   09   1   2   3   4   5   6   7   8   9   10

Contents

PREFACE
    DAVID B. LOTT

THE SEASON OF ADVENT
TIMOTHY J. MULDER

THE SEASON OF CHRISTMAS
TIMOTHY J. MULDER

The Season of Epiphany
Kim L. Beckmann

The Season of Lent
Margaret Aymer

HOLY WEEK
CHARLES L. RICE

CALENDAR

PREFACE

For over three decades Fortress Press has offered an ecumenical preaching resource built around the three-year lectionary cycle that provides first-rate biblical exegetical insights and sermon helps, a tradition that this new edition of *New Proclamation* continues. Focused on the biblical texts assigned by the three primary lectionary traditions—the Revised Common Lectionary (RCL), the lectionary from the Episcopal Book of Common Prayer (BCP), and the Roman Catholic Lectionary for the Mass (LFM)—*New Proclamation* is grounded in the belief that a deeper understanding of the biblical pericopes in both their historical and liturgical contexts is the best means to inform and inspire preachers to deliver engaging and effective sermons. For this reason, the most capable North American biblical scholars and homileticians are invited to contribute to *New Proclamation*.

New Proclamation has always distinguished itself from most other lectionary resources by offering brand-new editions each year, dated according to the church year in which it will first be used, and featuring a fresh set of authors. Yet each edition is planned as a timeless resource that preachers will want to keep on their bookshelves for future reference for years to come. Both longtime users and those new to the series will also want to visit this volume's new companion Web site, www.NewProclamation.com, which offers access not only to this book's contents, but also commentary from earlier editions, up-to-the-minute thoughts on the connection between texts and current events, user forums, and other resources to help you develop your sermons and enhance your preaching.

This present volume of *New Proclamation* covers the lections for the first half of the church year for cycle B, from Advent through the Great Vigil of Easter. This volume also follows the time-honored series format, including the following elements and features:

- *New Proclamation* is published in two volumes per year, with a large, workbook-style page, a lay-flat binding, and space for making notes.

- Each writer offers an introduction to her or his commentary that provides insights into the background and spiritual significance of that season (or portion thereof), as well as ideas for planning one's preaching during that time.
- The application of biblical texts to contemporary situations is an important concern of each contributor. Exegetical work is concise, and thoughts on how the texts address today's world, congregational issues, and personal situations have a prominent role.
- Although each lectionary tradition assigns a psalm or other biblical text as a response to the first reading, rather than as a preaching text, brief comments on each responsive reading are included to help the preacher incorporate reflections on these in the sermon.
- Boxed quotations in the margins highlight themes from the text to stimulate the preaching imagination.
- A calendar at the end of the book will help preachers plan their worship and preaching schedules through the seasons of Advent, Epiphany, and Lent, plus Holy Week.

As has become the custom of *New Proclamation,* the writers for this latest edition represent both a variety of Christian faith traditions and multiple academic disciplines. Timothy Mulder, an acclaimed homiletician with background in both the Reformed and Episcopal traditions, brings his engaging and lively insights to the seasons of Advent and Christmas. Kim Beckmann, a former parish pastor who is now working on ministry and vocational issues for the Evangelical Lutheran Church in America, draws on both those experiences and more in her congregationally anchored reflections for Epiphany. New Testament professor and biblical preacher Margaret Aymer's deeply considered comments on the Lenten texts announce her as a significant new voice for both biblical studies and preaching. And we are particularly delighted that Charles Rice, one of the leading thinkers of the "New Homiletic," returns to print here after an absence of too many years with his thoughtful take on preaching in Holy Week. We are grateful to each of these contributors for their insights and their commitment to effective Christian preaching, and are confident that you will find in this volume ideas, stimulation, and encouragement for your ministry of proclamation.

David B. Lott

THE SEASON
OF ADVENT

TIMOTHY J. MULDER

The Gospel according to Luke is the anchor for the readings for Advent and Christmas in Year C. Most of us who follow the lectionary gravitate to the Gospel readings, although we need to keep in mind that always preaching on the Gospel will impoverish our preaching. Advent is one of those seasons to remember that one of the primary purposes of any lectionary is to help us hear the dominant stories and themes of Scripture. During the season of Advent, it is usually the Gospel readings that carry the dominant story, with the other readings providing crucial theological foundations or insight. One might contend that during the summer months of, say, Year A the preacher should focus on preaching the Old Testament stories of Genesis and Exodus. But in Advent, to preach from the Gospel with a foundation coming out of the Prophets only makes sense. Especially in Year C, it makes sense to focus on the Gospel because Luke has a very particular perspective on the events we have come to call Advent and Christmas.

In his introduction to Luke's Gospel in his paraphrase titled *The Message*, Eugene H. Peterson talks about the exclusive nature of clubs. Peterson claims that the author of Luke is a "vigorous champion of the outsider."[1] There is special care given by Jesus to women, common laborers, the racially different, and the poor. Peterson claims that it was Jesus' welcome of these outsiders that is the primary theological emphasis of Luke. If that is so, then how we read the story of the one who came in to bring life to those who were out is crucial to us today in terms of our own matters of immigration, racism, globalization, and an increasingly class-segregated society.

As we move into a consideration of the texts for Advent and Christmas we also need to put something on the table right away. The texts for Advent, especially those from the Prophets, point us to the fulfillment of the promises of God and God's reign. We will rightly sing, "Lo, he comes in clouds descending," as we hear the eschatological message of Advent. We have been reminded over and again that Jesus was already born and we don't need to anticipate that anymore. What we anticipate is his coming again. Yes, yes, but the reality is that the preacher is not only a theologian, but also a life and faith partner to one's people. While we have every right and even the obligation to tell people what they ought to consider, we cannot do so at the expense of ignoring where they are. We are doing well in our culture if we can consider expectancy, hope, and longing, and not rush with the post–Labor Day crowds into the gift-giving frenzy. So we deal with both Jesus' birth and the promise that he will come again in glory. Both are fulfillments of God's covenant and promise.

One other tension for the liturgically minded—who often feel as though our endeavors to truly celebrate Advent are like the finger in the dike as the flood of consumerism threatens to flood the souls of all in the naves of our churches—is in the area of hymnody. We have managed to hold off singing carols until Christmas Eve, much to the satisfaction of ourselves and our organists. But a few years ago I found myself out of parish work and in an extremely dark chapter in life. I went to a church with a friend who had all but sworn off God because of all the extreme cruelties experienced at the hands of church folk. It was an Advent Sunday, and to be honest, in the vulnerable and weak state we both were in at that time, I almost dreaded hearing the dire Advent warnings of judgment. And yes, some of that did come through in the sermon because that's what the text said. But the surprise came when a Christmas carol snuck its way through the Advent border security patrol. Those notes of grace and promise fulfilled did not feel like a theological or liturgical capitulation. Instead, they were like Paul who refused to let the cross and the resurrection be separated, two sides of the same coin, never one without the other. On that dark Advent day, a Christmas carol along with a warning to return was honestly the experience of "already but not yet." In fact, I could hear the hard word so much better because it came with the assurance of pardon conveyed in that hymn, which reminded me why Calvin always put the reading of the law after the confession and assurance of pardon. We confess, already knowing the answer to our confessions. So we enter Advent already knowing. A realized eschatology is not a bad way for people of faith to deal with the evils, principalities, and powers of our day. As Desmond Tutu so often said during the darkest days of apartheid, "The devil is already defeated. He just doesn't know it yet, but we do!"

Note

1. Eugene H. Peterson, *The Message: The Bible in Contemporary Language* (Colorado Springs: NavPress, 2002).

FIRST SUNDAY OF ADVENT

November 29, 2009

Revised Common (RCL)	Episcopal (BCP)	Roman Catholic (LFM)
Jer. 33:14-16	Zech. 14:4-9	Jer. 33:14-16
Ps. 25:1-10	Psalm 50 or 5:1-6	Ps. 25:4-5, 8-9, 10, 14
1 Thess. 3:9-13	1 Thess. 3:9-13	1 Thess. 3:12—4:2
Luke 21:25-36	Luke 21:25-31	Luke 21:25-28, 34-36

FIRST READING

JEREMIAH 33:14-16 (RCL, LFM)

"The days are surely coming . . . when I will fulfill the promise" (Jer. 33:14). According to Old Testament scholar Walter Brueggemann, the big surprise is that Jeremiah is so convinced of God's faithfulness to the covenant that he announces that even the Davidic dynasty will be a vehicle for bringing justice and righteousness.[1] Why is this a surprise? No sane person would think there was any reason for hope. The nation was already past the point of survival. Things had gone far too far. Nothing good could possibly happen. And yet, this prophet speaks. The city and the land will be saved and new life made possible when obedience leads to blessing. Then kings and rulers will do what they are supposed to do and corruption will turn to righteousness for the population. Might it be?

ZECHARIAH 14:4-9 (BCP)

Elizabeth Achtemeier, the late biblical scholar, puts it this way: "In the act that forms the goal of all human history God will take his throne as king over all the earth . . ."[2] But this takes place only after a battle between God and all the nations of the world that have allied themselves against Jerusalem. In that battle, the earth literally shifts, as if to make a path for God to enter the city in grand procession. The result is a new creation and the fulfillment of the covenant. The hard part for us to accept is the necessity of defeat before victory, and it is our defeat, our purging, and not our fighting back and winning the victory, that shows us that it is God who comes to our aid and is indisputably the only sovereign and our only hope.

RESPONSIVE READING

PSALM 25:1-10 (RCL)
PSALM 25:4-5, 8-9, 10, 14 (LFM)

The Tanakh translates verse 7 as, "Be not mindful of my youthful sins and transgressions; in keeping with Your faithfulness consider what is in my favor, as befits Your goodness, O Lord."[3] There is a difference between remembering (as the NRSV puts it) and being mindful. The petitioner comes to the Lord in hope of not being disappointed. It may be too much to ask for sins to be forgotten, but they certainly don't need to be the focus of attention. And why does the petitioner dare to ask God to do this for him or her but not for one's enemies? Why should they be disappointed, empty-handed? Because of the special relationship that exists between the petitioner and the Lord. God is the deliverer. But let's be clear that the key verse here is the conclusion of verse 7. God is asked to do all this as befits God's goodness. It is the same theme as in Jesus' parable of the laborers who are called to work at various times of day in the vineyard, yet at the end all receive the same pay. We so often make the point of the parable to be about the laborers, when it is in fact about the goodness of the vineyard owner. Our hope is in God because God is good, not because we have deserved a good response. Let that be repeated: our hope is in God because God is good. It is in God's goodness that we find our own. Here is the great surprise. The petitioner is fully aware that God will have to turn God's head in order to look away from what otherwise would demand justice. As theologian/activist William Sloane Coffin always said, "Somehow God's mercy always seems to outrun God's justice." There is our deliverance, our salvation, our only hope—it befits God's goodness.

> Our hope is in God because God is good, not because we have deserved a good response.

PSALM 50 OR 50:1-6 (BCP)

Here is the cosmic God sitting in judgment over a people who have broken the covenant God had with them. They can make all the excuses in the world and it won't change a thing. The people are guilty and the only thing that will help them is to offer their honest thanks and improve their ways. So this is not a matter of grace no matter what. This is grace in response to a truly thankful heart and repentant behavior. Don't dare to argue otherwise!

SECOND READING

1 THESSALONIANS 3:9-13 (RCL, BCP)
1 THESSALONIANS 3:12—4:2 (LFM)

Paul has heard a good report from Timothy about the Thessalonians (see 3:6) and now gives thanks for them: "For what thanksgiving can we render to God for you?" (American Standard Version). They have brought Paul joy because of their participation in—indeed, their exemplification of—the gospel. The "coming day" mentioned in Jeremiah will be a day of joy for Paul and the Thessalonians. Paul's thanksgiving for the Thessalonians spills over into and shapes his exhortation to them, for he can affirm that they are living lives pleasing to God: "just as you are doing, you do so more and more." Exhortation flows out of thanksgiving for those who are being exhorted, out of a confidence that the hearers of the message are, in fact, eager to "do so more and more." Knowing and believing the "good news" of the coming kingdom finds evidence in how we see that kingdom in the world around us—in others. Our own belief in the kingdom finds expression when we see it in others, when we name it in their lives and rejoice, giving thanks for the sometimes surprising ways that the people around us and in front of us reveal the coming kingdom in our midst.

THE GOSPEL

LUKE 21:25-36 (RCL)
LUKE 21:25-31 (BCP)
LUKE 21:25-28, 34-36 (LFM)

The account of "Vengeance Day" is a good news/bad news story with a warning thrown in. It will be a terrible time for some. But we also read that the Son of Man will be welcomed in grand and glorious style. Why doesn't the author elaborate on that? Why do we have such a vivid description of the terror and almost a passing mention of the point of all this? Is it because the author is a high school or college teacher who knows students don't prepare their assignments until the night before they are due? Eugene Peterson writes, "Don't let the sharp edge of your expectation get dulled by parties and drinking and shopping."[4] Does the author realize that few of us have a "sharp edge of expectation?"

While most will probably not agree, although the author paints a cosmic picture of Vengeance Day, I believe that apocalyptic moment is every moment of every day of each of our lives. I don't need to be warned to get my act together for some day when Jesus will return as my judge. Faith in God's gift coming into our lives is not something a few weeks off when the project comes due. It is about when I wake up in the morning and suck air into my lungs and put my feet on the floor and head out to meet people. There will be some terrible things out there, things in which I am horribly complicit. But I also want to be part of that welcoming party. Yes, I party too much, drink too much, shop too much. All of me gets dull, not just my expectation. But perhaps the worst of it is that the *expectation* is dull. How many of us go into the day and don't expect to see the kingdom in full sway before us or don't expect to greet Christ when we walk into the office each morning? Most of the world missed Jesus in the manger even with shepherds shouting and angels singing! If I resent anything these days, it is not those who point out the problems in our world, but it is the religious folk who act as though these are signs of things to come down the road. The coming of Christ is promised by God; it is not a procrastinated future. If we don't see Christ and welcome him and his kingdom today, then surely we will miss more than one more party, one more drink, or one more shopping day.

> The coming of Christ is promised by God; it is not a procrastinated future.

Notes

1. Walter Brueggemann, *To Build, to Plant; A Commentary on Jeremiah 26–52,* International Theological Commentary (Grand Rapids: Eerdmans, 1991), 98–99.

2. Elizabeth Achtemeier, *Nahum-Malachi,* Interpretation: A Bible Commentary for Teaching and Preaching (Atlanta: John Knox, 1986), 166.

3. *Tanakh* (Philadelphia: The Jewish Publication Society, 1985).

4. Eugene Peterson, *The Message: The Bible in Contemporary Language* (Colorado Springs: NavPress, 2002), 1904.

SECOND SUNDAY OF ADVENT

DECEMBER 6, 2009

Revised Common (RCL)	Episcopal (BCP)	Roman Catholic (LFM)
Mal. 3:1-4 or Bar. 5:1-9	Bar. 5:1-9	Bar. 5:1-9
Luke 1:68-79	Psalm 126	Ps. 126:1-2a, 2b-3, 4-5, 6
Phil. 1:3-11	Phil. 1:1-11	Phil. 1:4-6, 8-11
Luke 3:1-6	Luke 3:1-6	Luke 3:1-6

FIRST READING

MALACHI 3:1-4 (RCL)

Handel's *Messiah* rings in our ears with this passage of purifying the sons of Levi, but this is one of those times the lectionary has not done us any favors when it stops short of verse 5, which describes the vigorous nature of God's refining justice. God demands our all, our very best, but pastor and author James Harnish says that far too often our tendency is to get by with giving as little as we possibly can. Harnish's diagnosis is that the people back from exile have slipped from enthusiasm about their faith into spiritual depression. They are "burned-out skeptics"[1] who want to know from God what God has done for them lately. The only way to get out of this spiritually terminal disease is to respond to God with offerings of the totality of one's being, to offer one's best. Nothing short of that will be pleasing to God.

While that may be so, is it possible that our best may actually be what we think is our worst? When we are at our lowest point, when we think that everything has gone wrong or been taken from us, or that we've messed everything up, it is precisely then that we perceive the world around us more clearly and are capable of giving what is true. The season of Advent is full of reversals: lowly things and people are exalted, while the mighty are brought low. God continues to surprise by using or doing the unexpected. Sometimes this notion of purifying and refining means that we should be especially aware of looking for God in the midst of our very worst of times. For out of them may come the very best.

> The season of Advent is full of reversals: lowly things and people are exalted, while the mighty are brought low.

BARUCH 5:1-9 (RCL ALT., BCP, LFM)

This is an incredible hymn. The time to be sullen is over. The time is past when one takes hat in hand and pleads mercy before the judge. This is the time for celebration! Take off those old stinky rags and get decked out in the robes of righteousness: "Righteous Peace, Godly Glory," pop the champagne. Call to memory Judy Garland in *Annie Get Your Gun* when she sings, "Forget your troubles, come on, get happy!"

Several years ago a sociologist did a survey for a particular denomination. He discovered that it was the ethnic/religious norm among that group not to be too joyous in public. When something really succeeded, the leader or parent might offer one's congratulations by saying, "That wasn't too bad." Almost never would one hear, "That was really great!" There are times to be truthfully critical, when "not bad" may be all that can be said. But there are other times when it would quite literally be a sin not to affirm and celebrate. God has remembered God's children and brought them safely home. How great it is!

RESPONSIVE READING
LUKE 1:68-79 (RCL)

The magnificent *Benedictus* (because of the opening phrase, "Blessed be the Lord God of Israel") is divided in two parts. The first, verses 68-75, are Zechariah's prophecy interpreted here as Jesus being the one who will come to fulfill the promises of the covenant and the hope of the people. This is the one who is raised up and speaks the words of the ancient prophets in the modern context. This is the one who is full of mercy and who delivers God's servants from their enemies.

Then the second part, verses 76-79, are about John, and in response to the question on the minds of the neighbors in verse 66, "What then will this child become?" we are told he will be the one who prepares the way. In his time, it will be as though the dawn were breaking through the darkness and the pathway of peace is open ahead of them. Ask the choir to sing Randall Thompson's "Last Words of David," taken from 2 Samuel 23:4, as a beautiful echo of this thought.

PSALM 126 (BCP)
PSALM 126:1-2A, 2B-3, 4-5, 6 (LFM)

Long ago Leslie Brandt wrote a psalm paraphrase, *Psalms/Now*, in which this psalm began, "Let us begin this day with rejoicing. Let us acknowledge our

Lord's love and concern and allow our bodies to break forth into happy hilarity! Let us give our nerves and muscles the healthy exercise of Laughter! The Lord has done such wonderful things for us; let us be glad!"[2] Like the fairy tales that are too good to be true, God surpasses our best dreams to the point that we can only laugh in overwhelmed joy. But it is important to remember that the real fairy tales are often tales of horror, fear, danger, loss, and darkness. There are often tears before a happy ending. That was the major point of Frederick Buechner's book *Telling the Truth: The Gospel as Tragedy, Comedy, and Fairy Tale*.[3] Sin comes before salvation; Good Friday comes before Easter. Even Brahms was caught up in it. In his German *Requiem*, the music for "those who sow in tears reap with shouts of joy" is perhaps one of the most beautiful expressions of art ever composed. Only those who have hurt so badly can laugh or sing so fully, and know that anything this good can only come from the Lord.

Second Reading
PHILIPPIANS 1:3-11 (RCL)
PHILIPPIANS 1:1-11 (BCP)
PHILIPPIANS 1:4-6, 8-11 (LFM)

As in last week's epistle reading, the text this week is a thanksgiving. Indeed, Paul's thanksgiving here in Philippians is probably his most tender, if not even his most passionate. He says that he *yearns* for the Philippians with the *affection* of Christ Jesus, that he *holds them in his heart*. He expresses his absolute confidence that the one "who began a good work" in them will bring it to fruition. In short, this thanksgiving is something of a love letter between Paul and the Philippians. That affectionate tone is not something we perhaps expect from Paul—certainly it sounds like a different Paul than the one who wrote Galatians (where Paul gives *no* thanks for the recipients of the letter)! The other notable difference between this Pauline thanksgiving and what we find in other letters is the degree to which Paul here emphasizes that he is thankful for *all* the Philippians. Not just for the good guys. Not just for the leadership (the bishops and deacons; see 1:1). Not just for those who agree with Paul (see 1:15-18). He is thankful for each and every one of them. Here, at least, Paul got the message of the gospel clearly—Luke's message that God's glory is for *all* people.

> Here, Paul got the message of the gospel clearly—Luke's message that God's glory is for *all* people.

The Gospel
LUKE 3:1-6 (RCL, BCP, LFM)

Raymond Brown, in *The Birth of the Messiah*, says that this could easily have served as the original opening of the Lukan Gospel.[4] He goes on to say that if the Gospel had started here without ever having had the infancy narratives, we might never have suspected their existence. But Fred Craddock, in his commentary on Luke for the Interpretation series, points out that there is no known manuscript of Luke without its first two chapters.[5] Still, for our purposes, it is good to begin here and work our way toward the birth of Jesus.

John's call takes place in the wilderness. So much happens there. It was in the wilderness that God formed Israel as the covenant people. It was in the wilderness that the people experienced not only idols of their own making but also the manna of God's providence. It was in the wilderness that Hosea found a place of early romance between God and Israel.

John's call to prophesy in the wilderness results in his call to the people to return to God: repentance for the forgiveness of sins. In echoes of Isaiah 40:3-5, the prophet comes with a word of strength and of comfort. God remembers God's people. God loves God's people. And God's glory will be made clear and full by the reconciliation of the people with their god.

This new prophet foreshadows a new covenant. Here is a glimpse of what is yet to come: God's glory will be revealed not just to the house of Israel, but to all people. Luke's story extends God's favor beyond the covenant people. There is foreshadowing of a new covenant coming with this new prophet. This is more than a mere echo of Isaiah. John has gone beyond Isaiah with this vision.

> Here is a glimpse of what is yet to come: God's glory will be revealed not just to the house of Israel, but to all people.

But before there is the gift of *hope for all* comes the *hard word for all*. No one is excluded, not even those who have always assumed it or insisted on it.

Notes

1. James A. Harnish, *God Isn't Finished with Us Yet* (Nashville: Upper Room, 1991), 108–11.

2. Leslie F. Brandt, *Psalms/Now* (St. Louis: Concordia, 1973), 196.

3. Frederick Buechner, *Telling the Truth: The Gospel as Tragedy, Comedy, and Fairy Tale* (New York: Harper & Row, 1977).

4. Raymond E. Brown, *The Birth of the Messiah: A Commentary on the Infancy Narratives in the Gospels of Matthew and Luke* (New York: Doubleday, 1977), 240.

5. Fred B. Craddock, *Luke*, Interpretation: A Bible Commentary for Teaching and Preaching (Louisville: John Knox, 1990).

THIRD SUNDAY OF ADVENT

DECEMBER 13, 2009

Revised Common (RCL)	Episcopal (BCP)	Roman Catholic (LFM)
Zeph. 3:14-20	Zeph. 3:14-20	Zeph. 3:14-18a
Isa. 12:2-6	Psalm 85 or 85:3-13 or	Isa. 12:2-3, 4, 5-6
	Canticle 9	
Phil. 4:4-7	Phil. 4:4-7 (8-9)	Phil. 4:4-7
Luke 3:7-18	Luke 3:7-18	Luke 3:10-18

FIRST READING

ZEPHANIAH 3:14-20 (RCL, BCP)
ZEPHANIAH 3:14-18A (LFM)

Zephaniah was a prophet during the reign of Josiah (640–609 B.C.E.). The story of Josiah (2 Kings 22ff.) is of a reformer. Josiah outlawed pagan religions, had pagan artifacts destroyed, and had pagan priests killed. He destroyed pagan altars and images. After the rediscovery of the Law (Torah), he had it read in the square for all the people to hear and then commanded that the people get back on track. It was the most major "housecleaning" in the history of Israel. And this becomes a metaphor of what God will do for all creation. At the outset, the prophet Zephaniah foretells a housecleaning of the whole creation. It sounds like a variation on the flood. It is not only Judah that is in for destruction on account of its unfaithfulness, but all the nations. But after condemnation comes comfort in chapter 3. God forgives and is enthroned in the midst of the people. Shame is turned to praise and celebration is the order of the day. It would be interesting at this point in Advent to offer a sermon on shame. How can shame be transformed? Do we just hide our shame, repress it, ignore it, or become despondent or angry or bitter? The Gospel

> God forgives and is enthroned in the midst of the people. Shame is turned to praise and celebration is the order of the day.

reading for today encourages everyone to get in touch with their shame, not for the purpose of putting people down, but in order to breathe new life into them as Josiah did. Restoration results in rejoicing.

RESPONSIVE READING

ISAIAH 12:2-6 (RCL)
CANTICLE 9 (BCP)
ISAIAH 12:2-3, 4, 5-6 (LFM)

This canticle of praise proclaims that "surely it is God who saves us; we will trust and not be afraid." No doubt this poetry of Isaiah inspired the gospel hymn "Trust and Obey," which advises that to be happy in Jesus, we must trust and obey. We sing both the canticle and the hymn with uplifted hearts, but in the twenty-first century, as in the situation for First Isaiah, that is a lot easier to say than to do. Fear, not trust, propels nations to war and to financial absurdities in attempts to make ourselves safe. "Surely God is my salvation" needs to be more than a nice ditty we sing in church. This goes to the core of the covenant, and because of that, to the core of what faith is all about. Nor can we permit the admonition in verse 5b to be a mere nicety: "let this be known in all the earth." In an age of growing awareness of the power of religion around the globe and our interconnectedness with the entire planet, Christians need to struggle with the manner and character of just how it is that we will proclaim God as "salvation in all the earth." This is the truth we wrestle with every day. I'm not just singing this; I'm having to learn it every day. It becomes descriptive of who we are and our proclamation arises out of that.

> Christians need to struggle with the manner and character of just how it is that we will proclaim God as "salvation in all the earth."

PSALM 85 OR 85:7-13 (BCP)

Although things are not going well in verses 1-6, the promise of peace and salvation is near for the faithful. Once God was good to the land and people, and that day will come again. This is the psalm with that wonderful line, "righteousness and peace will kiss each other" (v. 10). This psalm, as Old Testament scholar James Limburg points out, reminds us that "when the Old Testament speaks of salvation, it is not ordinarily referring to life beyond death, but to a life in this world, lived in freedom and shalom . . . ,"[1] or as the modern bumper sticker puts it, "No peace without justice." This is about the here and now of this life's pain and joy.

SECOND READING

PHILIPPIANS 4:4-7 (RCL, LFM)
PHILIPPIANS 4:4-7 (8-9) (BCP)

Paul writes the letter (or letters) to the Philippians from prison. And it is in this short "prison epistle" that Paul repeatedly uses the word *rejoice*. He uses

it more times in these four chapters than he does in any other letter. Prison—
rejoice! Somehow, in Paul's mind, those two things connect. As he says in chapter
1, "For it has been granted to you that for the sake of Christ you should not
only believe in him but also suffer for his sake" (1:29 RSV). Or, to put it more
directly, "You not only get to *believe* in Christ, you get to *suffer* for him! Hooray!"
Thus, when Paul writes, as he does here in chapter 4, "Rejoice!" he means it. In
any and all circumstances, "Rejoice!" We might even try using the antonyms of
the words found in 4:8-9 and asking if even *then* we can rejoice: When others
are false? Rejoice! When others are dishonorable? Rejoice! When we are faced
with impurity? Rejoice! When ugliness appears? Rejoice! Someone lacks grace
or excellence or anything worthy of praise? Rejoice! We rejoice not, of course, in
the false, the dishonorable, the impurity, the ugliness, and the like. But our joy is
not found in "perfect circumstances." Our joy is not
dependent upon others being what we want them to
be. Our joy, and our lack of anxiety, comes from our
confidence in Christ's power to transform us—both
others and ourselves—into true, honorable, excellent,
beautiful human beings. We rejoice because we see this happening, even in the
midst of this world. We are patient, and not anxious, when we trust that Christ's
work in and around us will not fail to produce the fruits of righteousness. We give
thanks because we can't help but see the good work that God is doing around us
in the lives of others.

> We are patient, and not anxious, when we trust that Christ's work in and around us will not fail to produce the fruits of righteousness.

The Gospel
LUKE 3:7-18 (RCL, BCP)
LUKE 3:10-18 (LFM)

Everyone is a viper. In the documentary produced by Kristina Browne,
Traces of the Trade, she tells the story of learning that her ancestors, the deWolfes
of Bristol, Rhode Island, instituted the idea and practice of the Golden Triangle
between the shores of New England, the western coast of Africa, and the slave
markets of Savannah and Charleston. Human flesh was sold for rum and linens.
The descendants protested that they didn't sell any slaves, but the movie points
out how they are still benefiting all this time later from the ripple economy that
business started. So, just because one's family tree is connected to power—even
the power of God, in the case of Israel—doesn't absolve one from complicity in
sin and the need to repent in our own day. It's not just one's ancestors who need
to repent. The ax is laid to the root of any tree that doesn't bear fruit. So while
Luke's Gospel expands the notion of salvation beyond the old ideas, it also assigns
blame and the need for repentance to all.

TIMOTHY J.
MULDER

The crowds then wondered what they should do, the Gospel reads. What would repentance look like in their lives, or, we might ask, what would it look like in ours? The reply that John gave the crowds that day—that they share their material goods with those in need, be fair to those with whom they conduct business, and not misuse the power of their office—may be a bit unsettling to some Protestants. If repentance is required for righteousness, being right with God, then John's response clearly links right works with a righteous relationship with both God and neighbor. This is so very different from the way our culture deals with things and people who have gone badly off course.

Late in 2008, it was discovered that one of the giants of Wall Street, a man named Bernard Madoff, had deceived scores of people out of billions of dollars they had thought he was investing on their behalf. Many charitable foundations went out of business as a result. Lives were ruined as savings were depleted. One lawyer, who was asked if it would be possible for a judge to sentence Madoff to work the rest of his life to repay those he had wronged, replied that justice is more concerned with retribution than repentance. It seems this takes us back to the old "eye for an eye" system that rarely satisfies or builds anything up. But even as Paul writes to the Corinthians (1 Cor. 12:31), "I will show you a more excellent way," so in this passage John shows a more excellent way. Right deeds take us down the path of righteousness. No wonder people wondered if John were the Messiah. Of course not, John demurred, pointing instead to one who would follow. And that one would show us that in addition to right deeds would be grace rooted in love. But in this passage John gives an image that even the one who will judge with grace still takes our works seriously. He tells of one who will separate wheat from chaff, and to those who ask him what to do not to be cut off from God, he challenges them to live lives at a very high standard of conduct. If Jesus himself would eventually say that he came to fulfill rather than abolish the law and the prophets, might we also infer that he had no intention of abolishing righteous works as a requisite for salvation? Grace alone? Perhaps only in the context of John's description of how repentance gets played out in the lives of the faithful.

> If repentance is required for righteousness, being right with God, then John's response clearly links right works with a righteous relationship with both God and neighbor.

Note

1. James Limburg, *Psalms*, Westminster Bible Companion (Louisville: Westminster John Knox, 2000), 290.

FOURTH SUNDAY OF ADVENT

DECEMBER 20, 2009

Revised Common (RCL)	Episcopal (BCP)	Roman Catholic (LFM)
Micah 5:2-5a	Micah 5:2-4	Micah 5:1-4a
Luke 1:47-55 or	Psalm 80 or 80:1-7	Ps. 80:2-3, 15-16, 18-19
Ps. 80:1-7		
Heb. 10:5-10	Heb. 10:5-10	Heb. 10:5-10
Luke 1:39-45 (46-55)	Luke 1:39-49 (50-56)	Luke 1:39-45

FIRST READING

MICAH 5:2-5A (RCL)
MICAH 5:2-4 (BCP)
MICAH 5:1-4A (LFM)

Deep into Advent we come to a passage that makes us wish that sometimes the lectionary would have only one passage rather than four. This section of Micah assumes some knowledge of the story line of Ruth, which actually didn't come into its final form until Israel's return from exile. But the point is that Ruth's story is a subversion of Ezra/Nehemiah's command to put your foreign wives away from you. Without Ruth, we wouldn't have David . . . or Jesus. The story of Ruth is ultimately about the birth of a baby, but that birth does not come through expected or established ways. Once again, God subverts.

This pericope needs to begin with verse 1. The reality of life is harsh and seemingly hopeless. But, as James Limburg points out, God has done a reversal, a surprise. The Messiah does not come from the throne room of the big city, Jerusalem, but from little Bethlehem Ephrathah. "Ephrathah is the name of the clan of people who lived in the area of Bethlehem; the family of Elimelech and Naomi."[1] The reversal of greatness for smallness matters, as the story of Naomi

> God has done a reversal, a surprise: the Messiah does not come from the throne room of the big city, Jerusalem, but from little Bethlehem Ephrathah.

finds a stronger place in our infancy narratives. It was in pain and desperation that Naomi and her husband, Elimelech, left their home in Bethlehem and went to Moab, where their two sons married women from that foreign place. The final verse of the book of Ruth tells us that from her came the family line of Jesse, and from Jesse, David, and from David, of course—the shepherd from the town of Bethlehem—eventually Jesus. It is not only God's choice of the least likely and the small rather than the grand that should strike us this day, but how out of pain God brings goodness, especially when we are open to going beyond the borders of our previously held convictions of the way life must be. The family line of Ruth and Boaz is as unlikely as any story in history for its leading to the birth of a Jewish Messiah who would recast the image and work of a shepherd. It was in crossing these ethnic and religious lines that the universality of Jesus was prefigured and should move us today to do no less.

RESPONSIVE READING
LUKE 1:47–55 (RCL)

If, in his resurrection, Jesus is the firstfruits of those who will be raised from the dead (1 Cor. 15:20), then Mary, in her own way, is the first fruits of what God will do, because of Jesus, for the whole world. The poor, the powerless, and the oppressed will triumph. Of course, this song is patterned after Hannah's song in 1 Samuel 2:1-10, but it soars beyond that. Considering the mighty acts of God in the past gives Mary such reason for confidence in the future that she can already sing as though the future were an accomplished fact. This, then, is the model for prayer and praise, as we pray in the certain hope that our prayers are heard and answered before we even offer them.

PSALM 80:1–7 (RCL; BCP ALT.)
PSALM 80 (BCP)
PSALM 80:2–3, 15–16, 18–19 (LFM)

This lament of the community calls out over and again for God to come and save the people. "Let your face shine," means *be with us* and *let things turn out well*. "Give ear," means *we need God's attention*. The people are like the kids in the back of the car with their incessant chorus of "How long until we get there?" Even though God is acknowledged as the good, and therefore caring, shepherd, the people never get the answer they're looking for. They never find out how much longer the trip will be. The kids promise to be good, but that doesn't seem to hasten either an answer or the conclusion of the trip. They are left still wondering.

HEBREWS 10:5-10 (RCL, BCP, LFM)

We all make excuses for our errors and ways. We stack up all the wonderful things we've ever done on behalf of the kingdom and bring them to God like a child with a homemade work of art. God may smile at our good intentions, but must weep that we just don't get it. At the end of the day our offerings and our lives do not balance out the brokenness of our lives or the brokenness of the world. Verse 10 says, "we have been sanctified through the offering of the body of Jesus Christ once for all." But it needs to be repeated over and again, because no sooner has the author said

At the end of the day our offerings and our lives do not balance out the brokenness of our lives or the brokenness of the world.

it than the priests go back to making the same old offerings for sin. So the author comes right back and almost shouts this time, as if to say, "No! No! No! Aren't you listening? Christ's ONE sacrifice, Christ's ONE offering is it. Nothing else will do, nothing; don't you believe it?" The author repeats it over and again. We are pardoned, we are forgiven, through Christ's life and death and that alone. If one were to read on through verse 13, it becomes clear that Christ waits patiently or impatiently (we don't know which) in heaven until it sinks in to our belief system. Our forgiveness is assured. All that needs to happen is for us to acknowledge that message and for Christ's enemies to become his footstool. All the intervening good intentions and struggles (in other words, whatever we do) are pointless. One might wonder, What does Christ think? The cosmos could be having an agape feast every moment if it were ever to claim this text. Instead we keep striving and struggling. Even the cross wasn't enough to convince. Or was it?

THE GOSPEL

LUKE 1:39-45 (46-55) (RCL)
LUKE 1:39-49 (50-56) (BCP)
LUKE 1:39-45 (LFM)

All three lectionaries permit us to deal with Mary's encounter with Elizabeth without dealing with Mary's *Magnificat*. The BCP teases us with the first few verses. I think we should leave it at that. There are other times we can focus on that prayer/song. For now, let's be content to restrain ourselves, for there is more than enough here.

Whether it was fear and anxiety or excitement that propelled Mary to Elizabeth, we'll never know. Why she went to a relative rather than to her own mother, we'll never know. Perhaps it was for some of the same reasons that unwed pregnant teens today sometimes hesitate about going to their parents when learning of their condition. We also don't know whether Elizabeth was a first, second, or far-removed cousin. Perhaps the more distant the connection, the more at ease Mary might have felt to confide in her. It really doesn't matter. The stage has already been set. If young Mary's being with child is amazing, how much more amazing is old Elizabeth's? There are clear echoes of a woman laughing in a tent, "How can this be?"—and then Sarah names her child "laughter." For Elizabeth in Luke 1:25, we realize that pregnancy, while a surprise, was a blessing, because it took her shame away. Having not had a child up to that age had been a cultural disgrace. For young Mary, the disgrace is for the opposite reason; to be pregnant already would be harshly judged by her family and neighbors. Even though the angel Gabriel had told her she was favored to have all this happening, we don't hear that out of her lips just yet. We know she realized that this was of God and that she would be a participant in it all, but it's not until Elizabeth's encouragement and expression of joy in 1:42 that we hear Mary wondering aloud what all this is about. Is it a blessing? Why has this happened to me?

> If young Mary's being with child is amazing, how much more amazing is old Elizabeth's?

We can experience the wonder and tenderness of this scene when these two women were together. If Luke were writing a novel rather than a brief account, the time that elapses in this paragraph might have taken quite a while. As readers, we long for the author of Luke to fill in the story a bit more before Mary's words evolve into her song of praise and glory.

How similar to our lives throughout our days. It is rarely while things are going on that we can understand precisely what is happening with, to, because, for, or through us. In retrospect, we see the maestro God conducting the symphony of history, but in the moment, that is too hard to see. Yes, Mary was open to God, and we love her for it. But let's not diminish how hard that must have been, how frightening and how it probably didn't dawn on her at all as she sat listening to an angel. After all, how clearheaded would *you* be listening to an angel?

I don't think we need to put much stock in the speculation that Mary ran with such haste to Zechariah and Elizabeth's in order to live her pregnancy in secret from her home folk. I prefer to imagine that Mary is doing the healthiest thing any of us could do when life gets confusing, be it for wonderful or terrible reasons. She decided not to go it alone. She went to be with a person she knew loved her. In a way here is a preface for Emmanuel. We humans are not meant to go through the tough or the wonderful alone. Both need to be shared. Blaise Pascal, the French philosopher, once said, "One Christian is no Christian." That is true on so many levels and

> We humans are not meant to go through the tough or the wonderful alone. Both need to be shared.

for so many reasons. The same people who weep together celebrate together. In fact, the only justification I can find for so many church suppers is that the bonding that takes place there is what makes it possible for us to go to one another in times of grief or severe pain or turmoil.

Note

1. James Limburg, *Hosea-Micah*, Interpretation: A Bible Commentary for Teaching and Preaching (Atlanta: John Knox, 1988), 185–88.

THE SEASON
OF CHRISTMAS

TIMOTHY J. MULDER

The setting was the chapel at the convent of the Community of St. John Baptist. Barbara Crafton was the preacher for the day. She was preaching on the text from Luke 1 about the birth of John the Baptist. Most of us know the first few chapters of Luke so well that it is hard for us to listen. We hear the words, but they are just that: words, more words, familiar words. Once upon a time, I can't remember where or when, Fred Craddock suggested that we could learn as much from Scripture by listening to the spaces in between the words and paragraphs as we could by listening to the words themselves. That's great advice. But it is also true that we often move deeply into the story by paying attention to the little things that seem to be throwaway lines, unimportant phrases, offhand remarks. So in Luke 1:60-61, when Elizabeth tells her relatives that her child is going to be called John, they respond by saying, "Why, none of your relatives has that name." It takes the ears of a Barbara Crafton to hear in that simple line both the humor and the glory of what God is doing. This isn't the norm. This is counter to how our automatic pilots for life and faith function. It's more like the seven last words of the church: "We've never done it that way before." This one who has come into the world is not as things usually are. This one jogs us and we ask, What is happening here? John, who prepares the way for Jesus, is the preface to a new book, a new covenant. We have never read this one before. We don't know how it begins or the story it will weave or how it will end. John comes on the scene as if to say, "Never before . . . but now!" So pay attention.

21

With that as an introduction—really, his whole life is an introduction—John passes the baton of God on to Jesus. And if we thought things were different with John, we quickly realize that was only the beginning. God is doing what God has never done before. None of our relatives have ever seen the likes of this.

As the story unfolds in Luke 2, the author turns everything into a way humanity has never experienced life before. Shepherds, the ancient corollary of thugs, get the news and the point first. Angels don't try to trick humans, but to reassure them. Followers of the law and the authorities find themselves having to trust instinct, faith, and each other. Laughter abounds in the joy of old people on the edge of death. This wasn't how the Messiah was imagined, but this is so new, so new, so amazing.

It is not the preacher's task at Christmas to help one's people become more archeologically or historically educated. It is our task to share the awe. That in no way asks us to dumb things down; rather, it encourages us to tell the story of a child in such a way that helps us all realize that the one who came in Jesus, in a way that was so unlike our other experiences, still does. It is as "light to those who sit in darkness and in the shadow of death, to guide our feet into the way of peace."

NATIVITY OF THE LORD 1 / CHRISTMAS EVE

Revised Common (RCL)	Episcopal (BCP)	Roman Catholic (LFM)
		At the Vigil Mass
Isa. 9:2-7	Isa. 9:2-4, 6-7	Isa. 62:1-5
Psalm 96	Psalm 96 or 96:1-4, 11-12	Ps. 89:4-5, 16-17, 27, 29
Titus 2:11-14	Titus 2:11-14	Acts 13:16-17, 22-25
Luke 2:1-14 (15-20)	Luke 2:1-14 (15-20)	Matt. 1:1-25 or 1:18-25

Mass at Midnight
Isa. 9:1-6
Ps. 96:1-2a, 2b-3, 11-12, 13
Titus 2:11-14
Luke 2:1-14

A liturgical note: In recent years the church has rediscovered the power and joy of the Easter Vigil. It traces the story of humanity from bondage to freedom, from death to life, from damnation to salvation. Here, the Roman Catholic Church shows the power and joy of the vigil yet again as it waits in expectation for the dawn. The major celebration will come tomorrow. Protestants have made Christmas Eve to be the primary observation of Christ's birth.

TEXTS FOR THE VIGIL MASS (LFM)

Isaiah 62:1-5. It is not over until it is over. It does not happen until it happens. Dare we say it's not over until the pregnant lady sings?! The people have held on to hope for so long, but will that for which they hope ever happen? Some have already given up. Others barely cling on. For this reason the prophet says, "I won't keep silent. I won't rest . . . until everyone can see and know that the victory belongs to God and God's people have been honored the way spouses honor each other in marriage." There is an urgency here that lets all who hear it know that the ultimate is now at stake. Don't give up now!

Psalm 89:4-5, 16-17, 27, 29. This is a royal psalm about the king, and even though there are portions of lament here, the verses selected for this vigil are all refrains of praise. These are perfect refrains to be sung as we approach Christmas: "I will make him the firstborn, the highest of the kings of heaven." Although our reading for the night excludes verse 20, it is striking in this context that the king is anointed with holy oil, for the king is the Messiah. The king is a shepherd and God has turned the tables yet again.

Acts 13:16-17, 22-25. Paul is in Antioch of Pisidia, where he is preaching in the synagogue. In this passage of Scripture, then, Paul is proclaiming the "story of salvation" from the time of the exodus to the coming of Christ. The Law and the Prophets have been read to the congregation (see 13:15), and now Paul references the event of Christ to those same "Law and Prophets" (which is to say, the Old Testament). He tells of the story of the exodus, the wilderness wanderings, the "conquest" of the land and the judges, and the anointing of David as king over Israel. (He skips over the split of the kingdoms of Judah and Israel, as well as the exile.) And all of this long tale is simply preparatory to the coming of Jesus, announced by John the Baptist. This *is* the vigil: we await *one who is coming* . . . just like John the Baptist did.

Matthew 1:1-25 or 1:18-25. It is an easy verse to overlook. But it is perfect for Christmas Eve. Who thinks of verse 17 as part of the Christmas story? Instead, we are like children who can't wait to unwrap the Christmas presents under our parents' bed. We hate to wait, but there were fourteen generations from Abraham to David, and a second fourteen from David to the Babylonian exile, and guess what, there have been fourteen generations from Babylon to the very moment the curtain is scheduled to come up on the stage with an angel hovering over Joseph and telling him that a virgin will bear a son to be called "God with us."

A good appetizer never fills the diner up. Rather, it awakens the taste buds and makes us truly hungry for what is about to be served.

While there is beauty and devotion in this passage, especially the scene with Joseph and the angel, we can't afford to skate over the pain of the moment, the anxiety of the season. All is not well. What is being told sounds good, but all of us have been disappointed before. So often it is only in retrospect that we can look back and see God at work in our lives. At the moment it is hard to tell what is going on. We can say that Joseph should have plainly heard and understood what the angel said, but how often have you clearly heard and understood God? In the moment when we don't know what's going on, in the middle of our dreams, the disruptions

> While there is beauty and devotion in this passage, we can't afford to skate over the pain of the moment, the anxiety of the season.

of our sleep, even the visions, voices, and dreams of our waking hours—how hard is it to know if this is God talking to us, and if we are understanding what is being said?

FIRST READING
ISAIAH 9:2-7 (RCL)
ISAIAH 9:2-4, 6-7 (BCP)
ISAIAH 9:1-6 (LFM)

The Civil War anthem "Mine eyes have seen the glory of the coming of the Lord" proclaims as our lesson does in verse 5: the boots of the tramping warriors and all the garments rolled in blood shall be burned as fuel for the fire, for the child has been born who is the prince of peace. The oppressor is broken and justice and righteousness will reign in its place. . . . God's truth is marching on. Battle hymns are not popular now—in fact, we can hope that they would never be popular—but this is a story of battle. Generation after generation has called out, "How long?" and finally the answer comes. But, as biblical scholar Christopher Seitz points out, "The cause for joy is not so much pending military victory (*over the Assyrians*) but the 'birth' of a new ruler, in whose wake such a victory will come in due course."[1]

While most of us appreciate the pretty lights that get strung and the trees that get decorated and the presents from and for loved ones and the carols we can't help but sing as we drive in the car to the mall and listen to the radio—for all of that sweetness and light, we have missed something. Even if we "keep Christ in Christmas," it is not just the story of Jesus being born, but it is the context into which he was born that matters as much as his birth. There is a war going on here. To use evangelical language, there is a war for the souls of humanity. We don't talk or think that way anymore. But the world is at stake, the values by which we live, the things to which we devote ourselves and for which we sacrifice so much. In making Christmas so nice, we have lost the urgency—indeed, the desperation—of needing God to be with us to make it through all this and, in fact, to find and live a life that is worth living. Without the battle, all this comes down to little more than another holiday well-wishing. We need to feel deep within ourselves what is at stake for us and for all that this child comes to affect, things that otherwise could never happen.

> This child is born "for us," "to us," and "with us." This is Immanuel.

This child is born "for us," "to us," and "with us." This is Immanuel. On Christmas we stop there with the conviction that God has fulfilled God's promises. The historic reality is that the people in Isaiah's day still did not quite trust those promises, they still walked in darkness; the following chapters in Isaiah tell us so. For our preaching, perhaps that is a possible topic—how even with Immanuel we continue in our ways, doubting, following other voices and gods and powers. The call of Christmas is at least in part to invite the world to celebrate the reality in our midst and to be changed by it. Some will; others won't. Ours is the task to bear witness to the light.

RESPONSIVE READING

PSALM 96 (RCL, BCP)
PSALM 96:1-4, 11-12 (BCP ALT.)
PSALM 96:1-2A, 2B-3, 11-12, 13 (LFM)

"Joy to the world, the Lord is come. . . . Let. . . . heaven and nature sing!" While it is unlikely that anyone will preach on the psalm tonight, many will sing it; in fact, there would be nothing wrong with singing that favorite carol in place of the psalm. As in Isaiah 55, this psalm unites humanity with the rest of the created order in praising God. While a sermon on global warming is unlikely to succeed at this point, we would not be badly served to remember that the Christ of God has come as much to redeem the entire creation as to be the Messiah of the descendants of Abraham.

SECOND READING

TITUS 2:11-14 (RCL, BCP, LFM)

It's just no fun at Christmastime to hear these words: "training us to renounce irreligion and worldly passions, and to live sober, upright, and godly lives in this world." *This* is what the grace of God has appeared for? Really? No one wants to hear this. And yet . . . Christmas *is* a time to assess our lives. Joining in social revelry simply because we're *supposed* to, because it's expected of us (at office parties and the like), makes a mockery of Christmas. This does not mean, of course, that we are to go around with sour-prune faces. Rather, our celebration of Christmas needs to reflect the truth about our world, about its need for a savior. Our celebration is no blind revelry, but, rather, gives expression to a confident hope in the appearing of glory—even in our own midst. Our laughter and joy gives expression to that—to the godliness of God's own revelry of love for this world.

LUKE 2:1-14 (15-20) (RCL, BCP)
LUKE 2:1-14 (LFM)

Permit me to ride my little high horse for a moment on this consideration of Christmas Eve and the birth of our Lord. I love it that the Roman Catholic Vigil and Mass take as their readings *first* Matthew's account and *then* Luke's. Read these two texts sometime in October with your church board or education committee. Ask them to think about Christmas pageants. There are some wonderful ones. But over time most pageants, due largely to wanting lots of parts for lots of children, plus the accumulation of costumes, have succeeded in collapsing at least three great plays into one script. Like the sermon that doesn't know its focus or boundary, too many pageants use up all of the good stuff at once and leave nothing for another time. The sad result is that we never get to hear each evangelist's particular perspective and reason for telling the story. I know you know that in Luke we have a stable—not a house—and we don't have any Magi. Try telling your story that way. Let Jesus be born one year in an upscale birthing center for your pageant and see if it sparks questions. Where are the sheep, the cows lowing, the goats? How can Jesus get born without hay in a manger? How could Matthew depict such a royally concerned birth? And how about leaving the Magi for an Epiphany pageant? The script is easy to write and it's a way to rope families back to church after the holidays.

So on to Year C and Luke's Nativity. I think for a pageant in Year C, I would be tempted to have Jesus be born in a subway station. It would still take a kind-hearted station attendant to let them in (the modern counterpart to an innkeeper), and a cop to turn his back and police the others standing on the platform with a "Hey, let's give these two a little privacy, will ya!" Somehow we'd need to convey that in a setting that could be quite frightening, there will come the message, "Do not be afraid."

"Do not be afraid" is the message both on Christmas at the birth and on Easter at the tomb. We are afraid of terrorists, but what of God coming among us? Gods and angels are scary things. We think of them as soft harp players or Oprah-like gift givers, but that is not the reaction to angels in the Bible. Annie Dillard once wrote that we all should wear crash helmets in church. We could apply that anywhere we go. Bishop Paul Marshall once said that the point of preaching the gospel is to change the world and to change us. But many don't want to be changed. In that case, do they really want God? When God comes into your life, things

> This is a dangerous world, but as much because God enters it as because bad elements do. The difference is the outcome of that entering.

change, and not always of your own choosing. This is a dangerous world, but as much because God enters it as because bad elements do. The difference is the outcome of that entering.

Note

1. Christopher R. Seitz, *Isaiah 1–39,* Interpretation: A Bible Commentary for Teaching and Preaching (Louisville: John Knox, 1993), 86.

NATIVITY OF THE LORD 2 / CHRISTMAS DAWN

Revised Common (RCL)	Episcopal (BCP)	Roman Catholic (LFM)
Isa. 62:6-12	Isa. 62:6-7, 10-12	Isa. 62:11-12
Psalm 97	Psalm 97 or 97:1-4, 11-12	Ps. 97:1, 6, 11-12
Titus 3:4-7	Titus 3:4-7	Titus 3:4-7
Luke 2:(1-7) 8-20	Luke 2:(1-14) 15-20	Luke 2:15-20

FIRST READING
ISAIAH 62:6-12 (RCL)
ISAIAH 62:6-7, 10-12 (BCP)
ISAIAH 62:11-12

The sentinels on the walls remind God not to fall asleep until God's work is done. God has promised, but now let's see it. It's like the movie *Jerry Maguire,* where the football player client says to his agent, "Show me the money." At that point, in verses 10-12, the sentinels call down below to throw open the gates, for salvation is riding in. They have not been forgotten. They are redeemed.

When the postexilic people first heard the prophetic words, it was all still just a dream. But they took that dream into themselves and dreamed it passionately enough to be faithful sentinels keeping watch. They kept hope alive, until finally: The Lord is here! On Christmas we are glad to tell the sentinels they can stand down from their watch. For the Lord has come. The wait is over.

RESPONSIVE READING
PSALM 97 (RCL)
PSALM 97 OR 97:1-4, 11-12 (BCP)
PSALM 97:1, 6, 11-12 (LFM)

Psalms 96, 97, and 98 are all assigned on Christmas Day. In Psalm 96, creation sings for joy. In Psalm 97 the Lord is king, so all rejoice—again, including the created order. And finally, Psalm 98 celebrates the rule of the Lord as king. Look at the imagery: righteousness and justice are the foundation of God's throne; fire and lightning show the power and majesty of the Most High; heaven and humanity together proclaim God's glory.

SECOND READING

TITUS 3:4-7 (RCL, BCP, LFM)

Christ is not only the first fruits of the resurrection; he is also the firstfruits of true birth. We have been born because Christ was born. Think of how seeing a birth, or a newborn infant, can stir in you your own feelings of freshness and newness, of possibility. Oh, to live each birth as if it were, in fact, our own. As it is. All births offer us the opportunity to recognize afresh that we do not need to live in the anguish of malice and envy and hate (see Titus 3:3). We can allow the miracle of an infant's new life to regenerate our own lives. Christ's birth gathers up all births. The Savior has appeared, and through him, we have been regenerated, reborn into a life free from those destructive passions, freed into wishing the best for others, into a generosity of spirit and purse, and into love and being loved. And none of this has been by our own doing, but purely through the mercy of this God who has known our anguish. The Holy Spirit has been "poured out upon us richly through Jesus Christ." And thus, we are now free to pour out mercy and love and delight upon those around us. For in doing this, we become sure evidence that we have, in Christ Jesus, been reborn.

> We can allow the miracle of an infant's new life to regenerate our own lives. Christ's birth gathers up *all* births.

THE GOSPEL

LUKE 2:(1-7) 8-20 (RCL)
LUKE 2:(1-14) 8-20 (BCP)
LUKE 2:15-20 (LFM)

Only suburban and city folk confuse lambs and shepherds with fluffy, gentle little things and those who tend them as kindly nature enthusiasts enjoying an evening under the stars. Raymond Brown points out that "in Jesus' time shepherds were often considered as dishonest, outside the Law. This has led to the suggestion that for Luke they represented the sinners whom Jesus came to save."[1] Luke links the shepherds to the town of Bethlehem, the city of another shepherd, the shepherd/king David. It wasn't that he was a shepherd that made

David memorable. It was that he became the king. Bethlehem is God's choice for our Jerusalems. Remember, it was the people, not God, who decided to build a big capital city with a temple just like the neighbors had, and to have a king in the first place. You can put on all the airs you want. You can become a big, successful business tycoon or a Ph.D. or a surgeon, but you are still you. It is hometown, not the big city with all that implies, that was the choice for the coming of the Child of God.

Bethlehem is as much a part of the message as the child who was born there. It is the fulfillment of prophecy. In fact, for Luke, Bethlehem trades status with Jerusalem; it is there that humanity encounters its God. It is in the ordinary, not the extraordinary.

Luke echoes Isaiah. This is the child who will sit on the throne, not just as Wonderful Counselor, but as Savior, Christ, and Lord. This is the good news of Isaiah 2:7 that Luke would have known only too well.

> For Luke, Bethlehem trades status with Jerusalem; it is there that humanity encounters its God.

It has been noted that the multitude of heavenly host proclaim peace on earth at his birth, while the earthly disciples proclaim peace in heaven at his entrance to the holy city at the end of his life. Yes, it is an antiphonal song, bookmarks of a life recognized as the one who comes in the name of the Lord.

Note

1. Raymond E. Brown, *The Birth of the Messiah: A Commentary on the Infancy Narratives in the Gospels of Matthew and Luke* (New York: Doubleday, 1977), 420.

Revised Common (RCL)	Episcopal (BCP)	Roman Catholic (LFM)
Isa. 52:7–10	Isa. 52:7–10	Isa. 52:7–10
Psalm 98	Psalm 98 or 98:1–6	Ps. 98:1, 2–3a, 3b–4, 5–6
Heb. 1:1-4 (5-12)	Heb. 1:1-12	Heb. 1:1-6
John 1:1-14	John 1:1-14	John 1:1-18 or 1:1-5, 9-14

FIRST READING

ISAIAH 52:7-10 (RCL, BCP, LFM)

All the ends of the earth shall see the salvation of God. The sentinels on their watch saw it coming, but what joy for ruins to sing of restoration! Can you get an image of that—of ruins singing? I remember a trip to St. Andrews in Scotland. At the far end of the main street as one heads out of the town are the ruins of an abbey from long ago. As I walked through those outlines of what once was, it was as though I could hear a hymn being sung or bells being tolled. The walls of that abbey no longer provide shelter, but they still provide inspiration as thousands of students from that university town and thousands more tourists from all over the world walk those grounds and find it a holy place. I can imagine those ruins singing. Or there is the charred remainder of the altar at Coventry where the bombs and fires of war destroyed so much, but the words "Father Forgive" on the side of that altar still proclaim more courageously that ever. And not just ruins of stone or steel should be expected to sing, but what of human ruins, of life after cancer or divorce or being fired—can we hear those ruins singing, too?

The one who brings good news is so welcome. What great imagery: beautiful feet! We get a picture in our minds of the lean long-distance runner; each stride has a purpose. Instead of the panicked call, "The British are coming," it is the image of a loved one coming home after a long trip or tour of duty. "The Lord is coming; the Lord is near, the Lord is here!" Our nation has not enjoyed the announcement of peace after a war in a long time. The world wars had peace announcements. We have grown up with memories of helicopters lifting Americans out of Saigon, and we can only dream how we will eventually depart Baghdad. Perhaps we are closer to those ancients who heard the news that Jerusalem could be comforted by peace. It was not their military might that secured their restoration. Their oppressor had been defeated by a power other than themselves. God had been at work in and through history even despite them, but the result was the good news the messenger brought: "Your God reigns." Here's what we know about the beautiful feet of the messenger: it is not the feet themselves, but the message that makes them beautiful. On Christmas Day we proclaim that, with all that is still so wrong all around, we can see messengers of God's salvation everywhere we look. It is not the absence of conflict or problems that we naïvely await; it is the message that God reigns over and despite all that. And that still is great news.

> On Christmas Day we proclaim that, with all that is still so wrong all around, we can see messengers of God's salvation everywhere we look.

RESPONSIVE READING

PSALM 98 (RCL, BCP)
PSALM 98:1-6 (BCP ALT.)
PSALM 98:1, 2-3A, 3B-4, 5-6 (LFM)

Sing a new song! Why? Because of what God has done. On this, the final service for Christmas Day, we know we are celebrating something different than the original psalmist. On this day we know we want to thank God for the gift of Jesus. But the reality is that it is no less easy for us today to sing a new song than it must have been for those in the days of Jesus to accept that this finally was the one for whom they had been waiting. It is no less easy for the original singers of this hymn to sing new songs, because although they appreciated the victory of the Lord in that moment and were aware of God's faithfulness to Israel right then, we know that they knew that they were still surrounded by their enemies and that the temptations of other gods and other ways were always enticing to them. The kings in the days of the psalms may have won many battles, but they had many more enemies. The people believed the God of creation was on their side and that was reason for singing, but the final verse is still one to which attention must be paid. The Lord comes to judge. This is a mighty judge with demands of righteousness and equity. The Christmas songs we sing cannot only be of a helpless baby in his mother's arms but of one who comes in power to judge us.

SECOND READING

HEBREWS 1:1-4 (5-12) (RCL)
HEBREWS 1:1-12 (RCL)
HEBREWS 1:1-6 (LFM)

This first chapter of Hebrews is a marvelous hymn to the Christ, this one who is heir and creator both. All that we know of God is seen in this "Son" (he is never named in chapter 1). The author of Hebrews gathers up a whole array of Old Testament passages, from the Psalms, 2 Samuel, and Deuteronomy—all these treasures from the rich storehouse of the tradition find their fulfillment and perfection in this "Son" whose birthday we celebrate today. We love the angels at Christmastime—in the pageants, on our trees, even in TV shows and movies. But angels are nothing compared to the main event: none other than the King to whom all Israel's kings merely pointed. This one is *the* King, the one whose throne is "for ever and ever" and whose reign will issue forth in righteousness for all. We get stuck on angels, maybe because in our world they're imagined as soft and helpful and miraculous. But the angels are the sideshow here. The reigning King is what is needed.

THE GOSPEL

JOHN 1:1-14 (RCL, BCP)
JOHN 1:1-18 OR 1:1-5, 9-14 (LFM)

As in Hebrews, where the author opens the letter with a song to the glory of an unnamed "Son," so here in the Gospel of John the author opens his Gospel with a song to the "grace and truth" of the unnamed "Word." As in Hebrews, the Word has been with God since the beginning, participating in the very creation of the universe. Our English translations make it difficult to see the verbal "surprise" of the text here. Throughout John 1:1-13, the verb "is" (whether in its present-tense or past-tense form) always connects with either "God" or "the Word." Whenever creation comes into view, the verb shifts to "become" (present or past). Thus, "In the beginning *was* the Word, and the Word *was* with God, and the Word *was* God"; but "all things *became* through him, and without him nothing *became* that *became*." Even in verse 6, the text reads, "A man *became* sent from God," because the man, in this case, was John. The Word *is*—the Word does not *become*. *We* become, because we are part of the created order.

Until verse 14, when we are shocked by this statement: "And the Word *became* flesh." Even the grammar emphasizes the startling surprise, the unimagined event of the incarnation. That which is divine, that which *is* . . . has *become* flesh! The two realms—divine and human—have been brought together in this "Word made flesh." And we have beheld his glory—the glory of God *in* flesh. As my colleague Virginia Wiles has said, it's not so much that the Gospel of John has a high *Christology*; it's rather that the Gospel of John has a high *anthropology*. Human flesh has been revealed to be what God has always intended it to be—God's own work. The point in the Gospel of John is not that "Jesus was God," and thus *different* than we are. Rather, the point is that Jesus reveals the *way* (John 14:6) to true *human* life. God makes God's home here with us (John 14:23). The unity of Jesus and the Father is the same unity that Jesus and the Father have *with us*—the Gospel makes no distinction, as though one of those "unities" was a "trinitarian unity" and the other a "community unity." Our oneness *is* the oneness of Jesus with the Father. Through Jesus—and through the presence of the Spirit—we have been invited *into* the Trinity. And thus, washing feet (John 13) is not servitude, but glory. Death is not defeat or assault, but rather is Christ's "hour of glory."

> In this Christ, the Word, the God-made-flesh, God-with-us, we see ourselves "from God's perspective"—and that is both glory and responsibility, grace upon grace.

Neither the Gospel, nor this hymn (in 1:1-18), fits neatly into our categories. But then, that is the point of incarnation, isn't it? In this Christ, the Word, the God-made-flesh, God-with-us, we see ourselves "from God's perspective"—and that is both glory and responsibility, grace upon grace. It is almost too much to take in!

FIRST SUNDAY OF CHRISTMAS / THE HOLY FAMILY (LFM)

DECEMBER 27, 2009

Revised Common (RCL)	Episcopal (BCP)	Roman Catholic (LFM)
1 Sam. 2:18-20, 26	Isa. 61:10—62:3	1 Sam. 1:20-22, 24-28
Psalm 148	Psalm 147 or 147:13-21	Ps. 84:2-3, 5-6, 9-10
Col. 3:12-17	Gal. 3:23-25; 4:4-7	1 John 3:1-2, 21-24
Luke 2:41-52	John 1:1-18	Luke 2:41-52

FIRST READING

1 SAMUEL 2:18-20, 26 (RCL)

The old leadership has failed and the new one is coming, but to get from the past to the future there will need to be a leader of extraordinary stature. Samuel is the link between the old failed priesthood and the new monarchy he will consequently anoint for God. This is astonishing for several reasons. First, God had established the priestly order, promising that it would be "forever." As Walter Brueggemann points out, however, "responsive obedience is required even for God's most sweeping promises."[1] Eli's sons have so terribly violated their office that God needs to break the promise that was made with that tribe, that family, that nation. Although it has not happened by the time of our reading, Samuel will grow up to be the one who must overthrow the old order to replace it with God's new order. This is a prefiguring, then, of the role Jesus will play. While we may struggle with the concept of God bringing to pass the instrument that will undo and replace that which God has established in the first place, this may be an opportunity for the preacher to deal with all the variations on those who hold to theologies of "whatever is meant to be will be." Clearly, even God's intention can be changed by human behavior and attitudes. History is not locked on an unwavering course. Not even the will of God is absolutely destined to be fulfilled in the way God wishes (if we can even talk or think in those terms). The human interaction with the divine is a fluid relationship like any other. It is dynamic. How one grows up, then, matters.

On the Sunday that we consider the Holy Family, we have in this reading an image of a child growing up with dual influences: that of Eli in the temple, and of

Samuel's mother and father, Hannah and Elkanah, when they make their yearly visit. The stated reason for the visit is to make the annual sacrifice, something we know Hannah and Elkanah always did, even before Samuel's birth. But the conversation now as in those pre-Samuel days between the three of them was about a child who would be born and then "lent" to the Lord. In this reading there is a feeling almost like the old English boarding schools, with Mom and Dad visiting Junior on Parents' Weekend, bringing a new coat, patting the child on the head. Although we never have any reason to assume anything other than love and care toward their child, it is still a difficult passage for anyone who is a parent. It is unsetting to think that an old man who had utterly failed as a father would be acting as *parentus in locus* for the future hope for the house of Israel, and that the child's own parents would merely see him once a year to drop off a new robe. Samuel may be God's servant, but this is surely not a model for "family values" or parenting. Like Jesus, Samuel grew in favor with God and the people around him. That is surely despite the adult influence as he grew up and can only be attributed to the divine influence. Sometimes our kids turn out despite us, and sometimes they don't, despite us. If there is any lesson for parents in this passage it may be the comfort that we are not the sole determiners of our children's destiny. The purpose of this passage is to show Samuel growing into a man who would transform the nation and thereby all of history.

> The purpose of this passage is to show Samuel growing into a man who would transform the nation and thereby all of history.

ISAIAH 61:10—62:3 (BCP)

This is the song of the joyful haberdasher with its garments of salvation, its robes of righteousness, and its jeweled crowns and diadems. This is a bursting forth of praise in all creation, from the earth bursting forth in new vegetation to the nations bursting forth with praise. This is the joyful victory of all creation, joy in the God of all salvation.

1 SAMUEL 1:20-22, 24-28 (LFM)

Preachers should refer first to the notes above on 1 Samuel 2; but with that as background, even though this passage comes first, the theological point here is that one without hope now has hope, and even more than hope. A flesh-and-blood reality, not just a dream or a hope, comes into Hannah and Elkanah's life. There is no doubt that this would not have occurred without divine response to her prayers. Hannah is so convinced that this child, in a sense, is not even hers. She bore the son, but he does not belong to her. She offers him to the one to whom we belong, a sort of "We give Thee but Thine own, / what e'er our gifts may be. / All that we have is Thine alone, / a trust, O Lord, from Thee." This is high drama, but in fact, isn't this the case for every life? What is key here is that Hannah was so aware that the fulfillment of her hope could only come from God. She did not look to other sources or solutions. She did not just have hope, but she had hope in God. Her hopes fulfilled resulted in lifelong gratitude. As B. A. Gerrish once summed up John Calvin's theology, it was a cycle of "grace and gratitude."[2]

RESPONSIVE READING
PSALM 148 (RCL)

Sea monsters, fire and hail, young and old—let all praise the Lord. Paul Winter, the former music director at the Cathedral of St. John the Divine in New York, composed an Earth Mass that features the sounds of whales as well as humans.[3] It would be fun and effective to play a portion of this mass, especially the sounds of the animal praises, in the liturgical setting of the responsive psalm. Just let people listen for a minute or two and they will be caught up in the praises of a united creation.

PSALM 147 OR 147:13-21 (BCP)

The one who heals the brokenhearted and gathers the outcasts is great. The downtrodden are lifted up and the wicked cast down. Oh Mary, is this where you learned your song?! It is a song not just of praise, but of thanksgiving. Those who know the Lord will praise the Lord. There are so many reasons for praise and thanksgiving, and this psalm enumerates them.

PSALM 84:2-3, 5-6, 9-10 (LFM)

My soul longs for the courts of the Lord. I would rather be the door-keeper at God's house than live anywhere else. For, in God, desolation has turned to refreshment and the soul sings! This would be the perfect day for the choir to sing "How Lovely Is Thy Dwelling Place," from Brahms's *German Requiem*.

COLOSSIANS 3:12-17 (RCL)

The lectionary picks these apparently "gooey" texts for the Christmas season. And we're likely to glance at them and then push them aside, at most stealing a few sweet phrases from them for our conclusion. And perhaps that's best. But there are always nuggets here that can provide some energy for our musings on the other texts. This passage in Colossians is structured around a central imperative. Literally, it's central—halfway through this text: "And be thankful." That really is the key. We can try to be moral and upright (that whole list of virtues in verse 12: compassion, kindness, lowliness, meekness, patience). We can try to be forgiving. We can try to "put on love" in everything we do. We can work hard to be at peace. We can teach and admonish and sing. But all those things are nothing more than works of the law if we do them out of some desire to be "good" or upright. The life of virtue, of love and forgiveness, of worship—all these things are the natural fruit of gratitude. If we are *thankful*, the rest flows out without effort.

> The life of virtue, of love and forgiveness, of worship—all these things are the natural fruit of gratitude.

(This is, by the way, one of the central functions of the Eucharist, which is quite literally "thanksgiving.") But, of course, one can't force gratitude. The question to bring to the text, then, is "What do we do when we *aren't* thankful?" We wait. We admit that we aren't thankful—that there's hurt and disappointment and sadness in our lives. And we approach the table of the Lord anyway. We wait there honestly, without feigning a thanksgiving that we don't feel, but without denying the power of gratitude. Even when Advent is over, when we are already in the season of Christmas, we still need to watch and wait, to "ponder in our hearts" as Mary did—thanksgiving will come. And when it does, this text says, "Make it central." Notice it. Honor it. And the rest will begin to flow out of you.

GALATIANS 3:23-25; 4:4-7 (BCP)

It's quite fun to think about these texts from Galatians during Christmas. The little bit from chapter 3 could be read analogically, as another way of telling the Luke 2 narrative about Jesus going to the temple with his parents. Paul writes to the Galatians that "before faith came, we were confined under the law." The law is, in terms of Paul's illustration, our "nanny"—our *paidagogue*. Its purpose is to guard us unto faith. So, too, for Jesus and his parents. He was "confined" as a child to obey his parents. They functioned, actively and literally, as the "law" in his childhood. Their purpose, however, was to guard him *unto* faith—and that is, one might say, the purpose of Luke's narration in Luke 2. It narrates, with Jesus as the protagonist, what Paul is saying here to the Galatians in chapter 3. And so it is with each of us as well. We, too, have been "nannied" by the law of God. But when we mature, we no longer need the rope tied around our waist. We have, through baptism and the life of faith, been "freed from the law." We, too, can say, "I must be about my Father's business."

And how much more true this is when we recognize that we have been, as Galatians 4 tells us, "adopted" by God. Ideally, all parents would raise their children with the clear and happy knowledge that we as parents are no more than temporary custodians—nannies—for our beloved children are not, in fact, *ours*. They are God's children, for God has adopted them.

1 JOHN 3:1-2, 21-24 (LFM)

The first epistle of John emphasizes that we are all "children of God." The world may not treat us that way. But, then, the world doesn't know God, so why should the world know that *we* are children of God? Even Jesus' own parents didn't *fully* "know" that Jesus was God's child. They, too, had to learn that Jesus was here to be about his Father's business. The "Father's business" is *love* . . . and thus, to be the child of God is to be in the business of love. We do not know yet "what we shall be," but we stand in confidence because we *do* know that we are children of God.

The Gospel
LUKE 2:41-52 (RCL, LFM)

When Jesus was twelve years old, "his parents" brought him to Jerusalem for the festival of the Passover. We may wonder how Jesus thought of himself in those years. We wonder how Mary and Joseph thought of their son and their relationship to him. One of the things that is good to see is that no family, not even the holy family, gets through these years without frightening experiences, exasperation, glitches in communication. When Jesus is eventually found and Mary asks him why he has treated her and "his father" like this, Jesus answers that he had to be in "his Father's house." And it is clear that he is not talking about Joseph. So we wonder if Jesus played the game the children of divorce sometimes do of using one parent to condone what the other has not.

Personally, I don't think that's the reason this story is placed here. Rather, the author uses it as a transition between the infancy story and Jesus' baptism as an adult by this cousin, John, many years later. In this episode Jesus speaks. These are the first words we ever hear Jesus saying, as it is attributed to him in this Gospel, so we should pay some attention to what he says. There is something here that drives home the fact that this Jesus is a man of two families, and both are parental in nature.

Jesus grew up, as we all do, either looking for or taking some parental direction. This time it is unsolicited by him, but at the wedding in Cana, he will talk to this mother about the timing of the miracle he is to perform, and she tells him to get on with things. A bit of coaching, even for Jesus. He needed it. Our theologians may not like it, but there is no getting around the fact that not only is there character development for Jesus in the Gospels, but also Jesus had to struggle to think about who he was and who he would be.

> Not only is there character development for Jesus in the Gospels, but also Jesus had to struggle to think about who he was and who he would be.

And when he went to Nazareth following his time in the wilderness, he went, "as was his custom," to the synagogue on the Sabbath. After he read, the men commented that this was "Joseph's son."

Boys (and in our day, girls as well) do not go to the synagogue regularly by themselves. We don't want to confuse the temple in Jerusalem with the local synagogue here. But here was a child brought to the temple by his parents to be named even though an angel had already done that job. Here was a boy brought to Jerusalem, a long distance from home, for the festival of Passover. Even though it was written that this was supposed to be done, it is clear that many in Jesus' day did not go. It was Jesus' custom to go to the synagogue on the Sabbath and his family's custom to go the temple each year for the Passover. He didn't develop that custom by himself. His parents went to great extremes to engrain that custom in their son. Those who emphasize the deity of Jesus over his humanity might question, What was the point? Or to be more precise, What was the need? Did Jesus need to go to the synagogue every week to be in conversation with God, or to read from the prophecy of Isaiah? More than the need of Jesus was the need of Mary and Joseph to be doing this in order to define themselves as parents doing all they could for their child.

This is the text for the Sunday in which we consider the holy family, so we would do well to ask ourselves what habits and ways of living we are teaching our children. Clearly Mary and Joseph had no problem telling Jesus he'd messed up; he'd created a problem by staying behind in Jerusalem. I can imagine, "Young man, I don't care if you were about God's business, that's no excuse for your behavior. You of all people should have known how we felt these past two days when we were looking for you."

Partly this story is told by Luke to depict what later generations would call the fully God/fully man reality of Jesus. But it is equally about Mary and Joseph, who remind us that even if your kid is as good as God, your job as a parent is to still call him on it when he doesn't act as he should. The holy family had no fewer challenges in raising Jesus than any family ever has.

JOHN 1:1–18 (BCP)

For comments on this text, see the Gospel for the Nativity of Our Lord 3/Christmas Day, above.

Notes

1. Walter Brueggemann, *First and Second Samuel*, Interpretation: A Bible Commentary for Teaching and Preaching (Louisville: John Knox, 1990), 23.

2. B. A. Gerrish, *Grace and Gratitude: The Eucharistic Theology of John Calvin* (Minneapolis: Fortress Press, 1993).

3. Paul Winter, *Missa Gaia* (produced by Living Music Records, distributed by Windham Hill, 1982), LD.0002, ISBN 1048-80002-2.

HOLY NAME OF JESUS / MARY, MOTHER OF GOD (LFM)

Revised Common (RCL)	Episcopal (BCP)	Roman Catholic (LFM)
Num. 6:22-27	Exod. 34:1-8	Num. 6:22-27
Psalm 8	Psalm 8	Ps. 67:2-3, 5, 6-8
Gal. 4:4-7 or Phil 2:5-11	Rom. 1:1-7	Gal. 4:4-7
Luke 2:15-21	Luke 2:15-21	Luke 2:15-21

FIRST READING

NUMBERS 6:22-27 (RCL, LFM)

This passage is known as "The Aaronic or Priestly Blessing." Those who were priests had to, among other things, take a vow to separate themselves to the Lord. This nazirite law, which we also see for Samuel and others, is a consecration to be set apart for the holy work of God. If we place this reading in the context of Mary, Joseph, and Jesus, each of them in a way took a vow, not so much to live apart, but to do something for God that no one else had ever done. Mary as the God-bearer; Joseph as adoptive father; and of course, Jesus, who, in the total devotion of his life, is the ultimate nazirite.

There is another way that this passage is appropriate for this Sunday in Christmas, and that is the way God blesses God's people with grace and gives them a peace the world cannot give. The shining face implies the presence of God, and Immanuel is *God with us* in a way humanity had never before known.

EXODUS 34:1-8 (BCP)

"The LORD said to Moses, 'Cut two tablets of stone like the former ones . . . .'" J. Gerald Janzen compares the failure and grave sin of Israel in crafting and worshiping the golden calf to be like the failure of a first marriage.[1] How can those who have been married before ever make such vows again? These vows are supposed to be "as long as we both shall live," but that isn't what happened. There is failure compounded by guilt. But there is compassion, mercy, and healing in God's making it possible to vow once again, as one did the first time. The key phrase of "like the former ones" is a chance to start over, without prejudice. This is the possibility of a new beginning. This is resurrection, not by way of human improvement or sincerity, but by God's grace and power. This is not an easy forgiveness, but the steadfast love and mercy of God, which places humanity's sin and conviction within the context of God's faithfulness. Even as Moses had to write a new set of tablets of the Law, the people were able to move on, not as though nothing had happened to cause the destruction of the first, but to begin again without previous failure being held against them. And if this is the God who covenants with the people to be their God and for them to keep the commandments, then the new covenant in Christ becomes similar to that opportunity to "be raised with Christ." The one who comes into the world to save all people from their sins is God's new tablet, not of stone, but of flesh and blood.

> The one who comes into the world to save all people from their sins is God's new tablet, not of stone, but of flesh and blood.

Luther used to read the law before the confession of sin, to bring people to confession. But Calvin had the law read after the Assurance of Pardon as a way for faithful people to respond to the grace given them by God. A question to ask an adult discussion group might be, "Does the presence of Christ with us bring us to confession or does it inspire our living?" The answers would probably show both, even as Luther and Calvin would probably agree that the primary issue is the gift of the covenant from a faithful God to a people who repeatedly need to be raised from the death of our sins.

RESPONSIVE READING

PSALM 8 (RCL, BCP)

O God, when we look at all that you have made, who are we that you should care? This is a bit like the person in the boat who considers how vast the sea is and how small his little boat. And yet, even in the consideration of the majesty of the Almighty, there is a sense of the responsibility of humanity for the created order. Lower than God, but entrusted with dominion over all that God has made. This is a hymn of awe, a consideration of the marvels of creation and our own role and place in it. But as the hymn concludes, it is once again focused on the majesty of God.

PSALM 67:2-3, 5, 6-8 (LFM)

The psalm begins (even though this comes before our portion of it) with a blessing identical to the one given to Aaron. But the blessing is given with the goal that God's saving power might be made known to all the people and nations of the earth. For if they know, they will praise the Lord. Like a collect, it petitions God to continue to bless the people and concludes with a statement of reverence. There is no reason not to use this entire psalm. Eliminating only verses 1 and 4 serves no purpose. Many translations have this psalm conclude in seven verses rather than eight anyway. This is a psalm of thanksgiving, a simple prayer, a simple song, with a wonderful refrain: "Let the people praise you, O God; let all the peoples praise you."

SECOND READING
GALATIANS 4:4-7 (RCL, LFM)

For comments on this text, see the second reading for the First Sunday of Christmas, above.

PHILIPPIANS 2:5-11 (RCL ALT.)

The christological hymn in Philippians 2:6-11 fits well with Psalm 8. Indeed, one might argue that the hymn is, in some ways, an interpretation of Psalm 8. For the hymn here in Philippians emphasizes the *mortality* of the one whom we call Christ. Although this hymn is rich (like a chocolate torte, perhaps) in interpretive possibilities, one way scholars have read this hymn is that it uses the story of the creation of "Adam" as the backdrop for telling the story of Jesus, the Christ. This Jesus was "in the form of God"—just as we are created "in the image of God." But Jesus did not "grasp at" equality with God, unlike Adam and Eve who *did* "grasp at" the fruit, longing to "be like" God. Nevertheless, Jesus accepted the "form of a slave" and descended into mortality, even to the point of death (which is, after all, what "mortality" means). He fully experienced the humiliation that we all, in some way or other, experience. *Therefore*—the text says—"God has highly exalted him." *Therefore!* Because he "became human"? Yes, *because he became human*. As Genesis 1 says, "And it was *very* good." As Psalm 8 declares: "You, you who are *humans*—God has exalted *you!*" Oh, if we humans could ever grasp the reality—or be grasped *by* the reality—that God *exalts* humanity! That God honors us and celebrates us and "gives to us a name above every name"—the name of "children of God." The story of Jesus in Philippians 2:5-11 is *our* story. Not just a story that we tell about Jesus. It is—at least this is what Paul asserts in Philippians—a story *about us*. What might break free in this world if we believed that, if we trusted that it were true?

> Oh, if we humans could ever grasp the reality—or be grasped *by* the reality—that God *exalts* humanity!

ROMANS 1:1-7 (BCP)

In Romans 1 we have yet another christological hymn—all of verses 2-4. And, as is the case in Philippians 2 (see above), the "hymn of Christ" is turned to a hymn for us. The story of Christ—promised by the prophets, descended from David, designated Son of God—results in Paul's apostleship. And not just Paul's, but ours as well. The life of faith is not something that happens because we cognitively "believe" some facts about the story of Jesus. The life of faith happens because the story of Jesus has become *our* story. We belong to him, and his story is now the story of our *own* lives. We, too, have been raised *with* Christ; we, too, have been designated "son or daughter of God." We, too, then, are sent forth and give our lives for others.

THE GOSPEL
LUKE 2:15-21 (RCL, BCP, LFM)

And so the poor go to Bethlehem, these descendants of the shepherd king who have had good news proclaimed to them. For Luke it is important that the first to get the news of this birth are the lowest of the lowly. And when they find Jesus, he is not a baby in a crib as in Matthew's house version of the birth, but in a manger. The lowly come to one born into lowliness as well. From the very start, Luke's word of good news is that even as God has condescended to identify with humanity, so humanity can identify with God. In Calvin's eucharistic theology it is precisely in Christ's condescension that humanity is lifted up. This is what gives hope to the world in all its suffering, pain, and corruption. As Howard Thurman put it, this is the Jesus of the disinherited who, by his coming to share life with them, assures them that they are heirs with him of the kingdom of heaven.

> From the very start, Luke's word of good news is that even as God has condescended to identify with humanity, so humanity can identify with him.

In verse 21, when the infant was taken to the temple on his eighth day to be circumcised and named, he is given the name of Joshua in Hebrew or Jesus in Greek, which means "salvation." Mary has done what the angel had directed her to do before his birth in naming him in this way. Let's go back for a moment to that ancient Hebrew notion of speaking one's name. That the ancient Hebrews did not speak God's name was a sign of respect, humility, and awe; they believed that God was so vast as not to be able to be contained within a word or name. The name was like a magic incantation: "There's power in the name." That is something we have lost. To speak the name was to give definition. To speak the name was to hold the essence of that being. And so to be given and to call on the name of Jesus as the one who would save his people from their sins moves this focus of history to this point. For the people of Israel, the exodus had been the central story to show how God cared for God's people and liberated them. But now history shifts. This one whose name is salvation becomes the focus around which everything else turns.

Note

1. J. Gerald Janzen, *Exodus*, Westminster Bible Companion (Louisville: Westminster John Knox, 1997), 250–51.

SECOND SUNDAY OF CHRISTMAS

JANUARY 3, 2010

Revised Common (RCL)	Episcopal (BCP)	Roman Catholic (LFM)
Jer. 31:7-14 or	Jer. 31:7-14	Sir. 24:1-4, 12-16
Sir. 24:1-12		
Ps. 147:12-20 or	Psalm 84 or 84:1-8	Ps. 147:12-13, 14-15,
Wis. Of Sol. 10:15-21		19-20
Eph. 1:3-14	Eph. 1:3-6, 15-19a	Eph. 1:3-6, 15-18
John 1:(1-9) 10-19	Matt. 2:13-15, 19-23 or	John 1:1-18 or 1:1-5,
	Luke 2:41-52 or	9-14
	Matt. 2:1-12	

FIRST READING

JEREMIAH 31:7-14 (RCL, BCP)

"I will turn their mourning into joy." This is the promise to those in exile and it is given in both the future and the present tense. *God will do what God is already doing.* The condition of exile is one of depression and slavery, but the redemption and return of the people to both their geographic and spiritual home frees more than merely their bodies. Imagery of the good shepherd leading the flock home evokes both memories to the past and foretells things yet to come. In verse 9 we have the blind, the lame, those in labor, the sad, the weak, the marginalized—exiles who in all their sadness and hurt will be gathered and brought home. Many of us know that we are blind in various ways. What we fail to see is that God is already changing our blindness. God will do what God is already doing.

> God comes to all and each of us in our own experiences of exile and infirmity.

In his commentary on this passage Walter Brueggemann underscores five imperatives in verse 7.[1] The community, not just individuals, is invited—in fact urged—to "sing aloud, raise shouts, proclaim, give praise and say!" Here is the outline for a fine sermon in the season of Christmas. God comes to each and all of us in our own experiences of exile and infirmity. God gathers us as a people loved by God and brings us to our spiritual center, to a place that is safe, and our despair is transformed, by God's activity, into joy and hope. Our response is to sing aloud (not just to ourselves or within the walls of our temples). We shout to be heard in the public square. We announce a God who cares about the poor, the refugees, those without homes, and even those yet unborn—a God who carries the aged and the sick. What are the public policies of that kind of God and of that God's people? And we praise God and tell the stories, not just of ancient liberation and return, but of our own liberations and renewals. The gift of Christmas is the one who comes to turn mourning into joy.

SIRACH 24:1-12 (RCL)
SIRACH 24:1-4, 12-16 (LFM)

Wisdom, the creator of all, surveys the entire creation and chooses to make a home among Jacob and Israel. Wisdom takes root and grows in the city and Jerusalem becomes the beloved city; its people will inherit the blessings of Wisdom.

How does any of this pertain to the Second Sunday of Christmas? Perhaps in the fact that the dwelling of God is among mortals. Ours is not a distant deity, but one who is located in specific places—those places where people live their ordinary lives. Life is made holy by this one coming to live among us and share our lot.

Also significant in this hymn of praise is all the language of growth. Life is not stagnant, but grows and spreads in beauty, like rose bushes in Jericho. Beauty shows up in the most unexpected places. I don't know about all the seasons of the year there, but the one time I was in Jericho, there were no rose bushes. Nothing was in bloom.

> Because Wisdom has chosen to make her home among us, we are the beneficiaries of the company she keeps.

It was dry and hot, and so I wonder if the writer intended for the reader to be shocked at the unlikely but marvelous imagery of a thing of such beauty springing up in such a place.

From time to time parents will tell their children that they will be known by the company they keep. Often this is a parental admonition not to hang around with the wrong kinds of kids. But here the opposite is the case. Because Wisdom has chosen to make her home among us, we are the beneficiaries of the company she keeps. We are blessed by her life with us.

As we naturally focus on the birth of God's Son, Jesus, it is a wonderful thing to have another verse in our hymn of worship for this day bring to us the feminine side of God. We aren't trying to box God into gender roles so much as having one verse of a hymn be about the Son who has come to live among us and another about Wisdom coming to live among us, which creates a good theological as well as artistic harmony for the morning.

PSALM 147:12–20 (RCL)
PSALM 147:12–13, 14–15, 19–20 (LFM)

TIMOTHY J.
MULDER

Two things come to our attention in the concluding section of this community hymn of praise. The first is the preference of God for Israel. God has not dealt with any other nation as God has with them, and no other nation knows God's law as Israel does. Personally, I find this preference—this favored-nation status—troubling. It always seems to me that the new covenant in Christ moves us beyond any single nation or people. But perhaps that's precisely it. There is no getting around the covenantal relationship God established with Israel. The promises of God were not vague, but were specific. We cannot pretend that they were just "in theory." Even as God comes to us in the person of Jesus, a human of flesh and blood, so God's relationship with humanity was specific. The fact that the nature of a new covenant changes to move beyond a single place and people does not negate the earlier promises. And those promises have been fulfilled. Jesus himself said that he came to fulfill rather than abolish the law (Matt. 5:17). And what was the law but the contours of the relationship between God and God's people? This is a God who can be trusted, who fulfills what is promised, who keeps the covenant.

> The promises of God are not vague, but were specific. We cannot pretend that they were just "in theory."

Verses 15–18 remind us once again of the power of God's word. That word makes things happen. And it is not just causal. It has a life in and of itself. The line is too fine to separate this word between being the expression of God and being God's own self. The word is what it says and does and causes to happen. It is not a long jump from these verses to the prologue in John's Gospel.

WISDOM OF SOLOMON
10:15–21 (RCL ALT.)

Israel sings of its history of deliverance by the power of Wisdom. One has to chuckle, though, at the opening reference to Israel being "a holy people and blameless race." Holy, yes, by God's own choice and making, but blameless, hardly. Israel is no more blameless than we are today. In fact, the whole story of Israel and God's relationship is about how God does not give up on a sinful and wandering people. This passage recites the exodus and how, to use the expression so popular in the black church, God makes a way where there is no way. God puts down Israel's enemies and brings them through. It is even Wisdom that opens the mouths of the delivered who had been silent but now issue praise. If the people are blameless, it is only because Wisdom has taken away their blame, delivering them not only from their external enemies but from themselves as well.

PSALM 84 or 84:1-8 (BCP)

For commentary on this text, see the responsive reading for the First Sunday of Christmas/The Holy Family (LFM), above.

Second Reading
EPHESIANS 1:3-14 (RCL)
EPHESIANS 1:3-6, 15-19A (BCP)
EPHESIANS 1:3-6, 15-18 (LFM)

And yet again the epistle reading emphasizes that we have been "adopted" as children of God. It's always surprising how little connection we make between our adoption as "children of God" and Jesus' own standing as "Son of God." It's almost as though we're afraid to claim the status given to us by God, as though maybe it's heretical to claim to be a "child of God." The writer of Ephesians, however, shows no such hesitation. We have been given "every spiritual blessing." *Every* spiritual blessing. The inheritance is guaranteed (1:14). We live unto *exactly* the same purpose as Jesus: "to the praise of God's glorious grace." Yes, Christ is the one who mediates that grace to us. But then, are we not mediators of that grace to others? Is that not *our* calling? The one who called Jesus "Son" also calls *us* "son" or "daughter." The one who called Jesus to mediate grace calls *us* to mediate grace. If only we might begin to trust that we are, indeed, fully adopted *children of God*.

The Gospel
JOHN 1:(1-9) 10-19 (RCL)
JOHN 1:1-18 or 1-5, 9-14 (LFM)

For comments on this text, see the Gospel for the Nativity of Our Lord/ Christmas Day, above.

MATTHEW 2:13-15, 19-23 (BCP)

Joseph had a good relationship with angels, which is to say, with God. This is not at all or in any way to diminish our admiration for Mary's obedience to the angel's declaration to her that she would give birth to Jesus. That's the story Luke, not Matthew, tells us. But even so, in Luke's Gospel Mary is told she will bear a child; there really isn't much she can do about that situation. In Matthew's

Gospel, Joseph, as a result of the angel's first message, has to decide if he will stay with Mary. Can he get over his fear and other feelings? In fact, according to 1:19-20, because of his conversation with the angel, he changed his decision. Now, in this passage, Joseph, as a new father and soon-to-be husband, has to decide a second time if he will listen to an angel.—even if it means to run with his new family, to become a refugee family, away from both home and other family and, presumably, his profession as well. He does it. Then, finally, an angel comes to Joseph a third time (at least as far as we know, but who knows, there may have been many times Joseph talked with angels that were simply not recorded). This time Joseph is told to pack up his family and move yet again, this time to go home to Israel. But not quite home; because of political unrest they had to go make a new home in the area of Galilee, in the town of Nazareth. For Matthew this fulfills prophecy, but for modern readers, what we see is a person who makes family decisions based on conversation with God. Who knows, maybe it wasn't conversation; the angel may simply have announced what Joseph should do. The key of faith is whether we act on what we perceive is the will of God.

> The key of faith is whether we act on what we perceive is the will of God.

But I can't help but wonder if Joseph ever wondered if he had really heard God right. There is risk in the weight of decision making. Faith is not always tidy. We are not always sure, but need to take action anyway. Faith is not always knowing what is the right thing to do, but trusting that in God, whatever our decision or action, it will be all right, not knowing what "all right" might mean. Joseph bore the weight of making a decision for his family, trusting that he had listened to God as best he could and then knowing the freedom of acting on that conviction. That is all any of us can do.

LUKE 2:41-52 (BCP ALT.)

When does one come of age? For what? Timing was always a question that seemed important to Jesus. He didn't want to turn water into wine because it wasn't his time; but Mom knew better. He didn't want people to know he had healed or cast out demons or done other incredible things; it wasn't the right time. Finally, he set his face toward Jerusalem; the time to be delivered was coming. But when he was twelve years old, what time was it for Jesus? There's no indication here that it was time for his bar mitzvah. The family did not go to Jerusalem to celebrate Jesus' coming of age, his coming into adulthood. They went to Jerusalem because they went to Jerusalem every year. It was like turkey at Thanksgiving for us. They went to celebrate the Passover. But if the ancestors escaped slavery in Egypt long ago and that story was still ringing in this young adolescent's head, then perhaps he thought it was time for a little liberation of his own. We don't need to make too much of this, but he clearly knew what he was doing. After all, he was missing for three days. We can assume he wasn't in the temple in discussion with the teachers every minute, day and night, in a three-day marathon of theology. He had to go to sleep at night—somewhere—somewhere where his parents were not. If we want to talk about the full humanity of Jesus, we'd better include that it is part of every healthy human being to separate one's self from one's parents. The fact that Jesus did this at age twelve resulted in huge pain and anxiety for his parents, as Mary told him when he was finally discovered. They don't understand his "being in his father's house" statement because they're not supposed to understand that kind of talk. He was a child, one for whom they were responsible; this didn't make sense. We hear the story and say he was special; like the child who at age twelve astounds the audience with her violin on the stage at Carnegie Hall. But more is at stake than this. This is Luke's transition passage. How do we get from childhood to adulthood in one step? It's just too much. I would not read nearly as much into this passage as many scholars want us to see here. Jesus increased in wisdom and years and in human and divine favor, a wonderful way for the writer to echo Samuel's development. Life goes in stages and episodes. The stories of our lives are what make them more than a mathematical equation.

> We wish we knew more about Jesus' life. But sometimes all we get in life is a glimpse.

There is suspense, development, ups and downs in every human tale. We wish we knew more about Jesus' life. But sometimes all we get in life is a glimpse. It's like when Moses stood in the crag of the rock and the winds blew and God passed by, but Moses only caught a glimpse of God's backside; there was no face to face then. But the glimpse was enough to know that God was present, even though Moses had worried whether that would be so (Exod. 33:17-23). God was present. Here we catch a glimpse of an ordinary teenager, doing a wonderful thing while driving his folks crazy. Just like our kids. Isn't that the point of it after all? He was with us. We don't know much, but when times get tough and we worry if we're on our own, we catch a glimpse. Not many stories of Jesus' growing up made it into the book; I wish there were more, but this is enough.

MATTHEW 2:1-12 (BCP ALT.)

This is a little, soft, quaint story of a baby's birth, right? Yeah, sure . . . just as landing on the moon was only "one small step." Look at the cosmic conference of humanity that becomes involved in this scene. We have Herod, not just an individual, but a family dynasty that ruled Palestine for over 150 years. In our case that would be as though the Adamses or Bushes had had not just two family members in leadership, but a string of six for 150 years. That is a lot of power and a people's culture wrapped up in one name. Besides the ruler, there comes the entire entourage of advisors and courtesans and all the society that surrounds power in any age. That amounts to a lot of people.

Then we have these wise men from the East. Who knows how many of them? Their gifts fulfill the prophecy in the Psalms and Prophets. The main point is that they were *not* from the house of Israel. They were not the chosen people. What were they doing there? If the sun rises and sets every day, we can count on it, but Gentiles at the birth of the Messiah?—that throws everything that's ever been known out of whack. They don't belong. We take them for granted because they keep showing up in our pageants. But in those days they would never have shown up. But they did, and that's the point. And not only that, but they intuit what all the scholasticism of the chief priests and scribes could not comprehend.

"All of Jerusalem" was frightened by the news that the King of the Jews had been born and nobody knew about it. If knowledge is power, then who ever wants to be the last to know anything, let alone this? Well, the sad fact is that they knew all the facts, but just knowing the facts, in the same way that saying the Bible is the dictated word of God, just doesn't help much. Knowledge without understanding and understanding without corresponding and faithful action doesn't amount to anything except danger. Religious extremists know all kinds of things. But for faith to have integrity calls for more than knowing the facts.

> On some level the Magi represent those who perceive who Jesus is and then respond with true worship in the giving of themselves.

It has often been said that the epiphany of the Christ to the Magi is that at Christmas God gave God's gift to the world, and then the Magi, representing humanity, gave their gifts to God. But here is the crucial distinction. Even as Jesus would later warn that not everyone who says "Lord, Lord" will enter the kingdom of heaven, in a similar way the Magi do not represent all humanity. Nor do they simply represent the Gentiles. On some level they represent those who perceive who Jesus is and then respond with true worship in the giving of themselves. But even faith is a gift from God, so pray for the gift of faith that we might see Christ in the world in the most unlikely of places. Pray that we would ask questions not only with our intellect, but also with our perceptions and intuition and following those mysteries that guide us. Pray that we would seek knowledge that has a goal of receiving life and newness on many levels and not just the power or advantage that knowledge itself can sometimes bring.

Finally, the cosmic gift and learning is that there are more ways than we can ever imagine to travel once we have received God's gifts and offered our worship. God acts beyond our imagination. The delight of faith is not to presume we know what, through whom, where, or how things will happen. Faith is traveling wherever, resting in hope that it is God who is leading us, and our travels are not in vain.

Note

1. Walter Brueggemann, *To Build, to Plant: Jeremiah 26–52,* International Theological Commentary (Grand Rapids: Eerdmans, 1991), 61.

THE SEASON
OF EPIPHANY

KIM L. BECKMANN

Light was the subject of my first "All-School Theme Night" at my godsons' grade school. One February evening, the extended family was treated to artwork exuding light, skits about light, and experiments involving light that we could get our own hands into. We walked around light, all its dimension, all of its aspect, seen through the eyes and mediated through the imaginations of children and their teachers.

The season of Epiphany and the dimension of light is the winter-into-spring "all-school theme" of the year of grace. We are invited into the bright array produced by the art, lives, and experience of our ancestors in faith who, through a variety of media, grappled with the theme of revelation in the school of covenant life. In the texts of this season they leave behind these multifaceted testimonies to the evidence of God's grace for the world—a series of true stories revealing God's cosmic glory, sovereignty, and love—and the enfleshed shape it takes in our human space and time.

This season employs the rhetoric of revelation: prophecy, poetry, miracles, parables, autobiography, and wisdom—the literary arts of making known and revealing meaning through the power of images, insight, and the ordinary world of metaphor. Though we don't have any parables per se, Joseph Sittler once wondered if parables are simply spoken miracles, and miracles enacted parables.[1] In the Gospel stories of the wedding at Cana and the great catch of fish we are astonished by God's abundance. By keeping our eyes on our world, and that world which

55

is transformed by God and by Jesus' entry into its materiality, we come to know God and come to know our world as sacramentally blessed.

The readings of Transfiguration Sunday help us appreciate an indirect gaze upon and speech around God's glory. The rhetoric of revelation gives us a way of seeing what is not perceivable directly, and experiential grappling points for coming to some terms about what it means to say that Jesus, the chosen one of God, is the Savior of the world. In this way the season moves through texts full of luminous mysteries. They are shot through with light in a way that reveals without resolving a will and way of a God at once transcendent and immanent, disclosed and too wonderful to attain.

If this sounds a little dreamy, that may be just what's in order this season. Faith shaping—through sign, symbol, playfulness, and the power of metaphor as a way of knowing—aligns with what has been discovered about the human brain's wiring for insight and epiphany. Revelation and analysis register differently as a journey through cortical circuits. While we work our way through logic, possibly moving toward a solution, the brain is considering other options for us. When our mind unclenches, when we relax and let ourselves be taken on a journey out of environments that force us to produce . . . the breakthrough of insight may occur. Brain cells are actually changed in the moment of epiphany. "An insight is a restructuring of information—it's seeing the same old thing in a completely new way. Once that restructuring occurs, you never go back."[2] Scientists point to our drowsy alpha rhythm as we awake as a time when the brain gets unwound and becomes open to unconventional ideas. The dream state is a time for epiphany.

We explore dreams and awakening in the stories of the wise men and the disciples at the glory of the transfiguration. In biographical narratives, we learn something about God as God shines through the lives of our faithful ancestors.

Our Gospel readings reveal that marginality, liminality, and the sense of God's people being "at home" with themselves, their world, and God is not a settled affair.

We explore the nature of call in the vocation reports of Isaiah, Jeremiah, Nehemiah, Peter, Paul, and Jesus, as a portion of earthly reality makes a claim on them. We reflect on spiritual gifts and vocation in the body of Christ through Paul's letter to the Corinthians. We discover our individual and corporate calls through a sacramental life that recognizes both sanctuary and community as sacred space where God's hope for the world is revealed.

If metaphor is the primary language of insight and revelation because it "moves us," themes of Epiphany also include journey, itinerary, exile, displacement, diaspora, immigration, and restoration. Isaiah, Trito-Isaiah, Jeremiah, Nehemiah, psalmists, prophets, and historians of exilic and postexilic Israel explore these themes with us in the poetic prophetic. Our Gospel readings from Luke reveal that marginality, liminality, and the sense of God's people being "at home" with themselves, their world, and God is not a settled affair. Restoration remains elusive, with little agreement about whether the way home can be found through a return to ancestry, purity, and old programs or through some other new pathways and criteria for faithfulness. Jesus does little to settle the issue, but opens up and reveals an expansive, radical, and inclusive hope for the world and its salvation.

Epiphany is the season of glory. The Hebrew roots of the word *kabod* connote weight and mass. The costly, heavy, precious metals that are the accorded tribute of royalty gleam. The heavy-duty armor of kings and queens shines with fierce protection, strength, and might as part of that glory. Rich-woven robes, jewel-encrusted crowns, and other accoutrements of majesty and wealth hang heavy. Glory also suggests an ethical *gravitas* and relates to the weightier matters of justice. The righteous "shine like the sun." When we move into the New Testament and bring these aspects of glory into the word *doxa,* we gain the suggestion of the "weight of public opinion," a reputation that carries clout, the currency of praise. We begin to feel the weight of time for the blessed who enter eternal glory. The glory of the Lord may be related to light-producing phenomena of nature, such as thunder and lightning. Some references to the bright cloud may reference volcanic phenomena. With Moses, we discover that glory is what we see and experience of God, even as we never really experience *Godself,* the holy, holy, holy Yahweh of Isaiah's seraphs who remind us that the fullness of the entire world is God's glory.

Our first, responsive, and festival readings speak of creation as revelatory agent. The world as we know it tells us something about the unknowable God. Theologian George Tinker points out: "The imagery of divine rule in the Hebrew Scriptures is essentially creation imagery. That is, the ideal world symbolically represented in the Hebrew Bible builds on the divine origin of the cosmos as an ideal past and points to an ideal future. American Indian readers would assume that the ideal world is the real world of creation in an ideal relationship of harmony and balance with the creator."[3]

> We become more deeply aware in this season of a God who works through the rulers of nations, through social and political life, and the justice and righteousness that true worship calls forth through which the kingdom of God is revealed in Jesus.

We become more deeply aware in this season of a God who works through the rulers of nations, through social and political life, and the justice and righteousness that true worship calls forth through which the kingdom of God is revealed in Jesus. The themes of Epiphany give opportunity to be intentional in seeing these stories through the eyes and experiences of a multitude of cultures and peoples. Hebrew Bible scholar Hyun Chul Paul Kim gives us a small taste of what we can discover about God by seeing the world through the eyes of the nations:

In reading Isaiah, I am often reminded of my social history and location. As a Korean Christian, I recall the hardship Koreans had to endure during colonization and occupation in the first half of the twentieth century. One of Isaiah's theologically most difficult themes surfaces in the call narrative, when the prophet is ordered to harden the hearts of the people (6:10). The notion that YHWH would whistle to the northern army, sending it to invade YHWH's own people, does show that giant empires are mere tools of YHWH. However, it also presents the challenging question of *theodicy*. . . . Was Korea's hardship a divine chastisement? Was the imperial colonizer a divine instrument? If we turn to YHWH's divine pathos in rebuking the corrupt leaders and masses and listen to the brokenhearted, "Comfort, O comfort" (40:1), the text offers a profound message: Isaiah's God is neither immobilized by nor indifferent to historical and sociopolitical wrongdoings. This God does interrupt and disturb wrongful affairs with divine indignation. But if we carelessly moralize instead, applying this notion to the misfortunes of others, we fall into interpretive misuse.[4]

Our preaching lenses refocus in some life-giving ways when we conscientiously include lay members in our text study, gathering close to squint together for God's presence, and asking one another, "What do you see? What do you hear?" I give thanks to the pastor and people of Faith Lutheran Church in Homewood, Illinois, who gave me that opportunity over these texts. Other partners in enlightenment include friends and scholars, my partner in life and work Fred Kinsey, commentators published and unpublished, and now, all of you, who become the most important dialogue partners of all.

The priestly writers of Genesis teach that the stars are part of the sky lights that help us keep holy time and space. They don't give blazing light; they orient. The candles that grace our sanctuaries shine like Epiphany stars, guiding us to God's radiant love in Jesus. Christ's light is all around us, but if we're having trouble locating it, these sanctuary stars point us to altar, font, and word as places we will find God in Christ. May these stars guide you to worship, gift, and adore in your preaching vocation.

Notes

1. Joseph Sittler, "Moral Discourse in a Nuclear Age," in *Gravity and Grace: Reflections and Provocations*, Lutheran Voices (Minneapolis: Augsburg Fortress, 2005), 59.

2. Jonah Lehrer, quoting Earl Miller in "The Eureka Hunt," *The New Yorker*, July 28, 2008.

3. George Tinker, "The Bible as a Text in Cultures: Native Americans," in *The People's Bible: New Revised Standard Version with the Apocrypha*, ed. Curtiss Paul DeYoung et al. (Minneapolis: Fortress Press, 2009), 48.

4. Hyun Chul Paul Kim, "Isaiah," in ibid., 815.

EPIPHANY SUNDAY / EPIPHANY OF THE LORD

JANUARY 3/6, 2010

Revised Common (RCL)	Episcopal (BCP)	Roman Catholic (LFM)
Isa. 60:1-6	Isa. 60:1-6, 9	Isa. 60:1-6
Ps. 72:1-7, 10-14	Psalm 72 or 72:1-2, 10-17	Ps. 72:1-2, 7-8, 10-11, 12-13
Eph. 3:1-12	Eph. 3:1-12	Eph. 3:2-3a, 5-6
Matt. 2:1-12	Matt. 2:1-12	Matt. 2:1-12

A procession of stars dawns on our darkness, guiding the assembly to where our infant redeemer is laid. The eternal light hung in many sanctuaries is a constant star, drawing a people on the move into the mystery of God's presence tenting among us. The tabernacle light beckons us to worship and adore, and to ponder the mystery that our own hands may become the manger in which the Christ child is laid, perhaps a throne from which our king is pleased to reign.

FIRST READING

ISAIAH 60:1-6 (RCL, LFM)
ISAIAH 60:1-6, 9 (BCP)

"Bethlehem 2000" merchandise lay dusty in West Bank souvenir shops in January of 2005. Anticipated millennial-year tourists had never materialized amidst a worsening political climate and escalations of violence. Bethlehem had been all spiffed up for the arrival of the nations, the star a symbol of this initiative, but the gift shops had remained deserted.

I bought a camel figure from a sad-eyed Palestinian boy in the streets. Then I bought a whole caravan (apparently a lead donkey and three camels) from a thin man hawking them by our solitary tour bus. We had been discouraged from "encouraging" these vendors by our tour guides, who made dehumanizing analogies to feeding pigeons. But it was hard to resist the pleas of fathers who spoke of hungry children at home. It was hard not to notice the dust, disappointment, and desperation. It was hard not to connect with the hope that lit up these faces when we appeared. Perhaps they'd eat tonight. Perhaps tourism would pick up. Perhaps Americans could do something.

I ended up giving the lead donkey to my godson Joey. His brother Daniel probably got the sad-eyed boy's camel. I'm not sure where the rest of the caravan went, but when I presented the small gifts at bedtime we talked about caravans— the single files of pack animals, the merchants banded together to cross the desert with spices and treasures. In the morning, I noticed Joey had rearranged his bookcase. With the donkey proudly leading the pack, he'd lined up every animal in his room to form a stately caravan, switchbacking through the shelves. Plastic horses, stuffed bears, a wooden giraffe, a ceramic piggy bank, an onyx whale, all on an expectant single-filed upward march toward . . . something wonderful, surely.

The gloom is thick and deep in the opening verses of Isaiah 60. It covers the land, blankets the earth, enshrouds the people. Nobody knows when "the situation" will break. Those who remained through the privation of the exile, those who had come back to Jerusalem in the first wave of resettlement had . . . hopes. The hopes were fading fast as the anticipated stream of repatriates trickled. The economic outlook remained bleak. Rebuilding projects failed for lack of resources, but also for infighting about what kind of people of God they were called to reconstitute. The temple that would house God's glory, allow for God's own homecoming among them, clothe Israel with glory and prosperity, and so in turn glorify God to the nations . . . remained ruined. Is it always darkest just before the dawn?

"Arise! Shine! For your light is come!" Just the exclamation points will get you standing. Who wouldn't perk up? Put the dazzle on? At least look around a bit to see what all the fuss is about and sniff the wind for developments? The use of the feminine in these imperatives suggests it is Jerusalem itself getting this good news. So now imagine the very streets that had been forsaken, the walls that were rubble, the gates hanging useless off their hinges tingling with portent and possibility in this announcement. Imagine a collective upwelling, a single-filed movement in the direction of the light as the glory of the Lord rises.

As we lift our heads, as we ourselves become the beacon we seek, paradoxically ever more visible and welcome precisely because of the gloom, we see the salvation we have waited for coming. There they are! Our sons and daughters we thought would never come back. The life and hope and promise is right there on the horizon, cradled in arms, coming toward us! There are the caravans! There are those who will strengthen us, complete us. Our hearts enlarge and thrill to recognize these new kin. They are traveling with the wealth of all the nations. We are no longer covered in darkness. We are covered in camels! We are joining the procession of gifts to the altar, singing praise to God who breaks the darkness with light and the splendor of God's glory. We who were no people are brought into God's marvelous light, even as it comes to us and shines through us in those who arrive among us.

These feast-day texts set the stage for a season of Epiphany that recognizes we are people of God on the move. We consider Israel as journey as well as a people; diaspora fundamental to the church's nature. In these days of global migration, as millions are displaced, does the church of Christ migrate, and when it comes time for resettlement, resettle? We are a transient people here in the United States. Employment changes, natural disaster, urbanization, suburbanization, schooling—it's hard to build a stable church community on these shifting sands. How can we be more nimble and ready to mobilize? Can we be those in waiting as well as the caravan? What if those coming aren't the sons and daughters we expected? What if the ones returning are not the ones who left? What if the wealth of the nations *is* the nations?

> These feast-day texts set the stage for a season of Epiphany that recognizes we are people of God on the move.

The highest compliment to our congregation came from a woman who traveled much and worshiped only occasionally, whenever she dreamed of the Eucharist. She described the feeling she had coming up to our church doors as if she were on a hike in the woods and suddenly came upon an encampment of people along the trail! They were gladdened but not surprised to look up and see her. They smiled as though they were expecting people they didn't know, but were nevertheless one of them, to happen along. She was welcomed, for this portion of her journey, into the encampment. The people were relaxed and secure. They were happy to be camped together, to have come upon this gathering themselves, and in that joy shared a meal and whatever they had with others who came along.

That's my favorite description of the feel of our communities of faith. Provisional, always. Worship and other opportunities to gather, like an encampment. Looking up, to see who's coming, God's glory on the horizon. Our assembly ebbs and flows but has a core, a heart, a center, a hope—in Jesus, come to tent among us. There are dangers of a settled church in missing the promise of diaspora. At its best we are a sent people, as biblical scholar Francisco Lozada Jr. writes: "All diasporas are different, and every diaspora is poignant—but every diaspora also holds the possibility of leading new hybrid lives, filled with much hope."[1]

What is the good news for the sad-eyed boy on the street in Palestine and the merchants with dusty Bethlehem 2000 olivewood on their shelves, waiting for the restoration, for gates to open, the commerce to flow, the buses to roll, peace and prosperity to manifest? What is the good news for the lines of 1,500 job seekers in every American city waiting to apply for fifty positions? What is the good news for the lines for goods and services everywhere in war-torn countries? For hands outstretched at the food pantry while the newspaper takes to running

Great Depression images of bread lines? Or for our children at risk? Or for our aging congregations, still mourning for the glory days of robust Sunday schools and robed choirs? Or for the communities you serve? What is God up to? Where is God breaking through gloom, God's prophet announcing the wake-up call for us to sniff the wind, turn our heads, look for salvation, recognize true treasure? When and where will we stand up and shine for all to see as God's glory comes to us?

RESPONSIVE READING
PSALM 72:1-7, 10-14 (RCL)
PSALM 72 OR 72:1-2, 10-17 (BCP)
PSALM 72:1-2, 7-8, 10-11, 12-13 (LFM)

In this royal psalm, a king, the son of a king, is celebrated in the prayer and blessing of the people for a reign of shalom. This shalom integrates the full range of life's blessings, invoking a long-lived reign of wholeness in physical, spiritual, vocational, economic, and political well-being for all peoples and all creation.

SECOND READING
EPHESIANS 3:1-12 (RCL, BCP)
EPHESIANS 3:2-3A, 5-6 (LFM)

What I want you to know, says the writer of Ephesians, is something God knew all along but was hidden from former generations who hadn't yet seen the fulfillment of God's promises: Gentiles will be an inheritance with, a body with, and sharers with the promise in Christ Jesus through the gospel.

The claim that Gentiles are included in God's plan for salvation has lost its power to shock and bear the amazement of grace explored in these passages. When the council in Jerusalem meets with Peter to hear the account of the baptism of the Gentile Cornelius and his family you can almost feel the carpet burns. Now he'd gone and done it—made these unclean outsiders part of the new family in baptism without asking anyone if they could belong. These were people you couldn't even eat with, and now they were coming to dinner, part of the body, one with them. The dismay is palpable. This wasn't what they'd planned. Peter blames the Holy Spirit, who took it out of his hands, baptizing them practically before he could get a word out. "Remember what happened to us on Pentecost?" he says, "Well, I saw the same thing happen to them."

When the haggling starts about whether to let them in or not, and under what kind of cultural marks these Gentiles might need to conform to be incorporated, I always picture myself sitting in the inner circle of the council table as one of the deciders. The fact is, it's the other way around. We are the Gentiles. This is the moment that we, formerly unimaginable, unforeseen as part of God's apparently expansive and ongoing plan for salvation, got included in. Something totally new, an enlarging "with," is going to be taking place. The Spirit's action is good news for us, as revelation about what God continues to be up to. None of us are the deciders. God intends to bring all things together in Christ, through Christ's body. The readers of Ephesians would have known that community as the church, with Christ the exalted head. The church is God's plan both in its very existence, and in its ongoing life. The church is not meant to be static, but to hold a dynamic ethic toward growth, through Christ.

> The church is not meant to be static, but to hold a dynamic ethic toward growth, through Christ.

The writer of Ephesians calls this a mystery. While the word *mystery* is variously employed in the Epistles, in the letter to the Ephesians *mystery* refers to this intent of God's and the questions of unity that this joining "with" presents. Unlike the way *the body* will be used through many of this season's texts from 1 Corinthians to describe the diverse gifts necessary to make a local community work, in Ephesians "its vision of the church is set in the largest possible framework, the cosmic body of all the faithful united with its head, the risen Christ."[2] Throughout the letter, the body is described as growing into a sort of "new human being" and the gifts of this body literally incorporated into this "heavenly reality" rather than a local or even denominational vision of the church as "the agent through whom the growth takes place."[3] God has a plan to make salvation apparent even to the various powers of the universe, and we, quite collectively, are part of it through Christ, who was present at the creation. Those who are in Christ come to know each other as one clan. They hold this revelation: that everything comes together because one God has created everything.

You can almost feel the early church trying to figure this all out through their experiences. We can relate. It takes a lot of getting one's head around how God might dream this could work. Biblical scholar Pheme Perkins, quoted above, suggests the NRSV is limited by translating this as a cognitive task. "Getting people to see" the radically inclusive plan of the mystery isn't a cognitive act. It's not about changing minds (which usually creates heartburn) so much as it is about illumination that sets our hearts on fire. What it takes is Spirit-led imagination . . . a cognitive leap powered by eyes of the heart enlightened. It is such boldness and confidence won through faith that gives us access to God in revelation.

MATTHEW 2:1-12 (RCL, BCP, LFM)

Mikaela, six years old, colored stars through the entire service. Silver, gold, bronze, bright. That Epiphany was her first Sunday in worship, and the children were coloring stars to line the walls from the narthex to the altar. Mikaela didn't know much about church, but she knew her way around a Crayola box. She colored star after star. Concentrated, free to absorb whatever else was going on around her, I wondered how Mikaela's faith began to be formed, what she came to know of God, as she filled in the shape of these rays of light that dazzling January morning.

Dale had come to church Christmas and Easter, but truthfully found more of his communal and ceremonial groove as a volunteer fireman. Recently he'd had a dream, his wife told me, as she led me down the stairs to his workbench to show me something. In this dream, his sister-in-law, or perhaps God, told him to make crosses. So he did. Bird's-eye maple. Inlaid. Natural. Stained. Wall crosses. Altar crosses. He'd bring them up to her, one by one, and hold them out like a five-year-old with a creation to put on the refrigerator, or maybe like someone with an experience of God to share. "That's a great one!" she'd affirm. Back to work he would go. Dale wondered what this means, this shape that has taken such a powerful hold on him, come out of him, transfigured him. Revelation is still a journey, a leading we follow. He'd like to join a Bible study, maybe start coming to worship, explore the mystery of God who has come to him in the cross.

Though we have not yet gotten the Christmas tree down, the Epiphany texts already hint of passion. The wise men seek "the King of the Jews," which is the identity the governor questions Jesus about, the appellation Jesus is mocked with as rays of a thorny crown are beaten into his head with a scepter, and the title Matthew hangs above Jesus on Calvary.

Herod's own kingship was a bit shaky. He was an outlander from Edom, who had conquered his neighboring kin with the help of Rome. Though he outdid himself with magnificent public works projects, including renovation of the temple, he was bound to be resented by Judeans who wanted a king with Jewish blood who was not aligned with the occupying regime.

> The Magi may have been a little unsavory themselves—the same word is used in Acts for magicians and sorcerers.

Herod's rightful insecurity is exposed to almost comedic effect in the palace scramble when the three kings from the orient ring the doorbell one starry night, and, gifts in hand, ask where they can find the new king. Okay, so maybe the Magi weren't kings at all, but scholars, or astrologers, more of a priestly class of experts in the occult and interpretation of dreams. They may have been a little unsavory themselves—the same word is used in Acts for magicians and sorcerers.

In any event, the story has them cooling their heels in the foyer while Herod runs around trying to get a meeting with his own experts, the chief priests and scribes. Even that picture is striking—the chief priests who ruled the temple were related to the Sadducean party and the scribes tended to hang with the Pharisees, so all they had in common was their concern to keep the balance of power toward their own favor. Together they feverishly consult their scrolls and come to the conclusion: Bethlehem. A star rising out of Jacob. Herod sends the travelers on their way to a two-bit town in Judea. Whether he really expected a report back or not is debatable; he may have thought he knew enough.

At this point, beyond the hilarity, beneath the local politics serious enough to get all the under-two-year-old boys in the vicinity killed, there is an eye opener that should have been shaking their universe. The Sadducees and Pharisees coming together over the Torah, and the pagan astrologers reading a light in the sky, arrived at the same revelation. Now that's meant to tell us something new about Jesus the Christ, and what God is up to.

Would the star alone have gotten them all the way there? When the wise men resaddle their camels, the star stops and stays, and like a celestial GPS takes them directly to their destination. But as Matthew has it, these Gentiles now have not only natural revelation, but knowledge of Scripture to fill in the star's mystery with meaning. Divine comedy returns to the story as we feature the royal caravan pulling up majestically to the house of a peasant couple from Nazareth, ringing the doorbell, then worshiping and gifting an infant that few beside Mary and Joseph have been able to read as royalty, the sovereign God's own Word in the flesh. The three kings continue their sober obedience to the true king in a convicting dream.

> As Matthew has it, these Gentiles now have not only natural revelation, but knowledge of Scripture to fill in the star's mystery with meaning.

That Epiphany, Ed and Sarah, eighty years old, were ushers with a duty to take the offering. In a spirit of playfulness we had never seen in them before, they placed on their heads the Burger King crowns the acolytes had worn for the entrance procession of stars and kings and had left in the back of the church. Thus adorned, Ed and Sarah gathered the gifts of a startled and delighted congregation, and processed our gifts past crèche and font, to the cross-marked altar.

We begin the season with crowns and stars. Made kings and priests in our baptisms, we bear the light of Christ and make joyful offering of ourselves in a long processional journey. In the northern hemisphere, Epiphany is the season of photo-entropy. The sun, just returning in the twelve days of Christmas, grows stronger by the Transfiguration. Lent and its lengthening days are what we're headed for. We make the revealing turn from crèche toward cross . . . the way windowed tomato seedlings and sun-starved houseplants turn toward light. With Dale, we wonder. With Mikaela, we ponder. With Ed and Sarah, we joyfully engage the journey.

Notes

1. Francisco Lozada Jr., "The Bible as a Text in Cultures: Latinas/os," *The People's Bible: New Revised Standard Version with the Apocrypha*, ed. Curtiss Paul DeYoung, et al. (Minneapolis: Fortress Press, 2009), 43.

2. Pheme Perkins, *Ephesians*, New Interpreter's Bible Commentary (Nashville: Abingdon, 2000), 358, 410.

3. Ibid.

BAPTISM OF THE LORD

First Sunday after the Epiphany / First Sunday in Ordinary Time

January 10, 2010

Revised Common (RCL)	Episcopal (BCP)	Roman Catholic (LFM)
Isa. 43:1-7	Isa. 42:1-9	Isa. 40:1-5, 9-11
Psalm 29	Ps. 89:1-29 or 89:20-29	Ps. 104:1b-2, 3-4, 24-25, 27-28, 29b-30
Acts 8:14-17	Acts 10:34-38	Titus 2:11-14; 3:4-7
Luke 3:15-17, 21-22	Luke 3:15-16, 21-22	Luke 3:15-16, 21-22

The paschal candle rises over the baptismal font. By its light we see the fierce, tender love of God that calls out to us over the water, naming us sons and daughters. By its fire we enter the paschal mystery delivering us from sin, from death, and from the power of evil around us. At our baptism, our burial, and all remembrances of life and death in between, this light at the font helps us see our lives as coming from God and going to God. At evening prayer the Christ candle reminds us that God led Israel by pillars of cloud and fire dry-shod through the same Red Sea that drowned Pharaoh's army, into the wilderness, through the Jordan, to the freedom of the promised land.

First Reading

ISAIAH 43:1-7 (RCL)
ISAIAH 42:1-9 (BCP)
ISAIAH 40:1-5, 9-11 (LFM)

Lois politely let us get through almost an hour of the prebaptismal counseling for her three young adult sons and two preteen daughters before telling us about her brothers. That means we had gone through the whole spiel about the stories we tell of God's strong arm that had put boundaries on chaos, rescued God's people from a watery grave, renewed the earth, and drowned the wicked. We'd done the whole bit about drowning in the flood of baptismal waters, dying with Christ so we could be raised with Christ, reborn children of God forever.

That's when she finally told us she had a problem with all that imagery, what with her two brothers who had drowned in separate accidents on Lake Superior. This was a conversation we would have again, the night she called to tell me it had just come to her these drownings hadn't been accidents after all, but drunken misadventures that now struck her as casual suicides of meaninglessness. What could she do now with her life and work to redeem that tragic waste by leading others in a different path, all the children and youth she saw at risk? In many respects, she was far more comfortable with the smudging rituals of smoldering sweetgrass that had accompanied her Indian naming ceremony shortly after this realization. Restoring that part of herself that had been buried and shamed, she now took up work in her tribal community through Head Start programs.

Fire and water, generally speaking, is judgment language. But *now*, begins the salvation oracle in Isaiah 43, God is using these old, former things in saying something new. The oracle recalls Israel's birth experience, as well as the birth experience of the cosmos. This people is created and formed by God's own hand, just like the first human, in the calling and naming of Jacob/Israel, and now again in this calling by name. It was Egypt under judgment in the first exodus. The angel of death spared those with the lamb's blood on the lintel and Israel passed dry-shod through the same sea that drowned Pharaoh's army. Israel has subsequently experienced this judgment in the river of Assyria that swept up to their necks, though not over their heads. But now, as they journey back to the judgment-laden parched ruins of Jerusalem as a precious, honored, loved, redeemed, and ransomed people of exile gathered up from the four directions, welcome water will spring up for them in the desert. But it's costly. Biblical scholar Christopher Seitz explains it thus:

> This people is created and formed by God's own hand, just like the first human, in the calling and naming of Jacob/Israel, and now again in this calling by name.

> Israel's new life, its capacity to move through real fire and real tempest unharmed, costs something. God does not manipulate the created order and introduce entirely new categories—fireless existence. Rather, God redeems what God has made, and redemption involves an exchange within the created realm. A price is paid in order to set things back the way they were.[1]

Here it is nations in exchange for this nation. In Jesus, God offers the "great exchange," leaving the heavenly realm and taking on human form to redeem it by dying to make a way through death itself. In the baptism of water, John hints at the fire to come. The symbols remain ambivalent. The conditions of earthly existence are met; trials will come, but death won't have the last word.

Isaiah 43 was the liturgical accompaniment in the journey to the crematorium with my mother's body. A light sprinkle between the church doors and the hearse had taken care of the asperges. When we arrived at the mortuary, we opened the flimsy liner that had been in the rental casket. I'd put on her best striding boots, the ones that had always given her confidence for starting out the door. "When you pass through the waters, I'll be there. The flames will not set you ablaze," we read. I pressed the button myself to begin the cremation process, but the fiery sunset images with which they had adorned the furnace, meant to look warm and inviting, weren't comforting to me in the least. It all still takes a great deal of faith.

Christopher Seitz offers this intriguing perspective: fire and flame, God's own creation, are not hostile to God's rule but dispatched for them. Fire sent by God to punish is not now sent for that purpose, though it remains a trial. It is not removed from creation, just not now sent for judgment. So "how is this newly constituted people to know when adversity is sent in judgment or on our behalf?" Seitz posits. The answer: "because we have heard it from God." "To know that fire and flood are not acts of judgment entails a revelation, from God, to that effect; and with that comes the assurance of deliverance and protection."[2] After 9/11 folks flocked to church in an effort to discern the meaning of this catastrophe. 2010 marks the fifth anniversary of the overwhelming tsunami in South Asia. Hurricane and fire season will have passed for the year by this epiphany season, but these questions of "who and where God is" in the midst of violence, disaster, and tragedy are perennial.

> Fire sent by God to punish is not now sent for that purpose, though it remains a trial. It is not removed from creation, just not now sent for judgment.

Other lectionary selections for this day take on different aspects of this section of Isaiah. In *Reading Isaiah*, Edgar Conrad posits a restoration unity to the whole, representing the communal understanding of the survivors of the destruction of Jerusalem. They have the benefit of hindsight in moving forward. In this reading, all of these pericopes point to the role Judah/Israel shares as witness to God's plan to establish eternal sovereignty through the defeat of all the nations of the earth. In Isaiah 40, the judgment on Jerusalem has already occurred and they've received more than their share. They are to be comforted that their fight with the sovereign God is over. Now, as Babylon's fight begins, Israel takes up its role as witness to God's plan. In Isaiah 42, the servant receives this vocation. God has crushed the spirit out of these nations, but breathed God's own spirit of justice into the servant.[3]

Is the community of God's chosen this servant? Are the rhetorical questions omitted in the pericope God's continued vocational and catechetical schooling of those with a word to share about God's plan? Isaiah 43 reassures the servant sent in mission. On this day of God's revelation in baptism, particularly Jesus' baptism and identification as the Word with "the word," can we wrestle with these revelations of God, discernment of God's plan for the nations of the world, the nature and role of trial, our servanthood as witnesses? In claiming kinship through Jesus with all who have gone before us, can we see in their story our story, claiming strength for the journey into the future and God's "new things" because of what God has done for us in the past? Can we hear in this servant's commissioning our own commissioning? Does it sound both an individual and a communal note as we consider witness today?

Responsive Reading

PSALM 29 (RCL)
PSALM 89:1–29 or 89:20–29 (BCP)
PSALM 104:1b–2, 3–4, 24–25, 27–28, 29b–30 (LFM)

The "blow down," as they called it, became a windfall for the loggers. But in the moment, the straight-line winds had transformed a familiar forested stretch of the Net River properties into a disorienting woodpile. It was hard not to be in awe of the "voice of the Lord" that had broken the cedars and tossed them around like so many matchsticks. This reading of Psalm 29 aligns with the issues of sovereignty and the fearsome and awe-inspiring glory of the creator of the earth and its nations that we find elsewhere today. Psalm 89 works the themes of covenant and recalling to God the covenant promises made to the anointed king and chosen nation of God, as the nation of Israel comes to grips with the "blow down" of destruction and chastisement. Psalm 104 speaks to the cleansing force God's spirit provides within creation as a gift of renewal. Out of sorrow and penance, God brings new life. It is worth noting the environmental implications of acknowledging the interdependence of life—human and all created life—under God's authority and desire for shalom.

Second Reading

ACTS 8:14–17 (RCL)
ACTS 10:34–38 (BCP)
TITUS 2:11–14; 3:4–7 (LFM)

The pericopes from Acts snip doctrinal nuggets about baptism out of some very tempting blockbuster narratives! Philip's mission to "those beyond

Jerusalem" (i.e., the Samaritans) in Acts 8 includes the story of Simon the magician. Simon, in his attraction to signs and wonders, misreads the purpose of baptism and the priceless nature of the new life it means to bring, and he needs further instruction. The chapter continues with the mission to the "outcasts of Israel" in the story of an Ethiopian eunuch. The eunuch has been poring over Scripture. In the midst of Philip's instruction he experiences the sudden disappearance of any barriers that being a nonprocreating sexual minority might bring to his baptism and full acceptance into the community of the faithful and communion with God. The reading from Acts 10 breaks out of Israel altogether, teasing with just a few verses of the story of Peter's revelatory conversion on the Joppa rooftop and the beginning of mission with the once unclean Gentiles in the baptism of Cornelius. Gentiles remain Gentiles, eunuchs remain eunuchs, but the *believing* are newly drawn into the community of faith in the one body of Christ.

These three stories of powerful tradition-breaking openings to the gospel come courtesy of the Spirit and the sacrament of inclusion in God's household through baptism. They bear on this season's readings from Third Isaiah where God gathers the foreigners and outcasts. Jesus' own revelation of his mission picks up that same radically inclusive vision of restoration (see Epiphany 3). Religious, racial, and social walls and barriers built up over centuries crumble. Boundaries are redrawn expansively and citizenry in God's reign redefined. In wondrous, wild, and sometimes challenging ways to our dominant cultures and understandings, the Spirit of God is on the move to widen the circle, like the ripples that go out from the baptismal pool.

> These stories of powerful tradition-breaking openings to the gospel come courtesy of the Spirit and the sacrament of inclusion in God's household through baptism.

As read this Sunday, the Acts pericopes focus the importance of the Holy Spirit's work in baptism, the power of prayer, and healing that flows from Spirit-filled and prayerful living in Jesus' name. Luke brings "the church" into the story of the baptism of the Samaritans by calling Peter and John in to bring the Spirit through the laying on of hands and prayer following the baptism by water that Philip provides. We are cautioned not to read a baptism/confirmation split into this construct. Instead, we consider the gift that the community of prayer, and the power of the Spirit unleashed by fellow believers, bring to our common life for the transformation of lives and society.

Such is the thrust of the lectionary selection from Titus. Baptism is the sign of new life in Christ, renewal by the Spirit, and the revealed grace of God in Christ and in the lives of those joined to him. The verses from Titus also lodge in fuller context. Titus himself is a Gentile convert who sometimes accompanied Paul. The preceding verses exhort different groups to manifest the beauty of godliness, thereby attracting others to life in Christ. A quick tour of the Internet shows a number of homeschooling, home-keeping groups working under the title of Titus 2 to encourage Christian living, training, and mentoring in this vein. Grace, the revelation of the kindness and mercy of God and unmerited salvation in Christ, is both the transforming power and motivator for a life of love that begins now and is fully revealed in the life to come.

THE GOSPEL
LUKE 3:15-17, 21-22 (RCL)
LUKE 3:15-16, 21-22 (BCP, LFM)

The idea of having a baptism in the lake at our annual outdoor worship and church picnic had gone over easier than expected. Nobody blinked much at immersion: even little Eric, only six years enculturated in the wilderness of the Upper Peninsula, was able to articulate that God was in the water, that God had made the water, that his baptism in the lake would be like floating in God's belly just as he'd floated in his mom's. Plus, he loved swimming. So there was a surprising amount of joy involved in a way that I hadn't always experienced in the tense little groups around the silver-plated bowl at church.

We had given him a few choices. We could dunk him, or he could dive.

Like most six-year-olds, he wanted to do it himself. "Eric Mark is baptized in the name of the Father," we announced to the congregation perched on the slight rise above the lake, as well as the crowd gathered among other picnic-goers in this public space. Eric got ready to dive. He put his hands together to make the water-breaking wedge we learn when diving off the side of the pool . . . and also when we learn a more stylized version of prayerful hand-folding. He slipped into the water like a dolphin. Eric stayed under, floating in God's belly, until he couldn't hold his breath any longer and had to come out. He came up sputtering, gasping for air. "In the name of the Son." Once again we waited, while he lingered in a dead-man's float. Now, chest heaving, one more time, the prayer posture of baptismal readiness: "And in the name of the Holy Spirit."

The crowd cheered when he finally surfaced. A beach towel was draped around his shivering body. No lake is like bath water in the North Woods! But the little "Let your light so shine" candle, lit from the paschal flame borne by the acolyte from the shore out into the wavelets, seemed to warm him. Or at least it warmed us. We welcomed him into the Lord's family as God's own beloved child, to join us in bearing God's creative and redeeming word to all the world.

Such pictures of Jesus' baptism in the Jordan are so ingrained it might take us by surprise to note Luke's baptismal story is short on the water and long on the fire. It is after John's water baptism of Jesus and all the people, while Jesus was at prayer and "in Word" with God, that the heavens are opened and Jesus' baptism by the Spirit takes place. Unlike the Pentecost tongues of fire, it is in bodily, enfleshed form as a dove that the Spirit appears, while God fingers Jesus as the chosen one of God with whom God is pleased to dwell on earth.

Backing up to Advent sections of this chapter, we hear John's speech that neither the rights of birth nor the rite of new birth will ensure salvation. Bearing fruits of repentance in just living, turning toward the one to come in the Messiah of God, will keep us out of the winnowing fires of wasteful existence. It will also plunge us into the Spirit's baptismal fire that's none too safe, either. John, now in jail, proves it. These signs and revelations remain ambivalent for us. Is this our God of love who knit together all creation? What will being chosen by the Sovereign Creator do for us?

> Bearing fruits of repentance in just living, turning toward the one to come in the Messiah of God, will keep us out of the winnowing fires of wasteful existence.

God will offer these words of assurance and identity to Jesus and to us one more time at the transfiguration before the journey to Jerusalem's cross. Is this what is ahead?

Such pointing is the realm of prophets and of poets. T. S. Eliot captures baptismal fire's power and pain in this excerpt from "Little Gidding": "The dove descending breaks the air/With flame of incandescent terror."[4] Eliot composed this poem out of his experience as a nighttime fire watcher during the blitz of London. The descending dove he sees is inspired by incendiary dive bombers.

Eliot goes on to pose the dilemma for us in this way that's reminiscent of today's first reading: we're already in the fire, both hope and despair are contained in our choices about "fire," and we'll only be redeemed from fire's pain by fire. Eliot daringly names the "tormentor" in this dilemma: love.

The question is, can fire lead to something . . . . a fire of love and refining renunciation? Or the fire of death in wasteful violence and destruction? Napalm comes to mind for some of us. More of us are reminded of a perfectly blue "first day of school," when commercial airplanes dropped out of the sky as weapons of mass destruction. We've seen over and over the moment the fireball bloomed. What most networks spared us was the image of people, holding hands and clinging to one another as they jumped from the fire into the certain death below. What does the gift of Holy Fire bring to this moment? What does it reveal of God, and the love of God in human flesh?

We come again to Jesus' moment with God in prayer. Epiphany's revelation invites us to ponder our vocation: How will we draw near this love? What is the purpose of our lives? What value does this life have and how will we spend it? How can this be a moment of return and renewal in discovery? What is my role? Where is our common life involved?

Nathan Mitchell reflects on the Epiphany placement of this story of Jesus' baptism by John in the river Jordan:

> We are urged to move quickly beyond the intimate scene of Jesus' birth toward the more challenging vision of his baptism. In short, we are asked to move in the direction of life itself: from concern for intimacy to concern for community. A Christian parish becomes its best self when it accepts the challenge of community. The parish community, as the real expression of a local church, cannot limit its attention to the search for justice and intimacy among its own members. It must be prepared to take up the cross, standing against evil and injustice wherever they exist in the world. This may seem like a harsh message for the Christmas season, but in fact it is the church's message at all times, in all seasons. There is, ultimately, only one mystery Christians celebrate: the paschal mystery, Jesus' dying and rising in a new human community called "church."[5]

Notes

1. Christopher Seitz, *Isaiah 40–66*, The New Interpreter's Bible (Nashville: Abingdon, 2001), 381.

2. Ibid.

3. Edgar Conrad, *Reading Isaiah,* Overtures to Biblical Theology (Minneapolis: Fortress Press, 1991), 110.

4. T. S. Eliot, from "Little Gidding," in *Collected Poems, 1909–1962* (New York: Harcourt Brace, 1963), 207.

5. Nathan Mitchell, in *A Christmas Sourcebook*, ed. Mary Ann Simcoe (Chicago: Liturgy Training Publications, 1984), 144.

SECOND SUNDAY AFTER THE EPIPHANY

SECOND SUNDAY IN ORDINARY TIME
JANUARY 17, 2010

Revised Common (RCL)	Episcopal (BCP)	Roman Catholic (LFM)
Isa. 62:1-5	Isa. 62:1-5	Isa. 62:1-5
Ps. 36:5-10	Psalm 96 or 96:1-10	Ps. 96:1-2a, 2b-3, 7-8, 9-10
1 Cor. 12:1-11	1 Cor. 12:1-11	1 Cor. 12:4-11
John 2:1-11	John 2:1-11	John 2:1-11

Arms entwined, they drink from one another's cup. My beloved is mine and I am my beloved's. In the candlelight of the marriage feast, we can almost fathom the deep mystery of such a love where two remain even more wholly themselves as one. On Easter, we light the eucharistic lights from the paschal candle. We sing of the bees who have together made the wax that is the food for the flame, and of the light that does not diminish when it is shared. The altar lights guide us to such a place where God's love in Christ may be found and shared in abundance.

FIRST READING
ISAIAH 62:1-5 (RCL, BCP, LFM)

In Eugene Peterson's rendering, it is as if heaven and earth itself, the created universe and human creation, form a new creation in the light of God's unstoppable love for Israel:

> . . . *regarding Jerusalem, I can't hold my tongue,*
> *Until her righteousness blazes down like the sun*
> *and her salvation flames up like a torch.*

Transformed, Israel receives a brand new name!

> *No more will anyone call you Rejected,*
> *and your country will no more be called Ruined.*
> *You'll be called Hephzibah (My Delight)*
> *and your land Beulah (Married)*

Renewed and restored, Israel gets to start over again as a virgin! God has made public proclamation of this love! The watchers on the walls call God to remembrance, with no peace until God makes good on the engagement!

> *You'll be a stunning crown in the palm of God's hand,*
> *a jeweled gold cup held high in the hand of your God.*
> *Because God delights in you*
> *and your land will be like a wedding celebration.*

The story continues through verses 6–12. The promise is backed up by God's sworn oath and might. Watchers on the walls of God's fair city Jerusalem earlier derided for silence now boldly call on God to remember this passionate commitment. The land and its produce will no longer be allowed to be raped and plundered by any passing nation. Its grain will be eaten in praise of God and wine drinking will be regarded as a holy and sacred celebration. God forges a new relationship with the nations of the world and kingdoms of this earth in which Israel is honored. Indeed, paving stones need to be laid, rubble cleared off highways, the gates opened, and a welcome banner raised for the world leaders coming to see the glory God casts around Israel in a wedding embrace. So fling wide the gates, get ready for the open house, and

> *'Look! Your savior comes,*
> *ready to do what he said he'd do,*
> *prepared to complete what he promised.'[1]*

One wonders if you dare use this imagery of marriage anymore. Whenever these passages come up I try to hear them (and whatever I am going to extrapolate about God from them) from the point of view of young adults who, tick-tock-tick-tock, are agonized they will not find their life's mate. Or those damaged by love gone wrong in divorce and domestic violence. I squirm when I worship with my partnered gay friend denied this estate of matrimony in my state and in my church. According to the U.S. Census Bureau Fact Finder:

- 50 percent of all adult residents of the United States fifteen years old and up are unmarried
- 48 percent of all households are maintained by unmarried men and women
- 27 percent of those living in U.S. households live alone[2]

Then there is the curious language. One of my confirmands had never heard the word *bridegroom* before. Bride, sure. Groom, yes. But was a bridegroom some kind of gender-bend that allowed everyone equal opportunity to envision meeting their Beloved at the altar in Christ's marriage feast every Sunday, she wondered?

Women often have mixed feelings about being given a new name. Gender-role assumptions of the prophetic stream that metaphorically cast God in the role of male, Israel in the role of the female, are problematic. Can we use the exalted language of our pericope without bringing with it the baggage of the underlying characterization of God's sovereignty as male domination wreaking jealous violence and abuse in judgment against infidelity and exercise of human freedom? In this story, women are forced to "see it from his viewpoint" as just desserts. Men are punished and shamed by being cast as stripped and ravaged "women" chastened and humiliated by violent male power. After the violence, the wooing back begins.

> Gender-role assumptions of the prophetic stream that metaphorically cast God in the role of male, Israel in the role of the female, are problematic.

David Carr sees this depiction of lovemaking not as ecstasy and union, but passion and jealousy with long-lasting negative effects influencing human relationships and our understandings of gender, sexuality, spirituality, other people, and other faiths. In this extended metaphor of jealous exclusivity, "outsiders" are to be absorbed into the dominantly defined community or excluded as tempters to infidelity. Carr speaks to these malformations and the way forward. We can acknowledge the longing for deep connection as a powerful good, turned to separation and alienation by the brokenness of sin and the fear of loss of connection, going narratively back to the mutual desire and intimacy of Eden rooted in the freedom of fidelity.[3] Could looking forward to the cross also point to God's transformative, "ultimate end to violence"? Or, alternatively, to the cross ushering in a new relational covenant?

It's important to remember the language is not literally the relationship. If you are able to stick to *metaphor* and the ways the mutuality of human marriage relationship and erotic impulse to connection is both like and not like our relationship with God, responsibly address the culturally constructed gender assumptions and violence of patriarchal marriage, and straddle the delicate nuance of "created cocreator" relationship, the poetry may work. It also works well if, more broadly speaking, the metaphor of marriage leads us to expect *life*.

It's helpful to consider that this text comes from Third Isaiah. Most commentators date this poetry late into the restoration. God's hand had delivered Israel from captivity, but relatively few desired to uproot and return to the privations of the homeland. Jerusalem and its environs remained ravaged, its land barren, and national pride humiliated. Paul Hanson suggests that the inability to move forward reflects a huge rift within Israel.[4] Among other conflicts, one party of elite returnees were stumping for a repristinated holy city that had eradicated mixed marriages. Others, represented by Third Isaiah's voice or voices, heard a call to a radically open and inclusive mission to the outsider. In this time of rebuilding, God was doing a new thing that revisioned the law, putting out the welcome mat for others—more than just the children of Abraham—who had come to recognize the sovereign glory of God, thereby enriching all of Israel and increasing praise of Yahweh.

> God's hand had delivered Israel from captivity. But relatively few desired to uproot and return to the privations of the homeland.

Though there may have been disagreement about how to live together and achieve that peaceful and just future, there was also widespread disappointment that life was still so hard. By this time it had blossomed into doubt about God's power and resolve to deliver on the covenant promises. Had they been abandoned? Forgotten? The glorious future for Israel as the people of God that Second Isaiah had so poetically proclaimed had not materialized. Third Isaiah borrows deliberately from these phrases for our reading today to recast the vision and reinstill the strength of hope buoyed up by the remembrance that it is God who saves. God, their builder, brings life and reconstruction by binding Godself to the people and the land, in a ceremony to which the nations are invited.

The themes, then, are new creation, life, binding public covenant, abundance and fecundity, enlarged expectations . . . and delight. If heaven and earth itself can be joined in a common mission of bringing light, so can the relationship between God and God's people become one of union and desire aimed toward all the nations.

Responsive Reading
PSALM 36:5-10 (RCL)

Psalm 36 reinforces the first reading's themes. God's covenantal love is high as the heavens, deep as the sea. Under the canopy of its protection and the delight of its abundance, we clearly see the spring of all life.

PSALM 96 OR 96:1-10 (BCP)
PSALM 96:1-2A, 2B-3, 7-8, 9-10 (LFM)

Psalm 96 celebrates Yahweh's temple enthronement. Creation, Israel, all nations are called to sing praises. Themes of hope, encouragement, and faith once drawn for an exiled people far from the temple, wondering if God is far from them, are now applied to those who were returned but are nevertheless still awaiting restoration. "Lift Every Voice and Sing," written by African American poet James Weldon Johnson to commemorate Lincoln's birthday in 1900, will be sung by many today in celebration of Martin Luther King Jr.'s birthday. This hymn carries much of the same power of Psalm 96 as "new song," proclaiming the good news of God's establishment of justice awaiting fulfillment in heaven and on earth. Julian Bond wrote: "When people stand and sing it, you just feel a connectedness with the song with all the people who've sung it on numerous occasions happy and sad over the 100 years before."[5]

SECOND READING

1 CORINTHIANS 12:1-11 (RCL, BCP)
1 CORINTHIANS 12:4-11 (LFM)

"Spiritual gifts" is the third topic Paul addresses in response to the Corinthian community's questions about life together. Extending through 14:40, the passages about love at the "heart" of the segment inform the whole. Spiritual gifts are given to build up the community of Christ. Since it's the Holy Spirit doling them out for community wholesomeness, each is equally regarded. It's a potluck, if you will, where we don't want all desserts, all baked beans, or all pickles, so the Spirit personally ensures the food groups are covered.

In my daily work involving discernment of gifts for community leadership in gospel mission, our "catechism" goes like this:

Because of Christ, the world
Christ's extended arms call us to notice the neighbor in world awareness
Because of the world, vocation
The world calls out to our passions and gifts in service to the needs of the neighbor
Because of vocation, education
When the world God loves has called to us to serve our neighbor in a particular way we extend ourselves, becoming equipped for service

Our call from God doesn't come apart from our unique gifts: What do I like to do? What am I good at? What am I passionate about? What is needed in my community? How does my faith live and breathe every day?

Why is it that ordained ministry still seems the pinnacle of godly service? Though it's the doorman I pass on the way home from work who catches my preoccupied eyes and call me back to life by telling me to "have a good night," and the security guard who brings me to the new day by calling a "good morning" out of me, many people would not recognize this as a vocation or charism preferenced by God. What gifts have been preferenced in your community? Why? Which need lifting up? Today's epistle offers an opportunity to consider the gifts of the church as a community of believers gathered for edification and unleashed to bring life to all corners of the world through vocation as service to the neighbor.

The Gospel
JOHN 2:1-11 (RCL, BCP, LFM)

Water, wine, the wedding feast, brimming vessels poured out. The Gospel of John manages somehow to bear the load of the heaviest, richest tropes in literature and basic human experience and weave them in service to revelation of divine love and purpose so clear we can almost see to the bottom of the well.

In early church practice, the wedding at Cana story was read on the Feast of the Epiphany. It's possible that this appointment was a deliberate reframing of the legend of Dionysus, whose presence was manifested by a bubbling spring of wine bringing intoxication that led to . . . um, life. Picture today's sparkling champagne fountains. Or rivers of flowing chocolate and the perfect strawberry thrust into the stream with anticipatory delight of the mingled flavors overcoming the terror of dark, rich chocolate dribbles on your wedding finery. Picture the ancient biblical promise of the feast that marks the day of the Lord, a feast of fat things and wine on the lees well refined. Or water gushing from the rock.

In Eastern traditions, water is often blessed as part of the Christmas/Epiphany feast recalling Jesus' baptism. A bit of liturgical poetry captures the rich swirl of images around this first of the signs following Jesus' baptism, dreamily and unashamedly bringing the elements together as if they themselves were the gifts of this day of revelation:

> *Today the bridegroom claims his bride, the church,*
> *since Christ has washed away her sins in Jordan's waters;*

the magi hasten with their gifts to the Royal wedding;
and the wedding guests rejoice,
for Christ has changed water into wine, Alleluia![6]

KIM L. BECKMANN

Oh, that I was this poet, or a storyteller like John. Oh, that I was as accomplished as they in the rhetoric of revelation that understands how metaphor and poetry reveal the new truth not by explaining it, but by describing it in terms of like and not like. The reign of God is among us but not fully, in the clarity of that half-waking dream that seems so real but doesn't cohere when we try to make it conform to human existence bound by finitude, time, and space.

Homiletician David Schlafer offers a helpful tool when considering a rhetorical vehicle for our Sunday revelations. He suggests there are three basic sermon strategies: image, story, and idea. A sermon that will primarily employ a story, for instance, will often use images or ideas in service to the story. But the vehicle remains primarily a story.[7]

> The reign of God is among us but not fully, in the clarity of that half-waking dream that seems so real but doesn't cohere when we try to make it conform to human existence bound by finitude, time, and space.

Raymond Brown suggests we apprehend the wedding at Cana best when we understand John's primary motives that all these rich motifs and allusions serve. The primary emphasis is the revelation of the person of Jesus. Jesus is the one sent by God to bring salvation to the world. This is a story about his glory, the weighty splendor of God, and the disciples whose call is completed in their belief. Jesus himself is the real temple, replacing the motif of the feasts celebrated in Jerusalem. He is the sacrifice of God to end all sacrifice. The Spirit that Jesus gives replaces the necessity of worshiping at Jerusalem. God has done a new thing.[8]

This news will be shared with the Samaritan woman at the well who thirsts for living waters. The Samaritans and other people of the land who honored Yahweh, for whose inclusion Third Isaiah called, had been excluded from the worship in Jerusalem. The restoration that eluded Israel is effected in Jesus. The stone jars for purification have been empty, dry. In Jesus, they are filled to the brim with water that becomes the finest of wines and all that wine represents. Paired with the multiplication of loaves, this story can take on eucharistic overtones and the abundant life that Jesus' life for us, and our thanksgiving to God for that life, represents. The day is now but the hour is not yet. The hour in John always relates to the glory of God in a weighty sovereignty revealed on the cross, beginning with the lifting up of bread and wine. Each of the signs in John offers a preview; this is the first. It is the Lamb of God that will take away the sin of the world, and we are caught up in the delight of the marriage feast of God's Lamb. This transformation is indeed a luminous mystery whose bottom line is life.

Can the wedding feast, like the marriage, continue to be a useful image and symbol in revealing the God of life whose salvation in Christ brings life to the world, and of this life to which we are called in Jesus? I asked my gay and single young adult friends what I should do about marriage and weddings in my preaching. A common theme seemed to be fresh insight and excitement about the binding power of covenant they have experienced in interfaith, especially Jewish-Christian, weddings. The publicly attested promise of the signing of the Ketubah, and the visible beauty intrinsic to this contract, has been a powerful revelatory and celebratory act. Granted, the legal ceremony was often held elsewhere since it was difficult to get clergy to perform such a service jointly. But the possibility that God can join us across racial, family, and faith lines, witnessing this inclusive and expanding power of love, has resonated in ways that deeply touch their universal understandings of their place in the world.

Public promises are strong and necessary, they assert. Marriage is not just about what you do in the privacy of your own home. Our life in God and the covenant of love is not a private affair, either. We know this is true in the sign and sacramentally transforming reality of baptismal incorporation into the body of Christ. This leap of faithful belief in the power of promises made within the circle of God's covenantal promise to us and for the love of the world completes our calling as disciples of Jesus.

The Bible study group at Faith, Homewood, was also upbeat when asked to name the first thing that came to mind when I said the word *wedding*. The words and phrases characterized deep hope, faith, and joy in the possibility of new life.

> When asked to look at the story through the lens of a worker, they picked the servants. That much water would have taken a long time to draw, and been incredibly heavy. One woman was struck by the compliance of these servants, on the strength of Mary's order to do whatever Jesus told them to do, even when it turned out to be such a laborious task. "This is what Jesus asked of them, even if it required heavy lifting. But along with the disciples who believed, it was they who were privileged to see the glory of God! Not the wine steward. Not the bridegroom. Not the guests. They may have enjoyed the fruits. But these workers, working together, were brought into the miracle. It reminds me of the shepherds in Luke. God picked simple shepherds to be among the first to know what God had done in Jesus. When I think about what this means in terms of the heavy lifting of my work, my relationships, and even, frankly, my church life, I'm so blown away by this glimpse of Jesus, and so mindful of how drably dutiful I've felt about such a gift."

We explored the usual questions about Mary and her role. "What I think it means to have Mary in this story," one participant said, "is the role we have in bringing God's intent for new life to birth. Mary brings Jesus to birth and brings him out into the world. Now that he's out there, she forces the issue of his life! What is my role in bringing the birth of God to the world? We often don't feel our hour has come."

The place this story lives in their community is the Dairy Queen. "We wait through the winter for the spring opening with such longing and desire we can taste it. When the day comes, life comes back to Homewood! The whole community turns out and gets reacquainted. Dairy Queen gives away ice cream, and it's always the best ice cream of the season!"

These metaphors of marriages and wedding feasts seek to reveal that God's intent for us and for the world is life. Life comes to us now in Jesus, sent for the salvation of the world, who died on the cross and rose again to lead us in grace and faithfulness to joyful and abundant life with God forever. In these stories of abundance, celebration, and transformation, God is the great giver; all flowing from the gift of life.

> These metaphors of marriages and wedding feasts seek to reveal that God's intent for us and for the world is life.

Notes

1. Eugene Peterson, *The Message* (Colorado Springs: NavPress, 2002), 1330–331.

2. See http://factfinder.census.gov, tabs on people/households, accessed December 1, 2008.

3. David Carr, *The Erotic Word: Sexuality, Spirituality and the Bible* (New York: Oxford University Press, 2003), 75–86.

4. Paul Hanson, *Isaiah 40–66*, Interpretation: A Bible Commentary for Teaching and Preaching (Louisville: John Knox, 1995), 186.

5. Julian Bond, http://www/npr.org/programs/morning/features/patc/lift-voice, accessed November 30, 2008.

6. Morning Prayer for Epiphany in *A Christmas Sourcebook*, ed. Mary Ann Simcoe (Chicago: Liturgy Training Publications), 107.

7. David J. Schlafer, *Playing with Fire: Preaching Work as Kindling Art* (Cambridge, Mass.: Cowley, 2004), 60–69.

8. Raymond Brown, *The Gospel According to John I–XII*, The Anchor Bible (New York: Doubleday, 1984), 103–10.

THIRD SUNDAY AFTER THE EPIPHANY

THIRD SUNDAY IN ORDINARY TIME
JANUARY 24, 2010

Revised Common (RCL)	Episcopal (BCP)	Roman Catholic (LFM)
Neh. 8:1-3, 5-6, 8-10	Neh. 8:2-10	Neh. 8:2-4a, 5-6, 8-10
Psalm 19	Psalm 113	Ps. 19:8, 9, 10, 15
1 Cor. 12:12-31a	1 Cor. 12:12-27	1 Cor. 12:12-30 or
		12:12-14, 27
Luke 4:14-21	Luke 4:14-21	Luke 1:1-4; 4:14-21

A pair of torches flank the reading desk. They illuminate the word of Scripture, made translucent to us in joyful faith. Here, we come to see and know God and God's will as a steadfast, liberating love for our lives.

FIRST READING
NEHEMIAH 8:1-3, 5-6, 8-10 (RCL)
NEHEMIAH 8:2-10 (BCP)
NEHEMIAH 8:2-4A, 5-6, 8-10 (LFM)

The name Nehemiah means "Yahweh has given comfort." Theologically speaking, God paves the way to restoration in Nehemiah's story.

A cupbearer (or, as a slip of letters in the Septuagint would have it, a eunuch) for the Persian king Artaxerxes, Nehemiah was so overcome with grief over disrepair in Jerusalem that he got his boss to release him to rebuild the walls. He even talked Artaxerxes out of a bunch of royal timber to restore the gates.

By all accounts, Nehemiah was a gifted community organizer. Upon arrival as governor of Judah, he employed effective political strategies and rallied returnees to overcome the resistance of the Samaritans and other people of the land. He encouraged action meetings and used power to gain distributive justice for farmers (including women left behind to tend farms) exploited by the upper class. He agitated and inspired workers tired of picking through rubble. The gates were hung and Jerusalem "secure" within fifty-two days.

Any good organizer celebrates success and delivers public agreements. The timing of the Water Gate festival of the law after the delineation and securing of the boundaries of the holy city makes perfect sense. However, chapters 8–10 from which today's reading is drawn are not considered part of Nehemiah's memoir, but a continuation of the story of Ezra the priest. Nehemiah's role is probably a scribal insertion. Placed after the same list of returnees found after the rededication of the altar in Ezra 2, we are to note *which* community has restored the temple, built these walls, and is now gathering to hear the law of God and pledge covenental response. These three chapters illustrate the ideal response to the law: reading of the law, confession of sin, the firm agreement.[1] This is the way back home.

It was the congregation as "one man" who hungered for this revelation of God and God's will for their lives. They invited Ezra to read the Torah on the new moon of the new year. The meeting was held outside the temple area. Lay as well as clergy, women as well as men, were able to attend. Children may have been present—"all who could understand"—though interpreting this as a function of age or as ability to understand Hebrew is disputed. Elements of posture, response, and ordo may indicate the rudiments of synagogue worship we'll experience in today's Gospel.

Thirteen laypersons flank Ezra in the "pulpit" area to assist in the reading. Verses 4 and 7 containing their names are commonly omitted, which is lucky for today's lector, if unfortunate for underlining the importance of *all* gifts in the second reading. Levites came into the people's midst, met them where they were, and effected understanding. The reading lasted six hours and those who had invited this word listened with rapt attention throughout. *(You're permitted a heavy sigh here!)*

Did the Levites translate from Hebrew to a more familiar Aramaic, paraphrase for simplicity, or even interpret? We don't know whether the Law of Moses represented the Pentateuch, nor, since six hours would not have sufficed, what was read. Some of the trees from which they are to gather branches (olive and myrtle) for Tabernacles are not among those in Leviticus, though they are presented as "what is written."[2]

> The people respond with weeping, but are instructed to cease. The sweetness of the Law is cause for celebration and the relinquishing of any bitterness.

This small point argues against a "fixed" interpretation of the law, and toward the freshness of the word for changing contexts that will open us to Jesus' reading and interpretation of Isaiah in our Gospel.

The people respond with weeping, but are instructed to cease. The sweetness of the Law is cause for celebration and the relinquishing of any bitterness. As physical and spiritual walls have been restored, "the joy of the LORD is our strength." The encounter with holiness sets the day apart for generous feasting, though it's unclear whether this sharing is only for community members or for-eigners as well.

Themes for preaching explore the relationship between religious reform and political, social, and economic reconstruction, perhaps through faith and congre-gation-based community organizing. Many organizations today bear Nehemiah's name. This passage explores lay initiative, desire for the word, and the importance of lay and clergy working together in worship, Bible study, and generous living. Fresh interpretation and contextualization of a living word is key.

But any time I read about walls and gates these days I want to look deeper. When we examine "the community" that had built the wall and restored the temple gathered to hear and covenant with the law, we find it is the community of those able to establish lineage through the genealogies of those taken into exile who in the first place had been priestly families and Judean aristocracy. The "peas-ants" (Samaritans) left behind constitute the enemies of resistance to rebuilding that would allow priests and other elites to coordinate and reestablish their control over the land based on holiness codes, ritual and ethnic purity and purging, and the raising of children who understood Hebrew. "We didn't cross the border, the border crossed us," comes to mind as we consider walls at our own borders and the very present struggles regarding immigration. It's hard not to conjure the separation wall in today's Jerusalem.

Commentators believe Nehemiah's security was meant to prevent exter-nal threats, not impurity. With walls that could open and close, Sabbath cessa-tion of trade could be enforced and the marked character of Sabbath-keeping identity reinforced. The walls also separated Judah socially from her neighbors. Jewish marriages may have broken up to forge alliances with landholders who had not been exiled. Ezra required Jews to divorce and expel foreign wives and renounce those children. Nehemiah warned against the dangers of mixed mar-riages, enforced written covenants allowing for existing marriages, but forbade these alliances in the next generation, keeping property, kinship, and temple membership rights within the group. Families were divided. There is the religious ideology of restoring a holy covenant with Yahweh, but the story is complicated, as it always is, by fears for survival and alienating the empire and desires to control land, fertility, and economy.

Ched Myers and Clinton Hammock give alternative readings to the prevailing tradition defining the restoration of the Judean community and interpretation of God's will in the law as a closed society.[3] They propose a contemporaneous Isaiah 56:1-6 presenting a radically inclusive (and ultimately losing) viewpoint. Here, the Jerusalem Temple is meant to be a "world house," a home and house of prayer for all peoples. While every society draws boundaries, Isaiah's "wall" is not based on religious/national, ethnic, or cultic purity, but on ethical behavior and justice: obeying Torah, keeping a generous Sabbath, turning away from evil. As an example of how far God goes toward full inclusion, eunuchs (who may more broadly represent sexual minorities) and foreigners—anyone whose bodily identity has previously excluded them on the basis of race, ethnicity, or ability to procreate—are welcome members. Myers lifts up two Americas: rich and poor, inclusion and exclusion, one of which is honored in "liberty and justice for all" and "embodied whenever Indian treaties were honored, and in the embrace of civil rights, women's suffrage, or child labor laws"; the other exemplified by "a Constitution that originally enfranchised only white landed males" with conflict between the two erupting today in immigration issues. Where does the church locate itself?

> Isaiah's "wall" is not based on religious/national, ethnic, or cultic purity, but on ethical behavior and justice: obeying Torah, keeping a generous Sabbath, turning away from evil.

It is from Third Isaiah that Jesus will read in our Gospel lesson. Which structures are worth building? Which walls need to be dismantled? Who defines the conversation or writes law on who is inside and who is outside the boundary? Could a fresh word on God's rule for our lives today include the perspective represented by Isaiah 56?

RESPONSIVE READING
PSALM 19 (RCL)
PSALM 19:8, 9, 10, 15 (LFM)

That Easter Sunday I answered nature's call. You know how it is: special music, twenty miles between churches, next crowd already waiting for the Alleluia to come out of the box. I got it all rolling and discretely opened the door off the sacristy to make an exit. Inside, the congregation was belting out *Gloria*: "Sing with all the people of God and join the hymn of all creation." Overhead, an endless wedge of geese honked spring's call to new life. That's Psalm 19. The liturgy of universe and sanctuary echo one another. This song is ongoing, dynamic, relational; connected to the source of all life. Revelation is open to anyone with a wonder of God's glory.

PSALM 113 (BCP)

Psalm 113 is a *hallel* psalm. We may imagine responses pilgrims shout out to the questions posed by the psalmist, and prompt them ourselves! God sits enthroned over all, but cares for the seatless/homeless, scorned, and cursed.

1 CORINTHIANS 12:12-31A (RCL)
1 CORINTHIANS 12:12-27 (BCP)
1 CORINTHIANS 12:12-30 OR
12:12-14, 27 (LFM)

Were you a head, a foot, or a hand? No doubt you can recall a sermon or program that placed your gifts within the community of Christ. The immediacy with which even a child can relate the working of his or her body to the mechanism of community in this metaphor/parable of the body of Christ has made this passage revelatory and memorable for two thousand years.

This figure was popular in Paul's day to describe the body politic. Its roots lie in fables about the stomach and the foot. Complaints were lodged that the belly pleased itself while the rest of the body worked. Where in other segments of the letter Paul reproves the proud and privileged, here he also chides those who withdraw out of a sense of inferiority. The failing would be dissociating in either extreme. The moral is that the body doesn't get far without the nourishment the belly provides, but the belly needs the foot to get to the food. Or, we are members, one of another.

> Where in other segments of the letter Paul reproves the proud and privileged, here he also chides those who withdraw out of a sense of inferiority.

Paul's twist is explicitly sacramental. While at times he uses body as a literary device to help us understand what it's *like* to be in a body of Christ, verse 12b asserts as fact the mystery that in baptism we *are* the one body of Christ.[4] Our differences remain and enhance our community, but in the gift of baptism our story—specifically our story of salvation—becomes the same. We have been made to drink of one Spirit that joins us as one with Christ. We've been thinking water, and now we suddenly recall what it is to be joined shoulder to shoulder at the Lord's table. Augustine put it this way:

> If you want to understand the body of Christ, listen to the apostle telling the faithful, 'You, though, are the body of Christ and its members' (1 Cor. 12:27). So if it's you that are the body of Christ and its members, it's the mystery meaning you that has been placed on the Lord's table; what you receive is the mystery that means you. It is to what you are that you reply 'Amen.' So be a member of the body of Christ, in order to make that 'Amen' true.[5]

The remaining verses help us understand what it is to be that Eucharist in the world. The body of Christ sent forth from the mass, as retired Archbishop Weakland and Bishop Sklba proclaimed in the Jubilee year pastoral letter of 2000, is a "Eucharist without walls":

> We yearn for the day when all will be one in the Eucharistic Lord. Until then, we are anointed through confirmation to bring the fruits of the Eucharist into the world around us, making Christ's presence real to others. Those fruits are seen in our loving service of others, sharing Christ's healing and nurturing presence through reaching out in love and generosity. . . . The challenge of our generation is to reflect more and more on how Christians, those who live in Christ's Eucharistic presence, are to bring that presence into the work they do. Our lives must be integrated in Christ.[6]

THE GOSPEL

LUKE 4:14-21 (RCL, BCP)
LUKE 1:1-4; 4:14-21 (LFM)

Jesus comes home. One way of approaching Luke's account of Jesus' life is around identity: Who is this Jesus? What's he about? The annunciation gets us started in Galilee. The presentation tells us of his parents' piety and his messianic identity, and the story of young Jesus in the temple tells us of his family business of God-revealing. In baptism, Spirit and Voice mystically claim paternity. A genealogy roots Jesus in a common human history that goes back to genesis in God. In the desert, Satan tests divine sonship against human nature. Then, of an age to be considered his own man, Jesus comes home.

Nazareth of Jesus' time wasn't much. John Dominic Crossan and Jonathan L. Reed indicate a Jewish settlement of two to four hundred villagers, representing perhaps a dozen extended families, somewhat off the beaten track in a bowl in the Nazareth hills ideally situated for agriculture. Jesus grew up amidst the vineyards, olive trees, grain fields, figs and pomegranates featured in his teaching. A well bubbled up and meandered through the village. The famous grotto of Mary may point to "semi-troglodyte dwellings" of the residents of Nazareth.[7]

In Luke's Gospel the poor represent all the marginalized. Jesus proclaims the release of the captive, exile over at last.

There is no archaeological evidence of any public architecture in Nazareth of Jesus' day. Crossan and Reed consider a synagogue as more likely a gathering than a building. They argue against the likelihood that the peasant community at Nazareth had an elaborate ritual structure, scrolls, or anybody who could read them, including Jesus.[8] Is Luke simply contextualizing based on his own literate, urban experience? How would imaging Jesus as a second-class citizen with no formal studies change the picture for those hearing this word in your context?

In any event, Luke's details make this a profound occasion. Regional buzz culminates in this moment when the hometown son steps over the threshold of being the kid who grew up in this worshiping community to being the person who stands up with the authority of the word. What text will he bring? Luke's Jesus finds what he wants to tell them about himself, and what time it is in God's plan for salvation, in Third Isaiah.

Jesus brings the word, and interprets it in the midst of the people: today, this Scripture is fulfilled in your hearing. He *is* the interpretation; the time is now. God is at home in them. He is the anointed servant, set apart for special service by the Spirit of God, as kings, priests, and prophets were anointed. This might have been news to those gathered in Nazareth who thought the time of God's prophets must be over. The word *Messiah*, anointed one of God who would bring in the kingdom, wasn't being uttered yet, by the crowd at least, but possibly that is what the electricity of the room was all about, possibly what Jesus meant when he proclaimed his vocation.

Jesus sings Isaiah's song of good news for the poor, in the key of his mother Mary of Nazareth. In Luke's Gospel the poor represent all the marginalized. Jesus proclaims the release of the captive, exile over at last. Though Israel had returned from Babylon, it had never felt at home. Was it because of the repristination efforts themselves? Or because those efforts to live in the law failed? In Jesus, God's rule is among them. Debts are canceled, sins forgiven, and the people are restored, at home with the covenant God. The proclamation of recovery of sight to those who are blind bears the good news of healing, and may carry overtones of overcoming barriers to full inclusion in the temple. In restoring this one "part" of the body, Jesus was healing the whole community of Israel and reconstituting it as the people of God. Open your eyes and see!

Virgilio Elizondo, reflecting on the experience of Mexican Americans as rejected *mestizos,* sees Jesus the Galilean Jew as a "reject who rejected rejection." Societal norming based on purity of one sort or another is revealed as disabling blindness here in Jesus' own person when he fulfills this scripture. Jesus, a mixed boundary person, finds his home and center in intimacy with God, the *abba*, the "one absolute" who at his baptism has bestowed "the dignity, confidence, security, docility, and self-respect" out of which Jesus exercises authority. He invites diverse hearers into deep trust in "*our abba*" as the homing center, finding these a freedom to treat all with fundamental dignity and healing acceptance.

> God is revealed in choosing the poor and marginalized—not to stay that way, but to become in themselves agents of new creation.

God comes to us in Jesus, the Jew from Nazareth, a day-laborer's son—not the son of a Pharisee, a priest, the royals, the military, or the intellectual elite of his day. God is revealed in choosing the poor and marginalized—not to stay that way, but to become in themselves agents of new creation. The church is invited into this healing when it challenges social norms of acceptability based on wealth, power, and prestige, and by living this way "tells the poor they are beautiful, desirable and worthy of respect."[9] Restoration, home-coming, is living out God's intention to restore the dignity of all created beings in the face of dominant culture's tendency to deny worth, draw exclusive boundaries, and put up walls to protect power.

Jesus proclaims jubilee—the year of the Lord's favor. As the response of those in Nehemiah 8:8 had been to "share the wealth" and feast on the goodness of life in God, he will eat with sinners, break simple bread in abundance for a crowd, and engage the wealthy at private dinner parties. Jesus demonstrates what it means to live as though jubilee is here, fully himself, freely mixing with all sorts, and disregarding society's standards for belonging. Finally, because we know

> Jesus demonstrates what it means to live as though jubilee is here, fully himself, freely mixing with all sorts, and disregarding society's standards for belonging.

what's coming, we know that just as he *is* the interpretation of this controversial vision of Third Isaiah, he is also truly to become the Feast and Jubilee.

Is the prophetic age over in Jesus? Our second reading lists prophets among leaders for whom God has given charismatic gifts for the church. Where are these gifts encouraged and nurtured within our assemblies and among those whose vocations in community, family, and work give opportunity for proclaiming and enacting justice for the poor, and the release of jubilee as though the time of God's favor is now?

Martin Luther King Jr. lifts up the prophetic nature of our Sunday work with the same Isaian text:

> Who is it that is supposed to articulate the longings and aspirations of the people more than the preacher? Somehow the preacher must be an Amos, and say, 'Let justice roll down like waters and righteousness like a mighty stream.' Somehow, the preacher must say with Jesus, 'The spirit of the Lord is upon me, because he hath anointed me to deal with the problems of the poor . . .' Well, I don't know what will happen now. We've got some difficult days ahead. But it doesn't matter with me now. Because I've been to the mountaintop. And I've seen the promised land. Mine eyes have seen the glory of the coming of the Lord.[10]

From my view in the pew, the candlelight opening our eyes to the word at the reading desk is noticeable, though cool and distant as stars in a night sky. But something happened at church the other day. The torches accompanied the procession of the Gospel. My heart beat faster as their flames came into our midst with the word. The preacher was getting into the reading. He lifted his arms in praise and articulation and didn't remember the torches and the generous cut of his robes. We all saw him getting alarmingly close to the danger zone of preacher flambé. We all held our breaths. Just as someone made a move to pull him out of harm's way, he lowered his arms and announced: "This is the Gospel of the Lord." We fervently exhaled: "Praise to you, Lord Jesus Christ!" The word of God that has come to us is incendiary. The word of God is not symbolic, not decorative, not safe, but life and light giving fire. When was the last time you experienced it that way? Where has connecting with the longings of the people, the problems of the poor, and the justice and righteousness that shines like glory gotten you so close you played with fire and your people flared up with gospel life?

Notes

1. Ralph Klein, *Nehemiah*, New Interpreter's Bible (Nashville: Abingdon, 1999), 797.

2. Ibid, 802.

3. Ched Myers, "A House for ALL Peoples?" *Sojourners* (April 2006); Clinton E. Hammock, "Isaiah 56:1-8 and the Redefining of the Restoration Judean Community," *Biblical Theology Bulletin* (June 22, 2000).

4. Hans Conzelmann, *1 Corinthians*, Hermeneia (Philadelphia: Fortress Press, 1975), 211.

5. Augustine, Sermon 272, quoted in Gail Ramshaw, *Treasures Old and New: Images in the Lectionary* (Minneapolis: Fortress Press, 2002), 71.

6. Rembert Weakland and Richard Sklba, *Eucharist Without Walls,* Archdiocese of Milwaukee, 1997.

7. John Dominic Crossan and Jonathan L. Reed, *Excavating Jesus: Beneath the Stones, Behind the Texts* (San Francisco: HarperSanFrancisco, 2001), 31–35.

8. Ibid, 30.

9. Virgilio Elizondo, *Galilean Journey: The Mexican American Promise* (Maryknoll, N.Y.: Orbis, 1983), 58–64, 71, 93, 100.

10. Martin Luther King Jr., "I See the Promised Land," in *A Testament of Hope: The Essential Writings of Martin Luther King, Jr.,* ed. James M. Washington (San Francisco: Harper & Row, 1986), 282, 286.

FOURTH SUNDAY AFTER THE EPIPHANY

FOURTH SUNDAY IN ORDINARY TIME
JANUARY 31, 2010

Revised Common (RCL)	Episcopal (BCP)	Roman Catholic (LFM)
Jer. 1:4-10	Jer. 1:4-10	Jer. 1:4-5, 17-19
Ps. 71:1-6	Ps. 71:1-17 or 71:1-6, 15-17	Ps. 71:1-2, 3-4, 5-6, 15, 17
1 Cor. 13:1-13	1 Cor. 14:12b-20	1 Cor. 12:31—13:13 or 13:4-13
Luke 4:21-30	Luke 4:21-32	Luke 4:21-30

Candlemas is celebrated forty days after Christmas, on the Feast of the Presentation of Our Lord. Beeswax candles are blessed to assist in revealing Christ. Worshipers carry a candle as a sanctuary house-blessing illuminates places that Christ may be found in the assembly. The light is carried into the lives, homes, schools, and workplaces of those who bear them. We present the Christ child, revealed in lives of holiness, love, and grace, in all the spaces we live and move.

In popular culture, February 2 is celebrated as Groundhog's Day. Themes of light and shadow, the desire for the world's turning from slumber toward life, mark this halfway day between winter solstice and vernal equinox. Simeon rejoices in the light and sees within the present moment the future of God's salvation. In between is the dividing shadow of the cross: "This child is destined to cause the rising and falling of many in Israel, and to be a sign that will be spoken against, so that the thoughts of many hearts will be revealed." The light of Christ brings the polarizing effects of political realities in our own lives and times into sharp relief, revealing an opening to new life.

FIRST READING
JEREMIAH 1:4-10 (RCL, BCP)
JEREMIAH 1:4-5, 17-19 (LFM)

Hermann Hesse wrote, "There are many types and kinds of vocations, but the core of the experience is always the same; the soul is awakened, transformed, or exalted so that instead of dreams and presentiments from within, a summons comes from without; a portion of reality presents itself and makes a claim."[1]

Nehemiah's vocation to rebuild Jerusalem comes through heart-tugging eye-witness accounts of his brother, meeting Nehemiah's inner conviction that he possesses gifts to care for this need of his community. Next week, Isaiah's clarity of call comes in the exalted spaces of the temple. A profound "yes" wells up toward an appointment among the servants of God to bring a word for his time. Peter's transforming and career-reframing experience of discipleship occurs in the more profane arena of his workplace and public shore of Galilee. These spaces are consecrated in Peter's awakening to the holy there, and his response to Jesus' invitation to join him in a healing mission to gather up men and women from far-flung margins into the abundance and new creation of God's rule.

> Jeremiah's call appears to be bred in the bone. By virtue of lineage in the guild of Anatoth, priestly ministry is written into his DNA.

Jeremiah's call appears to be bred in the bone. By virtue of lineage in the guild of Anatoth, priestly ministry is written into his DNA. Jeremiah inherits the family business and in some respects simply takes his expected place. But it also means he will have been steeped in the language and the story of the people of Israel with its God. Jeremiah has this gift at his disposal. That his call to share this facility as prophetic gift is set in an explicit point in Israel's political and common life is marked (as with Isaiah, Nehemiah, and Jesus) by the coming and going of earthly reigns. A portion of Israel's reality makes its claim on Jeremiah.

That reality was apostasy and its aftermath—Jerusalem fallen to the Babylonian Empire. While the call may be set within a framework of earthly rule, God sets the agenda. The word of the Lord comes to Jeremiah in a revelation of his vocation and its specific shape—a prophecy of judgment carrying seeds of hope. The word of God is powerful enough to bring both judgment and salvation, life and death, plucking up and planting, building and pulling down. These metaphors are drawn from three spheres important to the hope of the exiles: agriculture, construction, and royal-military.[2]

> God promises to be intimate and powerful with Jeremiah in this calling to shape Israel's future through the plucking up and building up of the word.

While it may have seemed Jeremiah was born for this moment, the conventional resistance to the call rings truer for Jeremiah. Struggle-filled dialogue with God over the controversial word he's given to proclaim, and his vocation to proclaim it, recurs throughout his career. In the LFM pericope, God galvanizes Jeremiah for the fight ahead by making him an "iron man" to withstand the whole land.

God promises to be intimate and powerful with Jeremiah in this calling to shape Israel's future through the plucking up and building up of the word. But what happens in Israel was going to pull all nations into the story of God's future. It wasn't a word for Judah alone. That it's God's word means that while it comes to us in context, a word in particular time and space, it can also be a word for us.

What have we been born for? What portion of reality in our homes, lives, and communities is currently putting a claim on us as individuals and as an assembly? Like Jeremiah, we have "eaten the word" that shapes us and is shaping the world into which this word is carried. How is God revealed in the summons to such an awakened, exalted, transformed life?

Reflecting on Hesse, Kristen Glass writes:

> Vocation does not need to be "found," vocation needs to be lived. By nature of being born, you have a vocation. You are called to live in the world and be a person in the world. Developing your vocation is about answering the world's specific call to action as the person you are. Vocation is not a "thing," it's a calling. It's a call for reflecting on yourself, on your role in the world, and on the gifts given to you that in turn you can return to the world. Living into your vocation, your calling as a human being, is responding to the portion of reality that is claiming you. The world that says there is a need for peace, justice, mentoring, calmness, action, grace, activism. The world presents many opportunities for you and you respond with your gifts, talents, abilities and feelings.[3]

RESPONSIVE READING

PSALM 71:1-6 (RCL)
PSALM 71:1-17 OR 71:1-6, 15-17 (BCP)
PSALM 71:1-2, 3-4, 5-6, 15, 17 (LFM)

Psalm 71 underlines themes of God's provenance from birth, tangible hope, and God as refuge when the cruel and unjust undermine the righteousness of God in which the psalmist seeks to live. Praise, even through adversity, is the psalmist's constant and pervasive way of life.

1 CORINTHIANS 13:1-13 (RCL)
1 CORINTHIANS 12:31-13:13 OR
13:4-13 (LFM)

A professional preparations committee in the heartland reflected on gifts, traits, and formation most important for public ministries. Boundary crossing and bridge building were among the top characteristics for missional leaders:

- "We need leaders adept in focused ministry with youth and young adults, but with the trend toward aging baby boomers the church needs to take geriatric ministry seriously at the same time."

- "Too many of our pastors think they are ordained to *serve Lutherans*, as opposed to *serving in a Lutheran context*. In our area, there aren't that many Lutherans. We need leaders excited about coming in to serve in this extended way."

- "Diversity has got to be at the forefront. With the election of Barack Obama, racism and hatred will need to be addressed. I also have a concern for corrections reentry. Recidivism is high because we don't have programs that take into account the huge problems of return and restoration to the community. The church needs to prepare leaders for this."

- "We need leaders who will help congregations address real: HIV-AIDS. Immigration. Gay relationships. Our bishop is trying, but in this area we're not jumping on this. We need leaders who will help us talk and act as communities of faith."

- A pastor spoke of the challenges of being a "blue person in a red state": "The political dimension is the context we live in. Church leaders today need to have inner resilience as well as bridge-building skills to press on for inclusive views and justice."

- A farmer/rancher gathered up his courage to share how he often feels worn down on the "other side": "We need leaders who will bring us back to respectful understanding and can build trust."

- A seminary faculty member wrapped it up: "How can we work toward a certain disposition of leadership that allows communities to intentionally disregard popular categories, by making clearings that embrace open, civil conversation? What kind of leader can join and host this conversation? A connected leader: you can't influence that to which you are not connected. A differentiated leader: a leader with the capacity to speak the truth in love."

This conversation took place days after the election of the first African American president of the United States. In the days following this historic occasion it seemed to many as if we had experienced a breakthrough moment in nonpartisanship and unification so profound that even his opponent could give a concession speech with deep leadership marks of conciliation, grace, love, and truth. A pastor noted the change in a confirmand who had come in with blazing red-party rhetoric, whose only commentary the day after the election found compassion and common humanity: "Isn't it so sad Barack Obama's grandmother didn't get to see him elected president?" An African American woman interviewed on TV remarked on her experience of encountering a white man on the streets who had met her eye, and smiled deeply, "as if he saw me in my skin and still believed we had something in common."

Our lives of faith and the church's mission take place in a highly politicized arena. I find myself wondering if our collective hunger for reconciliation in the face of our nation's economic and moral crisis *effected* this moment. Or whether our hunger for reconciliation, for "one-anothering" across the polarizing divides of our lives, has been *revealed* by this moment I write of late in 2008. I'm struck by the number of older African Americans who can only attribute this breakthrough to the hand of God. Even faith and hope couldn't have prompted them to envision this in their lifetime, they believe, nor human will and agency produced this set of events absent God's activity. Projecting into the future, I wonder whether or not we'll have realized the reconciliation Christ brings more fully by the time we preach Paul's sermon on love as the greatest and most enduring of community gifts in 2010.

The fact that Paul writes this wisdom to a body of Christ within a pluralistic community divided by ethnic, economic, religious, and cultural differences about two thousand years ago argues we will continue to need this sermon as long as we remain in the already-but-not-yet of redemption from sin that Christ reveals as a basis for life together. The call for formation of leaders who can speak the truth to us in love as intelligible grassroots reconcilers

> The call for leaders who can speak the truth to us in love as grassroots reconcilers for the sake of the world God loves isn't only for the *ministerium*, but for the *collegium* of the baptized.

for the sake of the world God loves isn't only for the *ministerium*, but for the *collegium* of the baptized. Such leaders stand like Jeremiah in the swirl of polar opposites such as the plucking and the planting, the pulling down and the building up. They find the love and truth in the whole of the reality that claims them, and strength in their intimate relationship with and reliance on God who called them. Such leaders will need to have deep roots in Scripture and prayer, maturing in Jesus' own self-differentiation and outer-directed love to inspire and include rather than impose and exclude, to build such communities in Christ as light for the world. How will today's sermon call forth, equip, and inspire such leaders?

Paul addresses a cross-shaped prayer life that cares for the edification of the whole community. At issue is the language of worship. While tongues may not represent our crisis of intelligibility, we have other access issues. In what ways do our communities accommodate hearing- or sight-impaired worshipers, non-readers, or those not fluent in English? We might review our worship folders for buzzwords and insider info. Do our sermons just make music for our own ears? How might the life-giving word nourish a wider range of hearers and preferred learning styles?

THE GOSPEL

LUKE 4:21-30 (RCL, LFM)
LUKE 4:21-32 (BCP)

Previously on *Jesus at Nazareth* we left hometown crowds amazed at the announcement of God's day of jubilee and restoration fulfilled in their lifetime, reminding one another this was Joseph's son—a homegrown prophet. Carpentry isn't the guild position Jesus adopted. Luke has taken pains to establish creds for Jesus' prophetic voice in his custom of attending to synagogue, an adolescent Jesus teaching temple scribes as he goes about his "father's business." Jonah had come from Galilee. Elisha and Elijah had worked in Galilee.

In fact, it is with reference to Elisha and Elijah and the parable of God's concern for a penniless Gentile widow and a leprous Gentile occupier that the mood swiftly turns ugly. Much ink has been spilled explaining the abrupt turn and deliberate provoking of the listeners. Some of the literary crafting has to do with Luke's setup for the mission to believing Gentiles in Acts. But there is also something authentic about Jesus' truth-telling among neighbors with whom he has been deeply connected. And, there is something very true to human nature in the paradoxical reaction of the parochial crowd that welcomes the news about God's new world order for the downtrodden such as themselves but that can't extend that jubilee beyond their borders.

Sociologist and theologian Caleb Rosado considers the *Significance of Galilee to the Mission of the Church*.[4] Mission is both universal and ultimate (the rule of God extended to all nations and peoples) and relative and contextual (for our place and time). Why Galilee? Why not Jerusalem or Judea, within Nehemiah's walls? What does this have to do with Jesus' epiphany today?

Galilee was surrounded by Gentile nations, separating it from Judea. The name "Galilee of the Gentiles/Nations" reflects its multicultural, multiracial character going back to First Isaiah. Though scholarship is coming to a new consensus that Galilee was overwhelmingly Jewish in Jesus' time, this mix had been part of Galilee's history. By the time of Luke's Gospel the Gentile presence was again on the rise. Rosado follows Virgilio Elizondo in using the word *mestizo* to describe the racial and cultural mixing of the people in this area's history and suggests it affected language as well, creating the tell-tale "accent" of the rural Galileans.

Peasants, common people, 'amha-arez—the religiously uneducated and "unwashed" people of the land going all the way back to the exile—these were terms the upper crust of the South spat at Jesus and his fellow townspeople. Rosado observes that Luke mentions the inn at Bethlehem of Judea as having "no room" for Mary and Joseph, not as being "full," and suggests we hold in mind Jesus' family being received about the way a black family from the North would have been received in a white motel in the South of the 1950s. That's what being a Jew from Nazareth was like. Nothing good was expected to come from there. More Galilean Jews were crucified by the Romans than the Jews of any other region. Jesus was just one of them.

> The name "Galilee of the Gentiles/Nations" reflects its multicultural, multiracial character going back to First Isaiah.

Galilee was the home of Zealots. They thought armed rebellion was the way to restoration. For Judean Jews, old tapes about ancestral and racial purity continued to play as normative. This had everything to do with who held certain offices, but also with who would have salvation. Those with access to Abraham's lineage would have the merits of his faith credited to their accounts. This didn't hold much water with either John the Baptist or Jesus, who followed Third Isaiah in stressing repentance and ethical behavior as the inclusive standard, and explains why their prophetic word infuriated the powers that be who literally banked on this privilege now and in the time to come.

So why did this word infuriate the very townspeople who should have been buoyed up by news of reversal? Luke's Jesus makes it clear it's not just for the Jews of Galilee. Not even just for Israel. Striving for what the Judeans had wasn't the restoration God was bringing to pass, neither was armed rebellion to bring the state to its former glory, but concern for all those on the margins that made humanity whole. These weren't the terms they had in mind. They wanted the privileged, chosen status and the prosperity gospel that their brothers and sisters of Judah aspired to, and that the dominant culture had normed. Rosado quotes Leonard Harman Robbins's short poem:

> *How a minority*
> *Reaching majority,*
> *Seizing authority,*
> *Hates a minority!*

We might also call this internalized oppression. Elizondo observes that the townspeople of Nazareth were considered socially and psychologically inferior even by their own people, and culturally inferior by great powers of the world. Being chosen isn't that special to people who already belong. But if you're outside, you want to cement your gain.[6]

Jesus of Nazareth, the Christ of Galilee, lives out Simeon's prophecy in his controversial inaugural address that starts out speaking their language, but then transgresses the only ways they had imagined the kingdom coming. "He goes not against them, but beyond them. He goes to root causes of enslavement and deification of systems of enslavement, and absolutization of these systems making an absolute end of them."[7] The thoughts of hearts are revealed. Jesus identifies the polarizing effects of the political realities in his time. What political realities of our life and times are cast into sharp relief in this Gospel today?

The group at Faith, Homewood, tackled the question of vocation for their congregation in light of this question. They wished they were bigger. They sometimes felt invisible. What portion of reality in their neighborhood was making its claim? While many could personally speak of a controversial welcome they'd like to effect, a barrier they'd like to break, an aisle they'd like to cross, a visible presence outside the church walls for the marginalized, a hope they had for a thriving multicultural expression of their life of faith, still the "cliff" loomed.

> Jesus identifies the polarizing effects of the political realities in his time. What political realities of our life and times are cast into sharp relief in this Gospel today?

What exactly was the consequence they feared? What was holding them back? Finally, a visitor, a retired pastor's wife, named something. "The cliff is our fear of losing members. Which family members are we going to lose? What reputation will we have in the community?" In fact, we realized, violence is threatened but doesn't materialize. Jesus passes through the crowd and carries his message to other towns. In Capernaum, the movement blossoms on a lakeshore.

"Jesus lives and offers to us an opportunity of breaking through the sin of the world, structures and boundaries of rejection, by accepting we are all children of the same God-abba. . . . As such, everyone is called to cooperate with God in God's plan for the world not as superiors and inferiors but as children and friends."[8] Because of abba-God we can form a new "us." The church can become *mestizo* too, a new creation, what Tertullian identified as a "third world," an in/out group that was both and neither, "bound by intimacy and mutual concern beyond normal empire behavior."[9] Elizondo observes that while Americans long for intimacy, rugged individualism militates against this life. Even when the earthly basis for segregation can be overcome, another division can come about: those who cannot accept a universal belonging and those who, in Christ, can grasp it.

That morning I'd asked Bible study participants to give an impression of their growing-up church. In the course of our discussion, a mom realized her young son might someday be asked this question. What would be the "impression" he would share of his formation at Faith—in Scripture, worship, prayer, outreach, and community life? What would norm his life in the word? Now she knew what was at stake for her—a light had revealed an opening to new life in the way her son's, the church's, and the community's future were inextricably bound in the gospel of Jesus. Love ignited passion, not violence.

Notes

1. Hermann Hesse, *The Glass Bead Game* (New York: Holt, Rinehart, and Winston, 1978), 36.

2. Terence E. Fretheim, *Jeremiah*, Smyth & Helwys Biblical Commentary (Macon, Ga.: Smyth and Helwys, 2002), 51.

3. Kristen Glass, reply to forum posting, "Vocational Decision of Doom," on http://imagineyourself.ning.com, accessed October 2008.

4. Caleb Rosado, *The Significance of Galilee to the Mission of the Church,* http://www.rosado.net (1994, rev. 1995), 1, accessed January 19, 2009.

5. Ibid, 4–5.

6. Virgilio Elizondo, *Galilean Journey: The Mexican American Promise* (Maryknoll, N.Y.: Orbis, 1983).

7. Ibid, 65.

8. Ibid, 63–64.

9. Ibid, 106–10.

FIFTH SUNDAY AFTER THE EPIPHANY

FIFTH SUNDAY IN ORDINARY TIME
FEBRUARY 7, 2010

Revised Common (RCL)	Episcopal (BCP)	Roman Catholic (LFM)
Isa. 6:1-8 (9-13)	Judges 6:11-24a	Isa. 6:1-2a, 3-8
Psalm 138	Psalm 85 or 85:7-13	Ps. 138:1-2a, 2b-3, 4-5, 7-8
1 Cor. 15:1-11	1 Cor. 15:1-11	1 Cor. 15:1-11 or 15:3-8, 11
Luke 5:1-11	Luke 5:1-11	Luke 5:1-11

The newly baptized receive a lighted candle. These candles point to our own bodies, our own lives lived in the world, as places where God may dwell and others may see God's power and glory reflected.

FIRST READING
ISAIAH 6:1-8 (9-13) (RCL)
ISAIAH 6:1-2A, 3-8 (LFM)

Whatever happened to Isaiah in the temple, the epiphany was so compelling we have made it a core element of our family story. We can't stop telling it. Every Sunday, the *Sanctus* gives opportunity to stand with the prophet Isaiah in awareness and jaw-dropping awe of God's glory.

Putting my whole self into such a story, bowing low before the altar in the "Holy Holy Holy," doesn't do much for my singing. But whatever other attention, inattention, or posture I've brought to worship thus far dissolves in that moment when I imagine myself in the midst of Isaiah's experience of power and majesty so full of life it leaves room for nothing else.

Even if we aren't exactly sure what the pivots of the temple might have been, with Isaiah I feel them shaking. I'm sorry to say I imagine the train of God's royal robe in a rather passé spotted ermine. But if God filled that largest space of Isaiah's known world with just the hem, who can even imagine God's greatness? Now the *zimbelstern* on the organ conjures the antiphonal brightness of the seraphs' fiery flight and call to one another high in the rafters, giving voice and dimension to the whole host of heaven including our song. I have in mind golden feather wings against midnight blue backdrop in the illumination of this vision depicted in the *St. John's Bible*. An ambiguous spectrum of color in the design makes me wonder, What all, who all, can be included in this worship of holiness, all the myriad ways it is expressed? Who can even stand in this brightness, this rumbling power, this filling majesty, the glory that is not God, but all we can apprehend of the all-encompassing love and splendor of God?

> If God filled that largest space of Isaiah's known world with just the hem, who can even imagine God's greatness?

A seminary classmate left parish ministry on account of such trembling. The holiness of this presence that became so real when heaven brushed and then embraced earth literally undid her. In the days when my call put me behind the altar, the stage lights of the chancel bouncing off gleaming fair linens, metallic embroidery threads, and silver and gold of eucharistic ware did add in a certain way to the experience of "glory." The weight of the priestly moment ahead contributed to a glare and roar in which reason fled and there wasn't a thought in my head. I could wish for a sun-shielding pair of wings. You need to know the view from the pew is wider, somehow; more diffuse and volumized. It's a perspective no less awesome: enthronement not just in the heavens as Isaiah's contemporaries would have it, not only in the Holy of Holies with its cauterizing coals, but in the whole of creation and the everydayness of the world.

The matter of Isaiah's background divides scholars. While his presence in the temple could imply he was a priest, or at least a member of the religious establishment, others believe he was a walk-in off the streets. If the pivots were the lintels or threshold posts of the door, this would support a perspective "from the outside looking in." Whether he began as a member of the religious establishment or not, Isaiah now experiences God's call to prophetic public ministry.

In the wake of this call from God and God's entire entourage, Isaiah is revealed to himself as a man with a divine word on his lips. He says yes to the business of revelation.

The RCL allows for an honest and disturbing look at what Isaiah has said yes to, and what he is sent to do. The words God puts in Isaiah's mouth are to contribute to Israel's hard-heartedness toward God and God's will to care for the poor with justice. We see evidence in the next chapter, with Ahaz's reluctance to ask God for a sign. Ahaz has already decided against life with the God of Israel that would call for a change in his administration. God has already decided on punishment. They will be "cut off." Even the stump will burn. When Isaiah asks how long this is to continue, the word is harsh. Nothing will remain . . . but a holy remnant or seed, God's always-plan for new life.

In *Reading Isaiah*, Edgar Conrad reads Isaiah 6 from the perspective of a "first survivor."[1] Isaiah's description of his call then bears resemblance to the situation of the survivors. They dwell in the midst of a people who have strayed. Like the survivors, Isaiah claims his sinfulness. The survivors are ones who tremble at God's word. The survivors are sent, as Isaiah was sent, as a witness-bearing revelatory testimony of the Lord. They are offering an exhorting word, with a similar result (63:17). In this reading, the message of Isaiah relates to the present circumstance of the community, not its future, in a time when the land is laid waste and the consequences of the message have come to pass. Isaiah's words and actions are meant as paradigms for the present survivors, who "dwell in the midst of a people of unclean lips," living in a time of waiting and hoping.

In its centennial year, our parish considered installing glass doors. I had a vision of Times Square-area churches at Easter: glorious light, forsythia branch and cherry blossoms, high altars visible from the street for all passersby. But a council member got nervous about such transparency: "If we did that, anybody out there could see what we have!" Read this way, can Isaiah's call be paradigmatic for present life as a sent people, kings and priests, light to the world in our baptism, congregations open to the world?

> When Isaiah asks how long this is to continue, the word is harsh. Nothing will remain . . . but a holy remnant or seed, God's always-plan for new life.

JUDGES 6:11-24A (BCP)

Gideon is awkwardly threshing wheat, hiding from the enemy in the hollow of his wine press. Up on the hill the wind could blow the chaff, but the Midianites would see the harvest and swarm down like the locusts they were. You've got to love that the angel of the Lord chooses this moment to greet Gideon as a mighty warrior with God's favor. Gideon is bold in his back talk, in the tradition of frank give and take about what God's favor has gotten them lately. Gideon is challenged to do something about it: save Israel. "Am I not sending you?" the Lord asks, calling Gideon's bluff. In good call-story form, he then protests his weakness. Unlike Ahaz, Gideon is happy to ask for a sign: an offering he brings is toasted without flint. Gideon's story stands alongside the calls of Isaiah, Paul, and Peter. Our reliance on God's purpose and promise reflects God's glory all the more (see also the Gospel for Transfiguration Sunday/Last Sunday of the Epiphany, below).

RESPONSIVE READING

PSALM 138 (RCL)
PSALM 138:1-2A, 2B-3, 4-5,7-8 (LFM)
PSALM 85 OR 85:7-13 (BCP)

Psalm 85 contains beautiful poetry. Possibly set just as exiles were returning from Babylon, the psalm speaks to God's past saving acts and present pardon and blessing. It looks forward to the time when the Holy of Holies once again houses God's glory, visible and present in the worshiping community in Zion and in the covenant relationships of those who listen to and hear God's word.

Psalm 138's flatter prosaicism may reflect the hard lot and daily grind of those restored from exile. High art will have to wait, but praise and supplication for God's steadfast love are on their lips now. Unlike earthly kingdoms, God's rule comes close to those in need.

SECOND READING

1 CORINTHIANS 15:1-11 (RCL, BCP, LFM)
1 CORINTHIANS 15:3-8, 11 (LFM ALT.)

Our psalms remind us that glory is the recognition and celebration of God's rule of life, even when that life is not yet fully realized. We are always both professing and pleading for God's deliverance. This letter to the Corinthians places the hope and glory of ultimate deliverance at the rhetorical pinnacle of the epistle, reflecting on the meaning of the resurrection in the life of faith. Most commentators believe Paul is responding to rumored concerns that the Corinthians didn't understand the eschatological, communal nature of the resurrection. A for-this-life-only, privatized, nonembodied understanding could render Paul's work, and their faith, in vain.

Today's segment rehearses the power of "the tradition" received and transmitted, incorporating believers into the history of the chosen people of God. The creedal formula of verses 3-5 underlines this story as bedrock for faith. This is "what we know" about God and salvation in Jesus, confess in the company of the faithful, and share with others. As in all the early creeds, the anticipation of the *parousia* goes unsaid.[2]

Lines of commentary debate the origin and purposes of the subsequent series of *thens* defining the apostolic chunk of early church life according to appearances of the risen Christ. My favorite theory is that the "mysterious five hundred" relate to the Pentecost story. If we are to make use of these verses for today, the incorporation of all these strands of apostolic leadership can suggest a networked rather than linear approach to the circuitry and energy of proclamation, reception, and the spread of the gospel. Though unnamed here (indeed, Paul has just silenced the women of Corinth), we could include Mary Magdalene among these receivers of revelation and the women at the tomb as witnesses to the resurrection.

Today's revelatory genre seems to be narrative/autobiography: God's glory working through unworthy spokespersons. Paul is at great pains (going so far as to refer to himself as an abortion, premature, an abortive creature, deformed, a monster from birth, or stillborn) to say his apostolicity shouldn't have happened in any world we can rationally comprehend. After his review of what we know of Christ's resurrection, Paul wants them to glimpse what we *don't* know—the glory of our life in Christ to come. He embodies it, strives for it, and "works" toward that glory (harder than anyone!) in his proclamation.

The Corinthians are no strangers to rhetoric about gods and idols—but through the witnesses to Christ's resurrection, they connected with and deeply experienced the transforming power of this gospel. No longer in the apostolic age, not yet in the New Jerusalem, those of us after Paul live in the "age of grace." Paul Sampley identifies such grace as a code word for the "ongoing work of God" that continues

> No longer in the apostolic age, not yet in the New Jerusalem, those of us after Paul live in the "age of grace."

to work through us and transform us.[3] How have we been grafted into this tradition? How are those moving out of our pews to be lights in Monday morning's world connecting their faith autobiography through daily life in the age of grace as preachers in their own spheres?

THE GOSPEL
LUKE 5:1-11 (RCL, BCP, LFM)

The light breaks through the overcast, teases the fishermen's heads, and pours silver down the fish scales of an overflowing catch in Winslow Homer's *The Herring Net*. Herring were running in the waters off Prout's Neck, and Homer hired a boat and a local lad to row him out to sketch the men at their work. Such subjects sold well back in the cities. The privileged, upper-class collectors respected the authenticity of these working people and their deeply elemental knowledge of forests, waters, and mountains.

Peter wasn't exactly uneducated. He was fairly well schooled in the schooling behavior of fish. You have to give him props for restraint in his patient response to Jesus' suggestion that he go out deeper and let his nets down for a catch. He has (as he points out) been out there all night doing just that. Peter knows there are no fish there. If you consider that two boats in his co-op made him something of a manager in what was most likely barely more than a subsistence enterprise, this business concern for his margin makes a lot of sense.

But Peter also knows nature is unpredictable. You never know when the fish will show up. Jesus wasn't a stranger to him either. Jesus had been preaching in Capernaum, amazing everyone with an authority to preach good news backed up by the evidence of astounding acts of healing. In fact, Jesus had been in his home and cured Peter's mother-in-law of her raging fever so completely that she'd jumped up to put on the Sunday dinner. Peter wouldn't have been surprised, I suppose, if there had been fish in the net when he responded to Jesus'

> Peter saw God's glory on the sea first, that elemental place where both frightful chaos and teeming abundance meet, where God speaks a word and fills the world with life.

invitation. But what Peter had seen and heard thus far apparently did not prepare him for what he saw next: fish leaping into nets strained to the breaking point, boats sinking with their glorious weight—and God. He saw the glory of God that fills the temple with just the hem of the royal robe. Only, he saw it out of the box. He saw God's glory on the sea first of all, that elemental place where both frightful chaos and teeming abundance meet, where God speaks a word and fills the world with life. And, not incidentally I believe, Peter saw the beauty of God's holiness in his workplace the way he had seen it at home, in the person of Jesus.

"Lord," Peter calls Jesus, in a context of his sinfulness that not only resonates with the call narrative of Isaiah, but also harks back to Luke's infancy narrative where "the Lord" is synonymous for "God."[4] So in Jesus it is God who shows up, out on the sea, here in his workplace, where Peter scratches and claws all night for a meager living to keep the kids in sandals. Here where things are rough and raw and rugged, his manners aren't the best, and his language not so clean. That tells you something else about the kingdom of God and its glory being revealed in Jesus when God shows up here in Capernaum of Galilee. This doesn't happen on the Mediterranean, in Caesarea Maritima, where Herod the Great tamed wild waves by developing a port with enormous concrete blocks, brought in drinking water with impressive aqueducts, built up the seashore with palaces and plazas of marbles and mosaics, ordered the streets around it to show Rome and the rest of the world the glory of his regime, and then gated the area so the poor and other undesirables would be excluded.[5]

Many of our hearers will wrestle with the meaning of this contrast. A woman reported that she and her husband, who had attended Bible study for the first time in his life, had talked all week about Peter's lack of entitlement. "When he saw this miracle of abundance, he didn't say, 'Wow, lots of fish, awesome, how can I get more?' but felt his smallness and sinfulness in the presence of God. The story made us think differently about 'what fish are for.'" Another member at Faith was struck by the pre-study slides from Sadao Watanabe's *The Disciples Catch Fish* of people holding fish as big as they are, and graphs of the world fish catch. He remembered seeing six-hundred-pound tuna when he was a kid. The next week he brought in a magazine that showed nets full of progressively smaller fish. He'd like to hear a sermon about oceans being fished and polluted to the extent that if there did exist a big tuna, you wouldn't want to eat it anyway.

Peter's Capernaum sustained one thousand souls with subsistence fishing and nearby fertile farmlands. The village's "streets" meandered organically, with spaces here and there for net mending and animals. Except for a few hand-piled breakwaters, the lakeshore where Jesus taught was open space for socializing and selling fish, produce, and simple household wares.[6]

When the crowd backed Jesus into the boat, it wasn't into some luxury liner. I've seen the "Jesus boat" found stuck in Galilee mud for two thousand years. No brass and teak here. One of the things speaking to its authenticity is the fact it is composed of so many different kinds of wood. When the boat needed repair, the fishermen tacked in whatever they could find lying around. The kind of boat of the church where God's glory shows up is a working skiff, not a cruise ship. It's been around. It's got marks. It's sprung a few leaks. Its integrity is mosaic. The Winslow Homer boat in *The Herring Net*, some have noted, seems to have a cross at its back. Its gleam doesn't come from shiny appointments.

> Jesus calls us from an open shoreline for the long haul, for the deep letting down and hauling up of the baptismal life of dying and rising.

Jesus calls us from an open shoreline for the long haul, for the deep letting down and hauling up of the baptismal life of dying and rising. We have a tendency to imperialize, colonize, and "templify" God's glory. Ironically, the thing that brought order to Capernaum was the attempt to box in God's glory in Jesus and hold on to it in the house of Peter's mother-in-law. Pilgrim graffiti in a plastered wall tells us this place was revered and preserved as holy.[7] It was most likely an early house church, succeeded by a fifth-century octagonal basilica around which Capernaum became organized.

We also "gate" the glory when we clericalize it. Whether Isaiah was already a member of the religious establishment or not in this call story, he becomes a public leader. Paul might have been misconceived, but he makes the apostolic cut. Peter may have been a regular guy in the boat, but he ends up being pope.

Not everyone who experiences this call to follow will do so as a salary-receiving member of the religious establishment. Luke, who may have received some of the "tradition" he passes on from Paul, both conceals and reveals the community in this story and others about Peter in Luke/Acts. When the nets are full of fish, the partners are called in and it's all hands on deck. Peter gets the recorded speaking roles, but there's a cast of many, if not thousands, in the water and one wonders what their speech consisted of out there. In Acts, Peter once again gets speaking roles, but John, representing the rest of the community, is always with him.

A few years ago I stopped preaching in order to be the daughter of a mother with lung cancer. A colleague visited once at a local hospital. One brought communion. My bishop came to the wake. But every night in bedtime prayers my mom and I gave thanks for the ways Jesus had walked with us that day through the care of people living out vocation. I'd wait for the pastor to show up, and it was a chemo nurse who told me the truth and prepared me for death. The oncologist made a house call, spinning up to my mom's broken-down shack in his Audi, bearing a sack of protein drinks his office nurse had sent along. He prescribed a growing list of medications that the pharmacists kept finding ways to get covered. One of mom's former students was the home-health aide who gave her baths and reminded her of the ways her life mattered. A man came one day and set up the hospital bed in the living room with efficient respect for us and for the holy work that would take place there. The respiratory specialist showed up to whisper confidence in God's love and the power of the resurrection in mom's ear. A couple hours after the funeral my brother's company had a plate of cold cuts delivered: "Wanted to make things easier, from the APC family." I hadn't grasped the real power and strength of the church . . . at large!

On the day of our baptisms, new members of the priesthood of all believers are given a candle. In Christ, we are places where God dwells, revealing lights to the world. Where are our stories in the tradition of those called to bear witness to God's glory? How is the meaning of our everyday life ("what fish are for") transformed by the call to follow Jesus? How do we see ourselves *net*worked in community, the church at large?

Notes

1. Edgar Conrad, *Reading Isaiah,* Overtures to Biblical Theology (Minneapolis: Fortress Press, 1991), 110.

2. Hans Conzelman, *1 Corinthians*, Hermeneia (Philadelphia: Fortress Press, 1975), 257.

3. J. Paul Sampley, *1 Corinthians*, New Interpreter's Bible (Nashville: Abingdon, 2002), 977.

4. R. Alan Culpepper, *Luke*, New Interpreter's Bible (Nashville: Abingdon, 1995), 16.

5. John Dominic Crossan and Jonathan L. Reed, *Excavating Jesus: Beneath the Stones, Behind the Texts* (San Francisco, HarperSanFrancisco, 2001), 57–62.

6. Ibid, 88.

7. Ibid, 92.

TRANSFIGURATION OF OUR LORD

LAST SUNDAY AFTER THE EPIPHANY / SIXTH SUNDAY IN ORDINARY TIME

FEBRUARY 14, 2010

Revised Common (RCL)	Episcopal (BCP)	Roman Catholic (LFM)
Exod. 34:29-35	Exod. 34:29-35	Jer. 17:5-8
Psalm 99	Psalm 99	Ps. 1:1-2. 3, 4 + 6
2 Cor. 3:12—4:2	1 Cor. 12:27—13:13	1 Cor. 15:12, 16-20
Luke 9:28-36 (37-43)	Luke 9:28-36	Luke 6:17, 20-26

Torches accompany and light the cross at the recessional. This time, the glory is coming right at us. We are invited to go with this glory, let it lead us out. We think the epiphany is over, but it is just beginning. The recessional isn't so much the end of worship, as a procession into the world God loves.

FIRST READING
EXODUS 34:29-35 (RCL, BCP)

The backside of God's glory is all Moses can handle. At the tent of meeting, where God and Moses usually held one-on-ones, God appeared in a pillar of cloud. In this way, God spoke to Moses face-to-face the way you speak to a friend. But lately there'd been that golden calf affair, smashed tables of Law, plus the whole notion of wilderness wandering with a stiff-necked pack of people. Moses tells God he needs a different kind of face time. He asks to see God's glory. So God invites Moses to the mountain to see God's "total goodness."

Glory has to do with the sheer weight of God's splendor, power, and majesty, so God takes all due precaution to keep Moses from being crushed. Moses will stand on a rock right beside God. When God's glory passes by, God will push him in the cleft of the rock and cover him with God's hand. When God takes God's hand away, Moses will see the tail end of God's *kabod*.

While they're up there, God lays down the law again. But here's what I think gets Moses' shine on. At the burning bush Moses got "I am who I am." But the fullness of the name YHWH, by which God now self-identifies so Moses will recognize God in glory, reveals the top seven things Moses and the people need to know about God's essence: enwombing mercy, gracious favor, counting to ten in anger, all God will put up with in abounding steadfast love, reliability, loyalty in love over the long haul, lifting the weight of sin. Oh, and two more things: God won't ignore sin, and will hold generations accountable for it.

Moses bows down and asks God for pardon for himself and Israel to deeply enjoin this covenant relationship. He comes down flushed with the fullness of this glimpse. He's radiant over the thrilling particularity of God's disclosure of where God is with Moses/Israel, a presence that puts everything in a new light. God had Moses at hello.

The glow-on is for the whole community. The shining communicates something about the very nature of God. The brightness, splendor, and lively incandescence Moses discovered in the glory on the mountain became part of him in the covenant encounter. That Moses can embody this word speaks volumes about who God is, how God is recognized, what life with this God will mean, and how God chooses to communicate.

> The brightness, splendor, and lively incandescence Moses discovered in the glory on the mountain became part of him in the covenant encounter.

Not everyone has that reaction, or is ready for this relationship. Even this mediated brush with glory frightens Aaron and the other Israelites. When they see what has happened to Moses they run. Moses resorts to veiling the glory, except when he speaks for the Lord, if that makes any sense. Paul, in our second reading, has some theories about this veil. We can't determine the veil's exact purpose, but within it we see the ambiguous and ambivalent nature of God's shining: "in the person of Moses, a new contact between heaven and earth, between Yahweh and Israel has come about. Israel is rightly frightened, but Israel is also able to receive its life as God inscrutably gives it."[2]

JEREMIAH 17:5–8 (LFM)

As a fragment of wisdom poetry echoing Psalm 1 pasted in Jeremiah's book like a random sticky note, this pericope falls into the category of lovely, derivative idea. But what if it's read as a personal confession of Jeremiah? What if he is talking to you as someone who's been there, been to the shrubby desiccated salt flats of spiritual and social desert? What if he's like one of my professors warning me he'd been to the end of the deconstructionist road, sucked on the olive at the bottom of that martini glass with well-published and celebrated colleagues, and could tell me there was only deadly abyss there? "I'd turn back, if I were you!"

Knowing something of the struggle of Jeremiah's call and life, the loneliness and the bitterness he has freely expressed, this passage can be powerfully read as a call to repentance. Jeremiah will learn to trust his heart, Yahweh, rather than the court of human opinion. He gets an active role in this hardy new direction. He's not just planted by the stream, but yearns for life, sending out roots toward life-giving waters. If you're looking for a Valentine's Day text that involves hearts, this might not be a bad choice. Today we repent together in the *Sursum Corda*: Lift up your hearts! We lift them up to the Lord!

Responsive Reading
PSALM 99 (RCL, BCP)

God sits enthroned in the Holy of Holies of the temple. God's holiness is to be praised throughout the universe, and is revealed in acts of justice.

PSALM 1:1-2, 3, 4, 6 (LFM)

A blessed life involves deliberate orientation toward the ways of God. It's hard to beat Eugene Peterson's contemporization:

> *How well God must like you—*
> *You don't hang out at Sin Saloon,*
> *You don't slink along Dead-End Road*
> *You don't go to Smart-Mouth College*
> *Instead you thrill to God's Word . . .*
> *The road* they *take is Skid Row.*[3]

Second Reading
2 CORINTHIANS 3:12—4:2 (RCL)

Paul riffs on two stories about the covenant to make his point about revelation's embodiment in Christ: Jeremiah's new covenant written on the human heart, and Moses' veiled face after encountering God's glory.

It may be that Paul is a little preoccupied with the veil, making a bolder interpretation than the text bears. New Testament scholar David Fredrickson thinks the veil connotes shame.[4] Read in the context of his last painful visit to Corinth and subsequent "letter of tears," Paul makes a defensive argument regarding the basis for boldness in his speech. Paul, in his ministry, is unlike Moses who covers his face out of shame for the transitory effects of the glory he reflects under the law. Moses' veil/shame was removed whenever he was in the presence of God.

To be in Christ means to be always in the presence of God. To be without shame means freedom. We can engage in bold, truthful speech when we stand in this freedom. In this respect, Paul likens his ministry to that of Moses. The veil and our shame may be set aside in Christ's justification and the permanent access to God we have received through Christ's barrier-breaking death and resurrection.

Sampley interprets this passage to avoid "absolute contrast." There is much glory in the covenant of the law, which is "holy, just, and good" (Rom. 7:12), even if it led to condemnation and death when hijacked by sin. For those "in Christ," how much *more* freedom and boldness in speech, life, and glory might be available in the covenant of justification?[5] Paul uses this argument to bind himself and his ministry more closely to the Corinthians in a way that, if we avoid anti-Semitic pitfalls, will be life-giving for our communities.

> The veil and our shame may be set aside in Christ's justification and the permanent access to God we have received through Christ's barrier-breaking death and resurrection.

Paul invites Corinthian believers to join him in gazing at God's glory through the mirror or true image of God that Christ's face reflects. In Christ, God has found a way for the glory of God's face to be fully apparent without crushing us. Jesus, in the verses just prior to our Gospel today, suggests those ashamed of him and his words will not know glory. Unveiled, we can be confident of the glory of Christ.

We continue to live into and grow into this reality through life in word and Spirit as the means of grace transform us in this image. In baptism we are sealed with the Spirit. The shiny cross on our foreheads is radiant with a glory that gives us all a "ministry of reflection" for God's story. A seminarian recently noted a comment about his face lighting up when speaking of outreach: "I've been working on my 'brightening.' Thanks for reminding me I had that power to communicate visibly my passion for the gospel."

What if our own skins were the boundary between gospel and the world? What if we consciously let the light of Christ we've been given get as close to that surface as possible? What if we, as the body of Christ, were radiant in God's presence sent forth to the boundary spaces where God meets world, as a Eucharist without walls?

1 CORINTHIANS 12:27—13:13 (BCP)

See the second reading (RCL) for the Fourth Sunday in Epiphany, above. Valentine's Day will find themes of compassion and love as the greatest gift on everyone's hearts!

Whether or not individuals in Corinth doubted the resurrection of the body, I wonder if this is a question anyone in the pews is asking. As a preacher on this text, I'd be curious enough to ask around. Or, if you've considered "talk time" sermons, give folks a chance to reflect on and share what they believe about resurrection with their neighbors in the pew in the course of your delivery. We often ask hearers to share their faith, but never structure time for practice!

What's at stake in Paul's argument? If death is the penalty for sin, to deny our resurrection means Christ's salvation and forgiveness of sin has no real meaning. What's the point of faithful living and acting in the here and now? If there's no bodily resurrection of the dead, then all those who have already died, including loved ones, are out of luck. Thanks be to God that's not the pitiful case. In fact, Christ has been raised from the dead. God's point is to raise us up. Christ is the firstfruits offering that consecrates the whole harvest. That's grounds for a whole new approach to life.

THE GOSPEL
LUKE 9:28-36 (37-43) (RCL)
LUKE 9:28-36 (BCP)

What is this story and what are you supposed to do with it? Is it a misplaced resurrection/ascension narrative? A theophany, apocalyptic vision, epiphany, pronouncement, or scenic confession? Knowing what kind of story is coming assists hearers in apprehending meanings. John Paul Heil locates the revelatory genre of the transfiguration story as "pivotal mandatory epiphany," with multiple epiphanic appearances clarifying the meaning of the event.[6]

The transfiguration is *pivotal,* casting light in three directions. In each of the Gospels it closely follows the prediction of the passion and resurrection, challenging Jesus' disciples to take up the cross and life in God's kingdom. It's followed by the disciples' descent into that life, and Jesus' exorcism of a boy crushed mercilessly in ecstatic/demonic episodes that the disciples haven't been able to do anything about. God's revealed majesty doesn't seek to crush, but to raise up the suffering.

The transfiguration is *mandatory.* The climax is the revelatory mandate to listen to Jesus, even words about suffering and passion disciples don't want to hear, to share God's plan for salvation.

The transfiguration is an *epiphany.*

- In *theophany*, the divine being remains invisible and is recognized only by its effects upon nature (fire, whirlwind).
- A *vision* is seen only through the eyes of a selected viewer within a heavenly context (John in Revelation).
- A hallmark of the *epiphany* genre is visible form anyone could see (dove in bodily form at Jesus' baptism underlining earthly reality).

In Luke, Jesus is transfigured while praying. Moses and Elijah have already appeared as the disciples awaken from their sleep and see Jesus' glory.

The transfiguration story engages *multiple epiphanies* in service to revelation. Not only do we not get it the first time, but we can't. There's no one thing in our experience that encompasses all we need to know about God. That's why metaphor is the language of insight and revelation. It's what it is, what it isn't, and the new things we discover in the collision of worlds that moves us closer.

Heil uses the story of Gideon's call (see the first reading [BCP] for the Fifth Sunday of Epiphany, above) as an example. An angel appears, Gideon has a great conversation about his upcoming role in God's salvation story, but doesn't seem certain of the angel's true identity. Gideon asks for a sign, and tries to hold on to the angel by offering hospitality. As the angel turns food into a sacrificial offering accepted by God, Gideon recognizes the angel's identity but only as it disappears. God's presence terrifies Gideon, but God has a final word of peace and life.[7]

Luke's transfiguration follows this same pattern. Peter belatedly offers the hospitality of the booths in the midst of some confusion about what this is about. A second epiphanic action of the textually familiar vehicular cloud "tents" Elijah and Moses for him. Out of the bright cloud comes a clarifying voice, and Jesus is left standing alone (with a big underline, exclamation point) as the final word.

> Luke stresses silence, released when the resurrection and ascension provide additional clarity and the Spirit of Pentecost appoints them ministers of this gospel.

As a pivotal mandatory epiphany, this revelation gives us chances to see the passion prediction that precedes this story, and the healing that follows, in a light that casts new meaning on the entire Gospel. The possibility of deeper understanding of Jesus' identity as the Christ of God and God's chosen servant, as well as the role we are to play in God's salvific action with God's people, is illuminated. Luke stresses silence, released when the resurrection and ascension provide additional clarity and the Spirit of Pentecost appoints them ministers of this gospel.

Luke's specific features pack in more meaning for his community:

- *The eighth day* (ritual day of naming and of new creation);

- *Peter, John, and James* (always called to experience private kingdom-revealing events, Peter/John named out of traditional order together to foreshadow the witness of the whole church as they appear in Acts);
- *context of prayer* (role in the baptismal epiphany and other significant revelatory events later in Luke);
- *shining garments* (sign of those who live in royal palaces, Herod sends Jesus to Pilate in bright shining garment, men in dazzling garments reveal Jesus' resurrection, our garb to come);
- *discussion of Moses and Elijah* (glory placed in the context of suffering, exodus that spares/frees, Jesus suffers death spared Moses and Elijah).

No doubt there's more!

The transfiguration teaches us where to look and listen for signs of God's salvation. We look in this text, and in our context. We pivot in a 360-degree turn. Glory is all around us. God's light is cast not just on mountaintop events but in everyday encounters with God, in suffering we endure, the least whom we accompany in Jesus' name, and in the hopeful future we glimpse in fragmentary and anticipatory moments of revelation.

How can our proclamation cast light that teaches us where to look in listening to the chosen one of God? The cloud was a symbol of God's indwelling presence with God's people—where do we locate that presence today? Around which contemporary narratives can this epiphany pivot? What about life weighs us down? For what glory ought we be staying awake? What role has prayer played in revelation in our private and corporate lives?

LUKE 6:17, 20-26 (LFM)

Luke takes Matthew's Sermon on the Mount down to the plain. Where the mountain has signified the place where heaven and earth, God and human, meet, Luke's Jesus takes it to the streets. God exalts the lowly and fills the hungry with good things. The rich are sent away empty.

What if the Beatitudes are parabolic expressions of God's rule among us that don't take us out of the world to understand what's really real? In an independent study on the parables, the late theologian Joseph Sittler posed that question in the form of an exam. The final project was to preach a sermon on the Beatitudes as if they were a parable of the kingdom.

How about this: The rule of God is like going to a funeral for an eccentric white woman you've never seen in anything but a baggy T-shirt mouthing off about something. You knew her, barely, but didn't go much further on your way to meet your own cool friends. Still, she'd welcomed you in her tiny neighborhood congregation; it wouldn't take that much to walk around the corner and lend your presence to a small band of mourners. So you go out of pity and a sense of your own generosity. When you get there, you are stunned. The church is crowded with people of means and the poor. The multicultural royalty of your denomination is there. A wonderful preacher and renowned evangelist has flown halfway across the country to deliver the sermon and play the trombone. She had reach you never imagined. Person after person gets up to talk about the way her gifts were multiplied in making shalom. You're lucky to be there.

Or how about this: the rule of God is like communion . . . and taking the subway to work. At communion, whatever our stations in life, work, age, or educational achievement are leveled in our need before God and outstretched hand for bread. On the train, everyone's thrown together in a common enterprise of getting to their day. If you want a seat, you often sit with people you might not otherwise get so close to in life. Together we whiz past the more fortunate going nowhere on the expressway.

The train doesn't romanticize poverty. You don't want to wear open-toed shoes. You don't stare too long at the woman carrying three plastic bags, packing and repacking them all over the seats, mumbling. In the wee hours of winter mornings you ride the train with what looks like bundles of clothes that turn out to be the city's homeless. Maintenance workers begin sweeping out around them as if these lumps weren't even there. Which is a mercy, since I'm fairly certain everybody needs to get out of the train at the end of the line.

Luke's Jesus rides the subway. He knows what it is to be hungry, hated, in need, suspected of craziness—not self-sufficient and insulated. To sleep on straw when there's no room in the inn. Father Elias Chacour, a Palestinian priest in Galilee, believes you can translate this "blessed" as Jesus' invitation to "straighten yourselves up, get up, go ahead, do something, move."[7] Rejoice, be glad, you've been lifted up by the one who raises up and calls you blessed to be God's own. Uncurl your cold, dead self from the ignored lump of clothes that maintenance workers are sweeping around, and rise with dignity. *You* are counted in me.

The rich get to overhear about a new world order. If you are among them, you know who you want to be sitting next to on the subway on your way to "getting up, going ahead, and doing something" yourself when the kingdom comes and the feast that knows no end begins. What if Jesus wasn't talking about pie in the sky when we die . . . but the first slice opened up to us, revealed to us this deep Epiphany in the one that heals the gaps between blessing and the woe, the poor and the rich, by laying himself right across it and mixing up the dividing line? What does God's rule, God's kin-dom look like when it breaks in and bids us to "straighten ourselves up" and claim this gift of the life of wholeness God intends for human beings and all creation?

Mary Ellen Diaz trained at Le Cordon Bleu in France and began a soup kitchen called First Slice. She'll serve a salad of local organic greens, fresh tomatoes, black olives, garlic croutons, parmesan cheese. The main course is spinach and butternut squash lasagna. Chocolate–peanut butter pie for dessert. If it sounds like something people who shop at Whole Foods would eat instead of something dumpster divers might be grateful for, you'd be right. Families who can afford it subscribe for three gourmet meals a week. But from that one subscription, twenty homeless people get the *first slice* of the lasagna and pie. Not leftovers, not the crumbs. The same food, first. Dignity.[8]

> The world raised to life in Christ in this way moves us beyond just sitting next to one another, to deeply knowing one another as peers and kin.

If the kingdom of God is like this, it unclenches our mindsbreaks through our failures of imagination, returns us, restores us, strengthens us to resist a vision of the world that would continue to divide and deal death. The world raised to life in Christ in this way moves us beyond just sitting next to one another, to deeply knowing one another as peers and kin. This vision would extend beyond human beings and relationships to the four-legged, to the winged and all creation. So we move deeper into the paschal mystery, and the next season in the year of grace. May the Lord's face shine upon you.

Notes

1. Walter Brueggemann, *Exodus*, New Interpreter's Bible (Nashville: Abingdon, 1994), 954.

2. Eugene Peterson, *The Message* (Colorado Springs: NavPress, 2002), 912.

3. David Fredrickson, "Pentecost: Paul the Pastor in 2 Corinthians," *Word & World* 11, no. 2 (1991): 209–10.

4. J. Paul Sampley, *2 Corinthians*, New Interpreter's Bible (Nashville: Abingdon, 2000), 66.

5. John Paul Heil, *The Transfiguration of Jesus*, Analecta Biblica 144 (Rome: Editrice Pontificio Istituto Biblico, 2000), 22–33.

6. Ibid, 45–47.

7. This translation is from notes on my visit to his parish in Ibilin. For a fuller account, see Elias Chacour with Mary Jensen, *We Belong to the Land: The Story of a Palestinian Israeli Who Lives for Peace and Reconciliation* (San Francisco: HarperSanFrancisco, 1990), 143–44.

8. See http://www.firstslice.org brochures for more stories about how the kingdom comes (accessed Feb. 8, 2009).

THE SEASON
OF LENT

MARGARET AYMER

L ent marks a space in between two of the great feasts of the church: Christ-
mastide and Epiphany, and Eastertide. We Christians can overlook this peni-
tential season, stereotyping it merely as a time to prove self-discipline by "giving
something up." Or we can use Lent as a means of fostering our feelings of guilt
and inadequacy about our faith, feelings that can often paralyze us rather than
prodding us to action. However, the scriptures readings for Lent in Year C do not
support either of these impulses. Instead, they call us away from guilty self-doubt
and from showy self-discipline to the harder and ultimately more honest work of
discipleship. This call comes to us in two ways: by reminding us of who God is,
and by reminding us of the demands of "full-body discipleship."[1]

In Lent, we might expect the scriptures readings to warn us about the justice
and judgment of God. In fact, the Lenten texts for Year C do just the opposite.
They entice us, rather than shame or command us, back to the love and mercy
of our compassionate, reconciling God. God, in the lections for Year C, proves
to be faithful and trustworthy. God's presence brings clouds and darkness, so that
God's transformation and covenant may appear as light. God rolls away the disgrace of God's people, making them a new creation. In the face of danger, God,
in Christ, proves to have self-sacrificial, mothering love, even for the unjust. The
God who is and will be sees those caught in fire, but not consumed, those trapped
between oppression and neglect; and God acts on behalf of those in need, making
a way where there was no way. To this God, the Lenten texts bid us return, a

God whose thought and ways are far above our own, but whose faithfulness and compassion are enduring.

These texts do not only speak to us about the compassion of God; they also call us to a discipleship marked by a renewal of our focus on heavenly matters, by reconciliation within the community of faith, and by living into a just and compassionate "full-body" discipleship. We begin with a turn toward heavenly treasure and approval and away from earthly treasure and approval. The scriptures readings call us to put away all things dedicated to worldly idols, and encourage us instead to trust in God, to turn toward the heavenly call, and to live as friends, rather than as enemies, of the shameful cross of Christ. In this first mark of Lenten discipleship, we must turn our focus away from our petty complaints to name the places that God has been faithful to us, even as we practice our faithfulness to God.

Our Lenten discipleship also requires from us intentionality about reconciliation among the people of God. We, whom Christ has reconciled to God, must also be about reconciliation. As such, our vision must change, so that we may see our siblings as new creations. These Lenten lections counsel us to drop our stones of judgment, to give up our need to be right, and to forget past hurts. Rather, these texts call us, who are only leasing God's vineyard, to welcome and to listen to God's messengers and, most of all, to welcome the Christ. Only when we can live into reconciliation can we celebrate the feast, as siblings around one table, even in the face of mortality—our own mortality and the impending death of the Christ.

Finally, the Lenten readings for Year C require of us justice for the oppressed, even as we, like Christ, lament for the unjust. As disciples of the Christ, we must stand with those caught between oppression and neglect, and to see those burning with hardship, yet not overcome. We must honor the hungry as siblings and love as prodigally as God has loved us. As a result, our hunger for justice must overwhelm our hunger for honor. The narrow door, not the door of honor, should mark our discipleship. Our ultimate pattern for Lenten discipleship is Mary of Bethany, who, despising all honor and a year's worth of wealth, humbled and impoverished herself in a full-bodied act of discipleship, the anointing of Jesus' body for his burial. Like our sister before us, the Lenten texts call us to put our wealth, our honor, our very bodies at the service of the one we call Lord and Savior. For Lent requires of us far more than the giving up of a bad habit, the practice of showy self-discipline. Lent ultimately requires of us our very lives. Sisters and brothers, let us keep a holy Lent.

Note

1. See my commentary on the RCL Gospel reading for the Fifth Sunday of Lent.

ASH WEDNESDAY

FEBRUARY 17, 2010

Revised Common (RCL)	Episcopal (BCP)	Roman Catholic (LFM)
Joel 2:1-2, 12-17 or	Joel 2:1-2, 12-17 or	Joel 2:12-18
Isa. 58:1-12	Isa. 58:1-12	
Ps. 51:1-17	Psalm 103 or 103:8-14	Ps. 51:3-4, 5-6, 12-13,
		14, 17
2 Cor. 5:20b—6:10	2 Cor. 5:20b—6:10	2 Cor. 5:20—6:2
Matt. 6:1-6, 16-21	Matt. 6:1-6, 16-21	Matt. 6:1-6, 16-18

FIRST READING

JOEL 2:1-2, 12-17 (RCL, BCP)
JOEL 2:12-18 (LFM)
ISAIAH 58:1-12 (RCL ALT., BCP ALT.)

Understanding the Readings

Joel 2 is most likely a late fifth-century B.C.E. prophecy composed after a famine-producing locust invasion.[1] The prophet parallels this with a vision of the impending *yôm YHWH,* the "day of the LORD": a day marked by heavy clouds and gloom, and the force of the "apocalyptic army" of YHWH (vv. 1-2).[2] Nowhere in Joel is either disaster considered a punishment for sin. Instead, each causes sorrowing and shame in the face of apparent divine abandonment (v. 17b).[3] The sounding of the *shofar* marks the prophetic response to disaster: a call for communal fasting and mourning from which not even newlyweds are exempted.[4] Mourning, here, is an act of faith in YHWH whom Joel, quoting the Torah, affirms to be "gracious and compassionate, full of mercy and loyalty" (v. 13; Exod. 34:6; my trans.).[5] At stake is the honor both of YHWH and of YHWH's people who, because of their calamity, are in danger of becoming a proverb (*mashal*) among the nations (v. 17b).[6] And yet, even the prophet is uncertain of YHWH's response (v. 14). Joel 2:18 marks a turning point only included in the LFM, signaling the positive, indeed zealous, response of YHWH on behalf of the people and the land. In the end, YHWH remains faithful.

Isaiah 58:1-12 is found in Third Isaiah, the portion of Isaiah written after the return of the exiles to Palestine.[7] This passage also focuses on apparent divine abandonment; the people claim to worship YHWH in vain (v. 3a). But the prophet disagrees. Raising his voice "like a *shofar*," he utters a full-throated condemnation of the house of Jacob for its transgression and rebellion (v. 1). The people seem to delight (*yekhpatsun*) both in justice (*tsedaqah*) and in just judgments (*mishpete-tsedeq*) (v. 2). However, their delight (*khepets*) is achieved by oppressing workers and through community strife (vv. 3-4). The prophet's prescription is clear. YHWH's people must deprive themselves of oppressive practices that keep people in bondage, literally tearing apart every yoke (v. 6). They must tend to the hungry, the homeless, and the naked among them; providing from their own sustenance (*napsek*) for the hungry (vv. 7, 10).[8] Only if these practices are followed will healing come to these exiles striving to rebuild Jerusalem. But, as the community puts them in place, the prophet promises that they will become an oasis in the desert and a light in the shadows; and YHWH will go behind and before them, answering whenever they call (vv. 11-12).

> The people seem to delight both in justice and in just judgments, but their delight is achieved by oppressing workers and through community strife.

Preaching the Readings

These passages provoke two different kinds of Ash Wednesday sermons. Joel is a call for those in desperate times not to give up but to return to YHWH. It evokes a time of community mourning in the face of unavoidable disaster. Such a sermon would speak particularly clearly to persons recovering from drought or flood, tornado or hurricane, or the countless other unforeseen disasters with which humans live. It speaks to those who may be entering into the solemnity of the Lenten season with broken hearts and beaten spirits. To these, Joel offers the reminder that God can be approached not only with repentance for communal guilt but also with sorrow for communal loss, and with faith in a God who is "patient and kind, compassionate and loyal." It is critical to remember that at no point does Joel blame the people of God for the disasters coming upon them, and such a focus would not be in keeping with the message of this text. In this case, disaster is not evidence of sin. But, in the face of potential hopelessness and a loss of faith, Joel reminds us of our need to depend on our compassionate God.

> In the face of potential hopelessness and a loss of faith, Joel reminds us of our need to depend on our compassionate God.

By contrast, the Isaiah text calls to repentance Christians who have never allowed their Sunday observances to interrupt their working lives. Isaiah meddles in the nonliturgical lives of the faithful, calling busy, successful worshipers to consider how their lives and lifestyles oppress those who labor. In the face of careful external observations of correct worship, not unlike the "worship wars," ordination struggles, and other such contentious ecclesiastical matters of twenty-first-century churches, the prophet sounds a disruptive note, as he challenges people of faith on their strife-filled interactions. This passage also evokes sermons relating to global injustices in the economy of the twenty-first century, particularly as the poor of the global South make luxury items for the wealthy of the global North without adequate pay or protection. The prophet places a choice before the faithful, a choice that may sound uncomfortably like earned grace. If the community would be healed, it must change its interactions with its neighbors; only then will YHWH hear and respond to them, guiding and protecting them. Yet the choice is not truly between earned grace and free grace; rather, it is between worship in ritual only and worship that shapes justice in the community.

RESPONSIVE READINGS

PSALM 51:1-17 (RCL)
PSALM 51:3-4, 5-6, 12-13, 14, 17 (LFM)
PSALM 103 OR 103:8-14 (BCP)

Understanding and Using the Psalms

Psalm 51 is an individual psalm of lament found in the second book of Psalms.[9] Like other psalms attributed to David, it is attributed to a specific occasion: David's rape of Bathsheba (v. 1). The use of *Elohim* rather than *YHWH* here may reflect the distance between God and the poet caused by sin.[10] Appropriately, this psalm is commonly used as a prayer of individual confession for sins. However, care should be taken not to preach it as David's prayer about Bathsheba without considering whether the sin of David in that narrative is "only" against God (51:4; LFM 51:6).[11]

Psalm 103 is an individual psalm of praise, which might also be classified as a hymn.[12] As one of the psalms set in the exilic period, this psalm turns a personal song of thanksgiving for healing (vv. 3-4) into a communal call to remember the faithfulness of YHWH to all oppressed people (v. 6), especially to those who keep covenant (v. 18).[13] YHWH is to be praised as a God who does justice, and who is loyal and merciful to frail humanity. There is a natural affinity between the portrayals of YHWH in this psalm and the reading from Joel.

SECOND READING

2 CORINTHIANS 5:20B—6:10 (RCL, BCP)
2 CORINTHIANS 5:20—6:2 (LFM)

Understanding the Reading

Second Corinthians 5:20—6:10 is part of Paul's defense of his ministry to the contentious church at Corinth.[14] As part of this defense, Paul underscores his understanding of the work of God through Christ in the world. Both lectionary readings are preceded by Paul's assertion that, through Christ's death, God has done an act of re-creation and reconciliation with the entire cosmos (v. 18). As a result, all who are in Christ are a new creation (*kainē ktisis*; v. 17). It is of this gospel that Paul and those who have done ministry with him are "ambassadors" or envoys of the Christ (v. 20). An ambassador, here, would be the mouthpiece of the emperor, speaking not her own words but those of the one who sent her.[15] Paul argues out of this rhetorical position of strength that the Corinthian church must allow God to do an act of reconciliation in them also (v. 20). The passive voice, "be reconciled," is critical. In 2 Corinthians 5:18-19, Paul makes it clear that the act of reconciliation comes *from* God *to* the cosmos, rather than in the reverse order. The miracle of the divine act of reconciliation is akin to the divine act of making "him sin who knew no sin on our behalf" (v. 21; my trans.). Each instance is evidence of God's activity.

Paul's quotation of Isaiah 49:8 continues his argument. Quoting the eschatological vision of the "suffering servant" in Isaiah 49, Paul connects the coming salvific age of God with the actions of re-creation and reconciliation that God has *already* done through the death of Christ (6:1-2).

> The argument is clear: if God has done this great work, then the promise of Isaiah must be intended for the present hour.

The argument is clear: if God has done this great work, then the promise of Isaiah must be intended for the present hour. There is an urgency in Paul's appeal, an urgency born *both* out of his local struggle with the Corinthians *and* out of his firm belief in the immediacy of the appearance (*parousia*) of the Christ.

Paul's defense of his ministry in this section concludes with a hardship and virtues list, "a typical form found among Stoic and Cynic philosophers" (6:3-10).[16] These must primarily be understood as a form of self-commendation, even if it is tempting to see them as a "to-do list" for busy Christians. Paul commends to the Corinthians his ministry, a ministry that, though facing hardship and dishonor, is nevertheless being conducted in "the power of God" (v. 7).

When choosing to preach this passage, one should pay careful attention to the active role of God, both in the passage and in chapters 5 and 6 as a whole. It is God who reconciles; this is not a human action. The passage, then, is not so much a traditional call to repentance as a call to submission to the work of God as God acts to make the community of faith the embodiment of divine righteousness or, perhaps better, of divine justice.[17] This reconciliation is the "grace" that is not to be taken in vain (6:1). For this reconciliation, like the re-creation of humanity seen earlier in chapter 5, is not instigated by human will or human repentance. Rather, it is a result of God's choice to make Jesus "sin who knew no sin" (5:21). This may be difficult for Christians to hear who feel compelled to "do something" in order to receive God's favor.

Preaching this text also requires careful attention to the "fierce urgency of 'now'" underscored by Paul's quotation of Isaiah 49.[18] For, although the divine act of reconciliation is in itself miraculous, even more powerful is the eschatological hope to which it points: the promise of the coming "day of the Lord." Paul's invocation of the promise from Second Isaiah points to the continuing, active presence of God in the world, a presence that will ultimately bring about the divine promises of the age to come.

The final section of this passage may be understood in light of the part of the call of Saul in Acts in which God says, "I myself will show him how much he must suffer for the sake of my name" (Acts 9:16). Paul's catalog of hardships underscores the suffering that can accompany being an ambassador of God. Thus, it would be appropriate in an Ash Wednesday sermon to use this part of the text as a discussion of the cost of discipleship. But the cost is not the only focus of this long list of hardships. One must also note the response to the cost: truthfulness although charged as liars, living in the midst of dying, rejoicing although sad, having nothing but possessing everything (6:8-10). Paul does not just dwell on the difficulty of the work of discipleship; he underscores also the joy of discipleship. A faithful sermon on this passage should do no less.

> Paul does not just dwell on the difficulty of the work of discipleship; he underscores also the joy of discipleship.

THE GOSPEL

MATTHEW 6:1-6, 16-21 (RCL, BCP)
MATTHEW 6:1-6, 16-18 (LFM)

Understanding the Gospel

With the exception of the LFM, the Gospel reading for Ash Wednesday consists of two different rhetorical arguments excerpted from Matthew's Sermon on the Mount. In the section on preaching the text, I will suggest ways in which these two sections may be interpreted together. Here, I will spend more time on the characteristics of each of these two sections.

Section one, Matthew 6:1-6, 16-18, consists of three directives about lived piety that have as their overarching theme the question of one's motivation for the public worship of God. This theme is stated in the first two verses of Matthew 6: "Be careful not to practice your just acts before people *so that you might be seen by them*"[19] (my trans.). The emphasis in this verse is not simply the public nature of the acts of piety or of justice, but the rationale behind the public practice—so that others might see you. The warning is clear: actions with this motivation will cause you to lose your heavenly reward, or, more accurately, your heavenly wages.[20]

The Matthean author groups together three forms of public piety in section one: almsgiving (or acts of mercy), prayer, and fasting.[21] For twenty-first-century Christians, none of these three acts would necessarily be seen as public acts of piety. In the first century, however, piety was a public matter. The values of the ancient world included those of honor and shame, more accurately "honor precedence" and shame. "Honor precedence," according to Louise Joy Lawrence, "constitutes worldly honor *that validates itself before an evaluating public.*"[22] It as important, then, for a first-century person to have community validation of her piety based on her external activity. Within first-century Judaism, this was further reinforced by the challenge of the Pharisee party to become a living Torah in all aspects of one's life, apart from and transcendent of temple worship.[23] The combination of these two forces combined often to reserve the greatest honors for those who could be *seen* to be living out Torah in all aspects of their lives, giving ten percent to God even of mint, dill, and cumin (Matt. 23:23).

The response of the Matthean author to this culture of public piety is not to forbid acts of mercy, prayer, or fasting. To the contrary, the presumption in each of these three sections is that disciples of Christ *will* be participating in these activities. This is emphasized by the repetition of the subjunctive conjunction *hotan*— *whenever* you pray, fast, do acts of mercy. The issue is not *whether* you should act, but *how*. To this question of how, Matthew begins with a counterexample: that of the "hypocrites." "Hypocrite" here should be understood as a synonym for "actor."[24] "The term," says Lawrence, "seems implicitly to censure those who, like actors, perform a role for public acclaim."[25] The counterexample, then, is not those who participate in acts of piety, but those who do so "for public acclaim." Those whom Matthew calls "actors" blow trumpets before themselves, engage in long prayers, and disfigure their faces *for public recognition*. For these acts, they receive payment in full: public recognition and worldly honor.

In light of the rise in the Protestant observation of the mark of ashes on Ash Wednesday, a word ought to be said about the prohibition of "face disfiguration" found here. Etan Levine points out that in first-century Judaism, the practice of fasting was often accompanied by the placing of wood ashes on one's head as a sign of mourning.[26] This practice became theologically interpreted by the early rabbis as a call to God to remember the binding of Isaac (or *'aqêdah*) in Genesis.[27] Isaac's binding, in turn, was seen as a means of vicarious atonement for all believers. As the Babylonian Talmud reports, "it signifies that God will remember for our sake the ashes of Isaac and have mercy upon us."[28] As a result, it is not surprising that early Christians would want to distance themselves from a practice that signified in *their* day atonement through Isaac rather than through Jesus Christ. In the twenty-first century, it would be anachronistic to apply this prohibition to Ash Wednesday observations that serve to remind Christians of their mortality and of Christ's sacrifice.

> Those whom Matthew calls "actors" blow trumpets before themselves, engage in long prayers, and disfigure their faces for public recognition.

Matthew's alternative to the public expression of piety is that of a private worship of God. This also leads to a kind of honor, not honor *precedence* but honor *virtue*: honor that is "gained before one's inner being or before an omniscient divine figure, from whom nothing can be hidden and in whose eyes honor is ultimately vindicated."[29] For Matthew, this is the kind of honor that Christians are to seek: honor in God's eyes, the God who sees and who will reward the piety of those who have no need to put on an act.

The final portion of this lectionary passage (vv. 19-21) turns to heavenly economics. In it, Matthew counsels against storing up treasures on the earth; what is at issue is the ongoing habit of "storing up" or "making treasures," signaled by Matthew's use of the present active indicative form of the verb *thaurizō*. That such "treasures" can be eaten away by moth and rust, and can be stolen by thieves literally digging through (*diorussō*) the walls of the house, suggests that these treasures include precious metals and fabrics, the material wealth most likely reserved for the very wealthy. It also points to the futility of such hoarding, for even if one could keep one's house free from thieves, the ravages of rust and moth would have been unavoidable in the ancient world. Craig Blomburg points out that only such possessions that are not being used regularly by the household are in immediate danger. The text, then, does not critique possessions overall; it critiques excess possessions that must be "stored up." That is, the text is not so much anti-possession as anti-hoarding.[30]

By contrast, hoarding heavenly treasures—the nature of which Matthew does not spell out—should be an ongoing practice, as all such treasures are guaranteed to be secure from the vagaries of life on earth. But Matthew's rationale is ultimately not about the safety of these treasures in heaven in contrast with the vulnerability of the treasures one can hoard on earth. Rather, Matthew understands that the location and safety of one's treasure can consume one's heart. If one's heart is focused on the earthly treasures that one is hoarding, it is much harder for that same heart to be focused on heavenly treasures. It is in this spirit that Matthew's warning regarding the location of one's treasure and one's heart should be taken.

> The text does not critique possessions overall; it critiques excess possessions that must be "stored up."

Preaching the Gospel

The two themes of the Gospel reading—piety for divine rather than human approval and the hoarding of heavenly rather than earthly treasure—have in common the contrast between the focus on heavenly rather than on earthly matters. The parallel is easily made. Just as one can hoard wealth, one can hoard community approval. But just as vulnerable as material treasure is, so also is popular opinion. And, perhaps even more disturbingly, the Matthean witness is that the most honored or blessed disciples are those who are reviled, persecuted, and slandered for the sake of Christ Jesus (Matt. 5:10-11).

For preachers of this Gospel, questions of visible piety emerge particularly in light of the ritual of the imposition of ashes that marks most Ash Wednesday observations. The gift of this Gospel is that it allows the preacher and the congregation to wrestle with the question of "for whom" the imposition is done. Matthew warns the community sternly against entering into the ritual of imposition solely so that others may observe the piety of those who are worshiping. The community is called to eschew piety for the sake of status or honor. Rather, pious acts are and ought to be, ultimately, between the believer and God. This text thus can serve as a call to self-examination regarding being judgmental and seeking status as one enters the Lenten fast.

At the same time, preachers should resist the temptation merely to spiritualize the stern warning about economic hoarding in Matthew 6:19-21. The ethics of wealthy Christians in an age of increasing global poverty is one with which Christians must wrestle. It would not be honest to present this text as though it had no economic implications. Similarly, it would be dishonest to preach this text as though the hoarding of wealth and the obsession with that hoarding had no spiritual implications. Wealth and poverty may seem like an odd topic for the beginning of the Lenten fast, but they are at the core of this portion of the Gospel for the day. Matthew 6:19-21 pointedly invites Christian disciples to reevaluate the location of their hearts, which is determined by the location of their treasure. It is a call to a simpler, more just lifestyle as part of the Lenten fast.

Preaching the Gospel in concert with the first readings raises two kinds of questions. The first surrounds the blowing of a trumpet in the context of prayer. While the Matthean text counsels against it, both the Joel and Isaiah texts call for it. Here the issue becomes not whether or when to blow the trumpet. Matthew's counsel against blowing the trumpet is, as has been noted, counsel directed at those who would seek recognition for their piety from others. The blowing of the trumpet, here, is not for the believing community but rather to mark the difference between insiders and outsiders. By contrast, the trumpet in Joel is a call to the community for a time of mourning, fasting, and prayer. As the entire community is involved, even the typically exempted newlyweds, there is no outsider left to marvel at the piety of the ones in prayer. The whole community is in prayer because the whole community is in mourning. Similarly, the trumpet in Isaiah—the cry of the prophet—is not directed to the outside world as a sign of the piety of the people. Quite the opposite; it is directed into the community as a sign of the injustice of the people. A sermon on these texts for Ash Wednesday, then, could certainly beg the question regarding when and under what circumstances Christian disciples should trumpet the start of a community fast.

> It would be dishonest to preach this text as though the hoarding of wealth and the obsession with that hoarding had no spiritual implications.

A second consonance between the first readings and the Gospel for Ash Wednesday is the question of economic justice found both in Matthew and Isaiah. Each points the community to a sober examination of its relationship to wealth and work, and the impact of that relationship on its relationship to heaven and to God's people. Matthew's charge about hoarding gets expanded in Isaiah's question about whether a fast without community justice is a fast suitable to YHWH. In light of these readings, an Ash Wednesday sermon could reimagine the Lenten fast as a fast from hoarding and injustice on earth. Instead, the community could focus on questions of adequate provision and care for all of God's people as central to the Lenten fast.

Reading the Gospel in concert with the epistle for Ash Wednesday suggests two other themes. The first echoes the prior theme: that of the economic cost of discipleship. The passage from 2 Corinthians includes several costs of discipleship toward its end, among them, poverty and destitution. And yet, says Paul, in the face of what might appear to be hopelessness, we are rich and we have everything.

Paul's inventory of his costs puts into stark relief Matthew's critique of Christian hoarding and the placement of the Christian heart. If the call is to allow God to reconcile the church to God, the question that Paul seeks to answer in this inventory is, "At what cost?" He gives, in perhaps more disturbing detail, the same sort of answer that Matthew gives—at the cost of earthly wealth for the sake of heavenly reconciliation and focus. In different ways, both seem to be asking Christian people the same question: Your money or your life?

At the same time, there is a broader set of consonances raised by 2 Corinthians and Matthew. These revolve around the cost associated with allowing God to do God's act of reconciliation. Primary to these costs is status: status lost because one cannot as a disciple trumpet one's piety before the world, and because, as a disciple, one may indeed face hardships for the sake of the gospel. Preachers of these texts may choose, then, to enter the Lenten fast by weighing the costs of discipleship with their congregations, costs that may include but are not limited to questions of economics.

> In different ways, both Matthew and Paul seem to be asking Christian people the same question: Your money or your life?

Overall, these texts call the community of faith to a deeper Lenten fast than that of mere ritual observance. Reading all of these texts in concert, we find that the Lenten fast is not to be called for public piety but rather for community mourning and community challenge. The call is not to a discipleship that ignores injustice, but one that dismantles it. The call is not to a discipleship with no demands on one's money or one's life, but to a discipleship that demands all that one is and all that one has. And the call is not to a God who will not hear or see a community in mourning or repentance; rather, it is to a God who is faithful, compassionate, and ultimately forgiving.

Notes

1. James L. Crenshaw, *Joel: A New Translation with Introduction and Commentary,* Anchor Bible 24c (New York: Doubleday, 1995), 23, 26. As Crenshaw notes, it is notoriously difficult to say with any certainty exactly when biblical books are written; this is especially the case with Joel, for which we have very few historical clues.

2. Duane A. Garrett, "The Structure of Joel," *Journal of the Evangelical Theological Society* 28, no. 3 (September 1985): 291–94.

3. Ronald A. Simkins, "'Return to YHWH': Honor and Shame in Joel," *Semeia* 68 (1994): 45ff. However, I do not fully follow Simkins's argument that the entirety of 1:1—2:11 is about a locust invasion.

4. *yetse' khatan mekhedro vekallah mekhuppatah*: Wilfred Watson calls this a form of gender-matched synonymous parallelism in which the two masculine nouns (*khatan mekhedro*) are explicitly paralleled with two feminine nouns (*vekallah mekhuppatah*).

This sort of parallelism is to signal completion, that the whole community is called to the fast. Wilfred G. E. Watson, "Gender-Matched Synonymous Parallelism in the OT," *Journal of Biblical Literature* [hereafter *JBL*] 99, no. 3 (1980): 325–27. For all transliteration, I am using the general-purpose style recommended by the Society for Biblical Literature Style Guide.

5. This formula for YHWH is also found in Jonah. For more striking ways in which Jonah and Joel are reading anthologically, see Thomas B. Dozeman, "Inter-biblical Interpretation of Yahweh's Gracious and Compassionate Character," *JBL* 108, no. 2 (1989): 207–33.

6. Simkins, "'Return to YHWH'," 51–52.

7. Paul D. Hanson, *Isaiah 40–66,* Interpretation: A Bible Commentary for Teaching and Preaching (Louisville: Westminster John Knox, 1995), 191–92; Walter Brueggemann, *An Introduction to the Old Testament: The Canon and Christian Imagination* (Louisville: Westminster John Knox, 2003), 171–72.

8. Victor Hurowitz argues convincingly that the use of *npš* here should be understood as a cognate of the Akkadian *napištu,* "sustenance." Victor Avigdor Hurowitz, "A Forgotten Meaning of *NEPEŠ* in Isaiah LVIII 10," *Vetus Testamentum* (hereafter *VT*) 47, no. 1 (1997): 43–52.

9. The five groupings or "books" of the Psalms are Psalms 1–41; 42–72; 73–89; 90–106; 107–150. These groupings follow the history of the Davidic and Solomonic kingdoms, the exile of the people, their lives in exile, and their return from exile under the kingship of YHWH. Nancy L. deClaissé-Walford, *An Introduction to the Psalms: A Song from Ancient Israel* (St. Louis: Chalice, 2004), 78, 129–44.

10. Frank-Lothar Hossfeld and Erich Zenger, "The So-Called Elohistic Psalter: A New Solution for an Old Problem," in *A God So Near: Essays on Old Testament Theology in Honor of Patrick D. Miller,* eds. Brent A. Strawn and Nancy D. Bowen (Winona Lake, Ind.: Eisenbrauns, 2003), 45, 50–51.

11. Barbara Ellison Rosenblit, "David, Bat Sheva and the Fifty-first Psalm," *Cross Currents* 45, no. 3 (Fall 1995): 326–40.

12. Bernard W. Anderson and Stephen Bishop, *Out of the Depths: The Psalms Speak for Us Today,* 3rd ed. (Louisville: Westminster John Knox, 2000), 116.

13. deClaissé-Walford, *An Introduction to the Psalms,* 99.

14. Several scholars have noted the contentious nature of the relationship between Paul and the Corinthian church, including Luke Timothy Johnson, *The Writings of the New Testament: An Interpretation,* rev. ed. (Minneapolis: Fortress Press, 1999), 295–324; and Raymond E. Brown, *An Introduction to the New Testament,* The Anchor Bible Reference Library (New York: Doubleday, 1996), 511–40.

15. Ambassadors functioned as stand-ins for those who sent them. As such, their messages had the same force as if their patrons were speaking. This made ambassadors powerful people, and the rejection of them was a rejection of the one who

sent them. See Ben Witherington, *Conflict and Community in Corinth: A Socio-Rhetorical Commentary on 1 and 2 Corinthians* (Grand Rapids: Eerdmans, 195), 328. Jesus makes a similar argument in Luke 10:16b: ". . . and whoever rejects me rejects the one who sent me" (NRSV).

16. Dennis C. Duling, *The New Testament: History, Literature and Social Context*, 4th ed. (Belmont, Calif.: Wadsworth, 2003), 229.

17. The Greek word *dikaiosunē* is commonly translated "righteousness" in English translations of the Bible. However, it is perhaps more appropriately translated "justice."

18. Martin Luther King Jr., "I Have a Dream" (28 August 1963). http://www.americanrhetoric.com/speeches/mlkihaveadream.htm, accessed January 6, 2009.

19. See n. 17, above.

20. The Greek word *misthos* is the most common word used for payment given to a worker for services rendered. The theological implications of the concept "heavenly wages" will be discussed later.

21. From the Greek word *eleew*, the word *eleosune* suggests acts of mercy, one of which may be the giving of alms.

22. Louise Joy Lawrence, "'For truly I tell you, they have received their reward'" (Matt 6:2): Investigating Honor Precedence and Honor Virtue," *Catholic Biblical Quarterly* (hereafter *CBQ*) 64 (2002): 690.

23. Calvin J. Roetzel, *The World That Shaped the New Testament*, rev. ed. (Louisville: Westminster John Knox, 2002), 38–39.

24. Lawrence, "'For truly I tell you . . .'," 700.

25. Ibid.

26. Etan Levine, "The Theology of Fast-Day Cosmetics (Matthew 6:16-18)," *Journal of Ritual Studies* 13, no. 1 (Summer 1999): 2.

27. Ibid.

28. Ibid.

29. Lawrence, "'For truly I tell you . . .'," 690.

30. Craig Blomburg, "On Wealth and Worry: Matthew 6:19-34—Meaning and Significance," *Criswell Theological Review* 6, no. 1 (1992): 77.

FIRST SUNDAY IN LENT

FEBRUARY 21, 2010

Revised Common (RCL)	Episcopal (BCP)	Roman Catholic (LFM)
Deut. 26:1-11	Deut. 26:(1-4) 5-11	Deut. 26:4-10
Ps. 91:1-2, 9-16	Psalm 91 or 91:9-15	Ps. 91:1-2, 10-11, 12-13, 14-15
Rom. 10:8b-13	Rom. 10:(5-8a) 8b-13	Rom. 10:8-13
Luke 4:1-13	Luke 4:1-13	Luke 4:1-13

FIRST READING

DEUTERONOMY 26:1-11 (RCL)
DEUTERONOMY 26:(1-4) 5-11 (BCP)
DEUTERONOMY 26:4-10 (LFM)

Understanding the Reading

Although the book of Deuteronomy is framed as the last statement of the law by Moses (Deut. 1:1), clues in its style and emphasis suggest an authorship some six centuries later in the Northern Kingdom.[1] Deuteronomy rose to importance as a law book sometime in the late seventh century B.C.E. in the Southern Kingdom under the reign of Josiah where it was used to prescribe temple-based cultic worship of YHWH for the people of the Southern Kingdom.[2] Written in the structure of a "covenant-making or covenant-renewing ceremony," the bulk of the book consists of "a historical resumé of the Sinai events, a recital of the laws, a proclamation of the establishment of a covenant, and a recital of blessings and curses."[3]

Today's first reading is an excerpt from the end of Deuteronomy's law recital, a portion of the law regarding the tithe of the firstfruits that was to be paid every third year (Deut. 26:12). In a significant expansion of the command found in Exodus 23:19a, the Deuteronomist presents a lengthy description of the presentation of this tithe. Those who have inherited "the land that the LORD your God is giving you" are to bring the first of the harvest, in a basket, to the priest, and are to make two specific declarations in the presence of the priest (26:1). In 26:3, the faithful affirm, simply by their bodily presence, that "this day . . . I have come to the land which YHWH swore to our forebears to give us."[4] Then, in 26:4-10, they rehearse the first portion of the exodus narrative and the last portion of the conquest of Canaan.

Of particular note is the way in which the narrative of this ritual pulses with the actions of YHWH. Four times in 26:1-3, the narrator reminds us of YHWH's actions: in the gift of land (vv. 1, 2, 3) and in the choice of a seat for the Holy Name (v. 2). The actions of YHWH also make up the centerpiece of the declaration in 26:4-9, particularly as it relates to the deliverance of the children of the Aramaeans from the mistreatment of the Egyptians (vv. 7b-9). YHWH's actions are to be repeated aloud as part of the ritual of the firstfruits. In a smaller sense, this is an example of what Bruce Birch et al. call "the interweaving of law and narrative."[5] The basis of law and ritual is ultimately the story of the divine interaction in the life of the community.

> The basis of law and ritual is ultimately the story of the divine interaction in the life of the community.

The role of the priest in all of this is fascinating. For in Deuteronomy, the priest stands at the precipice between the altar and the believers, but he stands mute, acting only to bear the gift from the believer to the altar. It is not he who makes the ritual pronouncement; nor does he proclaim the acceptability of the gift. Rather, in this triennial ritual, the priest stands as a silent witness to the work of YHWH in the life of the believers.

Preaching the Reading

Deuteronomy 26 should be reminiscent of another important ritual in Christianity: the anamnesis (a word that means "remembrance") that takes place in the celebration of the Lord's Supper. As Aelred Cody points out, this text, like those depicting the Lord's Supper, "recalls to mind not a static attribute but an event, something done in the historical past."[6] In this lection, the acts of YHWH on behalf of the people are the subject of the anamnesis. Believers are called upon to "make a *confessio*" about the work of God in their lives and in their harvest.[7] The lection functions as a "performative utterance," a ritual through which "the Israelite 'owns' the story of God's saving acts."[8] The ritual of the firstfruits is performed "in memory of" the past and ongoing faithfulness of YHWH to the believing community.

In light of this, a sermon on this text would rightly call the Lenten community to acts that recollect the faithfulness of YHWH, even in the face of oppression and wandering. This text may even serve as a springboard to a reinterpretation of the

Lenten discipline of confession—for confession need not always be interpreted as the naming of one's sin. As the text demonstrates, it can also be the joyful proclamation of the faithfulness of the promises of God, both in word and in actions.

This text, however, does pose a danger. Like much of the writings of the Deuteronomist school, it has a tendency to paint ethnic groups with a fairly broad brush. Although Aramaeans and Egyptians are both near relatives of the Israelites, it is the latter group that gets stereotyped by the Deuteronomist.[9] It is not unusual for an Israelite writer to perpetuate the trope of the oppressive Egyptians, but Christian preachers should be careful not to repeat it uncritically. For the "wandering Aramaean" (or, according to J. Gerald Janzen, the "starving Aramaean"), Egypt would have been a place of refuge before it became a place of oppression, as is the witness of the biblical narrative (cf. Genesis 46ff.).[9] Only after it became a place of oppression would YHWH intervene in its history and in the history of the Israelites. The real truth about the Egyptians lies somewhere in an uneasy and unwritten middle ground. As Sandra Gravett et al. point out, "the biblical boundary of exclusion and inclusion between Israelites and Egyptians is not stable but shifts, marking Israel's ethnic identity as one of ambiguous coexistence with Egypt."[10] In light of this, preachers should be careful not to wholly vilify Egypt even as they reenact the anamnesis of the saving work of God.

> Confession need not always be interpreted as the naming of one's sin, but also be the joyful proclamation of the faithfulness of the promises of God, both in word and in actions.

RESPONSIVE READING

PSALM 91:1-2, 9-16 (RCL)
PSALM 91 OR 91:9-15 (BCP)
PSALM 91:1-2, 10-11, 12-13, 14-15 (LFM)

Understanding and Using the Psalm

Psalm 91 reveals nothing to us about its author, audience, or about the reason for its composition.[11] Scholars differ regarding its classification.[12] The text of the psalm poses additional challenges. Verse 1 is a third-person description of the one who has lodged himself (*yithlonan*) "in the shadow of Shaddai [*b'tzel shadday*]." But in 91:2, the psalm becomes a first-person testimony, "I will say . . . [*'omar*]." Verses 5-8 testify to the protection of YHWH in the second and third person alternatively. Indeed, verses 5b-7 read more like a challenge: "Let it fly from the arrow daily . . ."[13] (my trans.). 91:9a is a first-person confession of the protection of YHWH, but verses 9b-13 return to the second-person testimony from verses 5-8. The psalm ends with the very voice of YHWH, confirming that the psalmist is loved and protected.

On the First Sunday of Lent, Psalm 91 plays an important role in the tempta-tion narrative. But the psalm may be taken on its own merits as well. It may be read as a heavenly play—with a narrator reading 91:1; a chorus reading 91:3-8 and 9b-13; a single voice reading 91:2 and 91:9a; and another voice, or group of voices, reading the YHWHistic response. In so doing, as in the first reading, the faithfulness of YHWH is highlighted.

Second Reading

ROMANS 10:8B-13 (RCL)
ROMANS 10:(5-8A) 8B-13 (BCP)
ROMANS 10:8-13 (LFM)

Understanding the Reading

In order to understand today's second reading, a quick review of Paul's understanding of salvation may be in order; and this is best done by summariz-ing Paul's argument in Romans. Paul sees all of humanity as subject to sin—thus subject to the wrath of God (1:18)—and as living in enmity with God (5:9-10). The result of this is decay and death (8:24); this is not death of the mortal body, but ultimate oblivion caused by irreconcilable distance from God. Bart Ehrman reminds us that

> sin in these verses is not simply something that a person does, a disobe-dient action against God, a transgression of [God's] laws. It is instead a kind of cosmic power, an evil force that compels people to live in alienation from God. The human problem . . . is that people are enslaved to this demonic power and are unable to break free from their bondage.[14]

Further, and most dire of all, "when [this cosmic force] succeeds, it totally removes a person from the realm of God . . . all people are subject to the over-powering force of death, and there is nothing that they can do to set themselves free."[15]

Within this context, this lection describes what Arthur Dewey has termed "genuine access to ultimate power."[16] According to Paul, despite the long odds that face all of humanity, Jew and Gentile, it is possible to be rescued from the cosmic grip of sin and oblivion. And that rescue comes not from the just relation-ship made possible by the keeping of the law. Instead, that rescue comes from trust, a better translation perhaps of *pistis* than the more common "faith."[17] That trust is in the proximity of a God who affects rescue for all of humanity, a deity as close as one's own breath (10:8).

At the crux of Paul's argument is his use of Deuteronomy 30 as a means to argue against another legal formula found in Leviticus 18. Both texts, ironically, speak about the keeping of Torah. Leviticus 18 serves to differentiate the people of YHWH from their close relatives, the Egyptians, and at the same time to slander these Gentiles as somehow being deviant.[18] Such a text would likely have weighed heavily on Paul's almost certainly majority Gentile audience. In response, Paul reimagines the Deuteronomy text, a text which argues for the proximity of the law that leads to a just relationship with God. Paul intention-

> According to Paul, despite the long odds that face all of humanity, Jew and Gentile, it is possible to be rescued from the cosmic grip of sin and oblivion.

ally refigures this law not as Torah, but as the cosmic redefinition of "law" that, he argues, the Christ event signifies.

Paul's point is not that one must speak a certain mantra into the air in order to force God's hand. Such a theology misses the ultimate point of Paul's letter that it is God who, through the resurrection of the Christ, fights and wins the cosmic battle on our behalf (6:9-11). Even the grammar of today's lection points to the passivity of those who are being rescued; Paul says that those who call on the name of the Lord "will be saved" (*sōthēsetai*), a future tense, passive voice verbal form that should not be confused with the more reflexive "will save themselves." Rather, Paul's point is that those who have already come to trust in this new understanding of the relationship with God will experience *God's* rescue and reconciliation, regardless of whether or not the strictures and polemics of the Levitical code find them wanting. With this assertion, which may well be based on "common liturgical language" of the early Pauline churches, Paul is arguing that the Gentile believers are always already made just before God *by God's action* in Christ Jesus. Not only is their supposed deviance dismissed, but despite their supposed lawlessness, they will be saved.

Preaching the Reading

Once understood, the second reading for the First Sunday of Lent practically preaches itself. At the very beginning of Lent, in which both sin and mortality are highlighted, this lection calls us to hope: to hope not in our own actions but in our trust in God who, despite us, has called us into right relationship. Preaching this text, then, becomes a call to trust that we, who also confess that Jesus is Lord, will be saved. But, if we are to be true to Paul, we must be very careful not to make this a call to action. Rather, this is a call to wonder and to celebration. The people of God, who make this weekly confession, are called to the wondrous paradox of our own sinfulness and God's faithfulness to us despite this.

Another danger in preaching this text is to pretend that somehow Judaism "got it wrong" and misinterprets its own tradition. If we are to be honest, it is not that Judaism misinterprets but that Paul *reinterprets* the biblical tradition. He rereads it to include the polemicized, stereotyped other: the Gentiles. We who inherit this tradition should be very careful not to repeat the same sorts of polemicization that frequent the texts of our adopted canons, both Old and New Testaments.[19]

> One danger in preaching this text is to pretend that somehow Judaism "got it wrong" and misinterprets its own tradition.

Rather, we Gentiles should stand grateful for the holy imagination of a Paul of Tarsus, who allows us, with the bearer of the firstfruits, to stand before the holy place and, in the words of gospel songwriter Margaret Douroux, proclaim in wonder, "If it had not been for the Lord on [our] side, tell me, where would [we] be? Where would [we] be?"[20]

The Gospel

LUKE 4:1-13 (RCL, BCP, LFM)

Understanding the Gospel

Every First Sunday of Lent, Christians read one of the Synoptic temptation narratives. For year C, the assigned lection comes from the Gospel according to Luke. Luke's redaction of this narrative points to a concern for spiritual and cosmic realities, for the presence of Gentiles in the church, and for the centrality of the Jerusalem Temple.

Luke begins his narrative by saying that "Jesus, full of the Holy Spirit, returned from the Jordan and went, in the Spirit, into the wilderness" (my trans.). Already Luke's narrative differs from Mark and Matthew in that Luke's Jesus goes, of his own volition, to the place of testing. Matthew's Jesus is "led by the Spirit" (*anēchthē . . . hupo tou pneumatos*), and in Mark's telling, the Spirit drives (or *casts*) Jesus out (*to pneuma auton ekballei*). There is a kind of self-possession in Luke's Jesus, a purposeful decision to face the tempter, which is not present in the other two narratives.

> There is a kind of self-possession in Luke's Jesus, a purposeful decision to face the tempter, which is not present in the other Synoptics.

Jesus' self-possession is underscored by Luke's description of Jesus as "full of the Holy Spirit." The Holy Spirit is an important player in the beginning of Luke's narrative: present at the birth of John (1:15-17); the annunciation to Mary (1:35); the prophecies of Elizabeth, Zechariah, Simeon (1:41, 67; 2:26-27); and during the preaching and baptisms performed by John (3:16, 22). In invoking its presence before Jesus' testing, Luke portrays a more powerful Jesus than either of the other two Synoptic writers.

This powerful Jesus faces three different temptations, each connected to the history of Israel as recorded by Deuteronomy. First, Jesus is tempted to assuage his forty-day hunger, a number reminiscent of the forty-year Israelite desert wanderings, by turning a stone into bread. Jesus' response seems straightforward, "not by bread alone will the person live" (*ouk ep' artō monō zēsetai ho anthrōpos*). In this response, Jesus seems to be saying that he is stronger than the need for food. However, Jesus' response points to Deuteronomy 8:3:

> [God] humbled you by letting you hunger, then by feeding you with manna, with which neither you nor your ancestors were acquainted, in order to make you understand that *one does not live by bread alone*, but by every word that comes from the mouth of the LORD.

Hunger is, rather, a way in which Jesus lives into the covenant relationship between God and God's people; by remaining hungry, Jesus demonstrates his trust that the food he needs will be provided by the same God who was faithful to the Israelites in the wilderness.

And yet, unlike Matthew, Luke omits "but by every word that comes from the mouth of the LORD." This omission is, very likely, deliberate. The premise of Deuteronomy 8 is found in verse 1: "This entire commandment that I command you today you must diligently observe, so that you may live and increase, and go in and occupy the land that the LORD promised on oath to your ancestors." While this might be good news to a more law-observant community, Luke's two-volume saga, written to a Greek named Theophilus and focused on the Gentile mission, could not accommodate such a restriction. Thus, Luke omits this as part of Jesus' response. For Luke, one did not have to keep the "entire commandment" in order to rely on the God of the wilderness.

In the second Lukan temptation, Jesus is given a vision of "all of the kingdoms of the inhabited earth" (my trans.), and is promised "this power and their splendor" in exchange for prostration before the devil (4:5-7). Behind this scene are two subplots. First, the scene relies on ancient understandings of patronage, in which a person would swear allegiance to a patron in exchange for some benefit, in this case, the power and the splendor of the inhabited world. One of the subplots, then, is the question of whether Jesus will opt to become a client of, and thus a spokesperson for, the devil in exchange for the power and splendor of the known world. But there is also a second subplot, a barely veiled critique of the source of imperial power. By Luke's telling, the power to dominate the world is given by the devil (4:6); by extension, then, the Roman domination of the world would have to be characterized as diabolic.[21] The question undergirding this second subplot is whether Jesus will pattern his ministry after the Roman imperial order.

Jesus' response needs to be understood in light of these two critiques. The quotation that he chooses is taken from Deuteronomy 6, a chapter particularly dedicated to the sole worship of YHWH. Earlier in the chapter is the great *Shema Yisrael*, which Jesus would later call the greatest commandment (Deut. 6:4). And immediately after Jesus' chosen quotation is a dire warning to the people of Israel not to worship the gods of other peoples, lest YHWH "destroy you from the face of the earth" (Deut. 6:15). Jesus is tempted with diabolic, imperial power in exchange for the worship and service of the devil. And just as he decides earlier to trust God to provide for his physical needs, here he decides to maintain his reliance on God for his earthly power.

Luke's final temptation takes Jesus to the top of the temple in Jerusalem. The temple figures heavily in Luke's birth and childhood narratives, as the location of the annunciation of John's impending birth, of the messianic nature of the infant Jesus, and of the boy Jesus' "father's house" (1:5-23; 2:22-38, 41-49). However, this temptation serves as Jesus' last interaction with the temple, the center of Judaism, until his entry into Jerusalem in Luke 19. The essence of Jesus' third temptation in Luke is this: "If you are so sure that God is so capable of providing you with your needs and with power, prove it." Jesus is tempted to hurl himself from the pinnacle of the Temple; and the basis of the temptation is a misreading of the psalm for this morning, Psalm 91. If, intimates the tester, God has given the angels charge over you, then they will catch you if you jump off of the temple. This is a misreading because, as noted above, Psalm 91 is a psalm of protection when one is under attack. Rather than counseling the one who relies on YHWH to be rash, the psalm counsels that one to wait and watch for YHWH's response.

> Jesus is tempted with diabolic, imperial power in exchange for the worship and service of the devil.

Jesus' retort, a third quotation of Deuteronomy, makes it clear that he understands this to be the case. The full quotation from Deuteronomy 6:16 is, "do not put the LORD your God to the test as you tested him at Massah." The allusion is to the desperation regarding lack of water that the people of Israel expressed during their wilderness wanderings. At the heart of this desperation was the question, "Is the LORD among us or not?" (Exod. 17:7). At the heart of that quarrel and this temptation was the question of the presence and reliability of God. Jesus' response, the climax of Luke's temptation narrative, is the affirmation of the trustworthiness of God in all things, a trustworthiness that does not need to be tested.

Preaching the Gospel

A careful reader of the Gospels will note that Matthew and Luke differ in the order of the second and third temptations. Matthew's ultimate temptation is for Jesus to gain "all authority in heaven and on earth" by worshiping the devil. For Luke, authority is only the penultimate test; the ultimate test is whether or not one trusts and relies on God, even when God's presence is not immediately apparent. This assertion of the unassailable presence and care of God is one that runs through the entire Gospel of Luke: in the punishment of Zechariah for not believing Gabriel's annunciation of John; in the story of Mary's pregnancy with Jesus; in the stories of Anna and Simeon's faithfulness; and in stories only told in Luke, like the prodigal son and the road to Emmaus. The theme continues in the Acts of the Apostles, in the choice of the twelfth apostle, in the story of Ananias and Sapphira, and even in the stories of the Ethiopian eunuch and of the conversion of Peter at the home of Cornelius the centurion. Through all of these narratives, Luke threads a theology of the fundamental trustworthiness of God.

Preaching this temptation narrative, then, requires the sermon writer to follow Luke's lead, focusing less on Jesus' ultimate cosmic authority, as Matthew does, and turning to questions of the believers' fundamental challenge in the face of temptation: trusting the presence and power of God so completely that there is no need to test it. Such a challenge flies in the face of "name it and claim it" popular theology, in which the believer is called to fling herself off of a variety of temples, testing God's ability to catch her. The discipline for this Lenten season, however, seems to be far less showy, if ultimately much more difficult. The discipline is to show one's trust through trust. The believer does not keep a holy Lent by showing through his risk taking how much he trusts God. Instead, she through her faithful belief in the God who walks with her, sometimes unrecognized, steadfastly turns her faith toward Jerusalem.

Preaching the Gospel in the context of the other readings for the First Sunday of Lent only highlights this theme of dependence on God. At Massah, as Luke's third temptation alludes, the Israelites ask, "Is the LORD among us or not?" This, the testing of the Lord, is responded to by the psalmist: "I will say about YHWH, 'My refuge and my stronghold, my God. I will trust in him'" (my trans.). In response, the third temptation underscores the way in which the psalm can be misused by those who really don't believe that God is with them. The one who tests God by jumping off of the temple, literally or figuratively, stands in contrast with the believer who hides under God's wing.

> The one who tests God by jumping off of the temple, literally or figuratively, stands in contrast with the believer who hides under God's wing.

A similar confession of one's reliance on God is found in the Deuteronomic anamnesis assigned as the first reading. The confession of God's faithfulness to one's enslaved, displaced, and exiled ancestors for generations stands in harmony with Jesus' stance in the third temptation. God, in both, is ultimately trustworthy. The readings stand in contrast because, in Deuteronomy, the evidence of God's trustworthiness is the harvest brought to the altar. Jesus, by contrast, brings to the temple only words quoted from his Scriptures; but they, too, are a kind of anamnesis, an act of remembering and of trust in the God who is faithful.

Paul also practices a kind of anamnesis, rereading the Deuteronomic narrative to "re-member," to bring back together, God's people, Jew and Gentile. Paul's "re-membering" relies on the nearness of the word of faith for all God's people. As a result, the question becomes less of what you do and more of whom you trust. For, if your trust is in the Lord, on whose name you call, you will be saved. This trusting in the name and promise of God is ultimately the way in which Jesus responds to the temptation to jump. He chooses not to jump *precisely because he does trust God*, precisely because he already knows in his heart, and confesses with his lips, the faithfulness of God.

Sundays in Lent are always a contradiction: short rest stops on the solemn road to the cross, they nevertheless rehearse, weekly, the anamnesis of the faithfulness of God made visible in the resurrection of Christ. If this week's "rest stop" were to be named, it would be called Trust. For here, at this First Sunday of Lent, the call is not to charge ahead with Lenten disciplines in an attempt to prove the faithfulness of God. The call, instead, is to remembrance and trust. It is a call to gather together, in your heart if not in your hand, the good gifts of God that you have received, with thanksgiving. It is a call to trust the security of the shelter of God. It is a call to hold on to the promise that God is very near to you, without testing it. Ultimately, it is a call to be so certain of the faithfulness of God that you, too, will not jump.

Notes

1. Lawrence Boadt, *Reading the Old Testament: An Introduction* (New York: Paulist, 1984), 355–56; Norman Gottwald, *The Hebrew Bible: A Socio-Literary Introduction* (Philadelphia: Fortress Press, 1985), 138–39.

2. Ibid.

3. Gottwald adds that Deuteronomy contains "appended exhortations, poems, and narratives that adapt the document to its function as an introduction for Joshua–2 Kings" (*The Hebrew Bible*, 388).

4. The translation is mine. The point here is that the verb *ngd* is hiphil and thus can function like a perfect-tense English verb. Thus, when believers say, "This day, I have declared that . . . I have come in . . . ," they are affirming that their very appearance in the temple with baskets of the firstfruits of the field is in its own right a declaration of their possession of the land.

5. Bruce C. Birch, Walter Brueggemann, Terence E. Fretheim, and David L. Petersen, *A Theological Introduction to the Old Testament*, 2nd ed. (Nashville: Abingdon, 2005 [1999]), 162.

6. Aelred Cody, "'Little Historical Creed' or 'Little Historical Anamnesis'?" *CBQ* 68 (2006): 6.

7. Ibid., 8.

8. Ibid.

9. J. Gerald Janzen, representing a minority of scholars, suggests that *'obed* in this text might better be translated "starving" rather than "wandering." J. Gerald Janzen, "The 'Wandering Aramaean' Reconsidered," *VT* 44, no. 3 (1994): 359–75.

10. Sandra L. Gravett, Karla G. Bohmbach, F. V. Greifenhagen, and Donald C. Polaski, *An Introduction to the Hebrew Bible: A Thematic Approach* (Louisville: Westminster John Knox, 2008), 216.

11. Psalms 90–106 are sometimes called the "Royal Psalms"; Boadt, *Reading the Old Testament,* 282.

12. Boadt considers this psalm a "trust song" (ibid.); Gottwald, a "wisdom psalm" (*The Hebrew Bible*, 532).

13. *mechets ya'uph yomam*: the verb here is clearly Qal imperfect third person masculine singular; I have translated it as a jussive. The same pattern may be seen in the two stanzas of 91:6: *middeber ba'ofel yahalok, miqqetev yashud tsaharayim*. Clearly, the poet is repeating *min* in each case to make a poetic parallel; but the translation should not presume that the key verb of the section is "fear."

14. Bart D. Ehrman, *The New Testament: A Historical Introduction to the Early Christian Writings,* 3rd ed. (New York: Oxford University Press, 2004), 355.

15. Ibid.

16. Arthur Dewey, "A Re-hearing of Romans 10:1-15," *Semeia* 65 (1994): 109.

17. Ibid., 115.

18. Randall C. Bailey correctly points out that this polemic of slandering close neighbors with so-called sexual deviance is a common practice in the Hebrew Bible canon ("They Are Nothing but Incestuous Bastards: The Polemical Use of Sex and Sexuality in Hebrew Canon Narratives," in *Reading From this Place,* Vol. 1: *Social Location and Biblical Interpretation in the United States,* ed. Fernando Segovia and Mary Ann Tolbert [Minneapolis: Fortress Press, 1995], 121–38). Jennifer Wright Knust makes a similar argument for the New Testament canon ("Paul and the Politics of Virtue and Vice," in *Paul and the Roman Imperial Order,* ed. Richard A. Horsley [New York: Continuum, 2004], 155–74).

19. See n. 18 above.

20. Margaret Douroux, "If It Had Not Been for the Lord" (Margaret Douroux, 1980).

21. The theme of the diabolic nature of Rome is not uncommon in the New Testament world. Perhaps the starkest portrayal of Rome as diabolic is found in Rev. 12:7—13:18.

SECOND SUNDAY IN LENT

FEBRUARY 28, 2010

Revised Common (RCL)	Episcopal (BCP)	Roman Catholic (LFM)
Gen. 15:1-12, 17-18	Gen. 15:1-12, 17-18	Gen. 15:5-12, 17-18
Psalm 27	Psalm 27 or 27:10-18	Ps. 27:1, 7-8a, 8b-9, 13-14
Phil. 3:17—4:1	Phil. 3:17—4:1	Phil. 3:17—4:1 or
		3:20—4:1
Luke 13:31-35 or	Luke 13:(22-30) 31-35	Luke 9:28b-36
Luke 9:28-36		

FIRST READING

GENESIS 15:1-12, 17-18 (RCL, BCP)
GENESIS 15:5-12, 17-18 (LFM)

Understanding the Reading

Genesis 15 poses several challenges for interpretation: challenges of textual integrity, translation, and interpretation. But it offers some interesting insights also, insights about the nature and faithfulness of God.

To start, Genesis 15 is not one text; rather, scholars have shown that Genesis 15:1-6 and 7-21 are two separate night scenes (vv. 5, 17) interrupted by a sunset (v. 12).[1] The first scene narrates God's promise that Abram would have children "of [his] inward parts" (*mimme'eka*; my trans.). The second promises land to Abraham's descendants. The lection, then, should be understood as an amalgamation of two separately composed texts.

Two translational puzzles are found in the first two verses of chapter 15. One involves the translation of the Hebrew word *magen* (v. 1). Usually translated as "shield," the word could also be *magan*, or "benefactor."[2] YHWH as a shield hearkens back to the war in Genesis 14; YHWH as benefactor fits well the promise of a very great "reward." A third option is that of a double meaning. YHWH both shields Abram from war (Genesis 14) and delivers (*miggen*) his enemies to him (14:20).[3]

The second translational puzzle involves what to make of *ben-meshek* and *damesek*, the descriptions of Eliezer in 15:2. Taken literally, *ben-meshek* means "son of acquisition," a different word from "heir" (*yrsh*) found in 15:3. The verse gives us little help, as Abram's complaint trails off without a verb to anchor it. Claus Westermann proposes one of the best solutions to this challenge: "the son of Meshek (that is Damascus), Eliezar." To his proposal, I would add the New Jerusalem Bible's decision to render the incompletion of the sentence with an ellipsis. It is almost as though, in his grief and frustration, words fail Abram.

The first narrative also brings up an issue of social history: slaves becoming their masters' heirs.[4] As heir, it would fall to the slave to perform the rites of sonship for his master, including burial and perpetuating the line. As Richard Hiers points out, the slave is not necessarily adopted; he is, however, mandated.[5] Thus, this text points to an ultimate erasure of personhood: that a male slave of a childless couple is not even free to head his own household upon his master's death, but is instead obliged to perpetuate his master's.

> As heir, it would fall to the slave to perform the rites of sonship for his master, including burial and perpetuating the line.

Finally, the first narrative presents a riddle in the phrase "and he reckoned righteousness to him" (*vayyakhshebeha lo tsedaqah*; my trans.). The phrase, having no clear antecedent, could refer equally to Abram and to YHWH. Who, then, is righteous, and what difference does that make? I will discuss this further below.

In the second story, 15:7-21, a word should be said about the ritual depicted in verses 9-10, 17. Here, Abram takes animals traditionally sacrificed during the First Temple period, cuts them in half, and creates two rows of halved carcasses.[6] This is Abram literally "cutting a covenant," per the Hebrew idiom. The passing of the firepot and torch between the pieces represents YHWH's ratification of the covenant. And yet, as we will see below, no demands are put on Abram in this covenant. This, too, is a riddle.

Preaching the Reading

In preaching Genesis 15, pitfalls include contemporary geopolitical disputes and easy supercessionist readings. A less obvious pitfall is to follow too closely the logic that somehow adopted children are inferior to those born of one's own DNA.

Still, two important insights emerge from this text for our Lenten journey. First, the presence of YHWH is often experienced as inscrutable darkness. Both divine promises in Genesis 15 are made in darkness; indeed, the terrifying presence of God is experienced as darkness falls (v. 12). Against that inscrutable presence, God's actions appear as lights: star, torch, firepot. God, nevertheless, remains dark. The Lenten walk ends in shadow, the shadow of the cross. Yet Genesis 15 reminds us that the surrounding darkness often marks the presence of God, our shield and benefactor.

The second insight emerges from the assertion of Moshe Anbar that these narratives were composed during the exilic period by two Deuteronomic authors; and it causes us to consider the riddle, "Who is righteous?"[7] Genesis 15 presents two promises that "obligate God but demand nothing of humans."[8] What kind of covenant would leave out requirements for one party? One answer: a covenant for exiles. At a time in which belief grows thin and covenant keeping is difficult two Deuteronomic writers compose narratives about God's promises "in order to encourage the people to hope for the renewal of their former glory."[9]

Who then is righteous? One option is that *Abram reckons that God is righteous*, and so should the exiles.[10] The faith of the exile confesses that, like Abram, we reckon God to be righteous and a keeper of covenant. Therefore, we will survive as a people and we will be given a homeland.[11] An alternative exilic response is the response of Paul: *God reckons that Abram is righteous* because of his belief.[12] Thus, argues Paul, a righteous diaspora community, one in Abraham's tradition, must also believe the promises of God to be reckoned as righteous.

> The faith of the exile confesses that, like Abram, we reckon God to be righteous and a keeper of covenant.

One need not choose. This, like *mgn*, can also be a matter of double meaning. For, in the obscurity of the Lenten fast, one needs to hold on to a belief in the righteousness of God, even before the promises of Easter are fulfilled. And that belief, in itself, may well be an important Lenten discipline, an act of righteousness for a people a long way from home.

RESPONSIVE READING

PSALM 27 (RCL)
PSALM 27 OR 27:10–18 (BCP)
PSALM 27:1, 7–8A, 8B–9, 13–14 (LFM)

Understanding and Using the Psalm

Psalm 27 contains two clear movements: the assertion of the protection of YHWH (vv. 1-6) and a plea for YHWH's help (vv. 7-14), a "praise-followed-by-lament" form.[13] The psalmist begins by asserting that YHWH is light and salvation. Immediately a scene of battle is invoked—but there is shelter in God's *sukkah,* translated alternatively God's shelter and pavilion, and a hiding place in God's tent, the sanctuary.[14] Confidence turns to lament at the hidden face of YHWH; but the psalmist stands firm on YHWH's parental care.[15] The psalm's penultimate strophes underscore the importance of faith: "For they had prevailed against me, false witnesses and a testifier of violence, if I had not believed that I would see the good of YHWH in the land of the living"[16] (my trans.). The psalm ends with endurance: "Wait for YHWH."

Connections to this psalm can be found in all of the readings. In the first and second readings, themes of waiting and trusting in YHWH resonate with the beginning and ending of the psalm. Luke 13 invokes fearlessness, despite the threats of "that fox Herod." And Luke 9 underscores the hidden, indeed clouded and dark nature of God, echoing the lament in 27:9.

SECOND READING
PHILIPPIANS 3:17—4:1 (RCL, BCP)
PHILIPPIANS 3:17—4:1 OR 3:20—4:1 (LFM)

Understanding the Reading

The letter to Philippi was written while Paul was being held by the imperial guard (*praitorion*; 1:13).[17] Paul, uncertain about whether or not this imprisonment will lead to his death (1:20), writes a "letter of consolation" to the church at Philippi.[18] To the residents of this Roman military colony, Paul redefines for them honor and shame, and calls them, in particularly military language, to stand together, firm in the Lord.[19]

Imprisonment is rarely seen as an honorable condition, even today. In Paul's era, it was the cause of great shame. For, in Paul's society, "all the transactions of life, the decisions one made, the goals to which one aspired, all of them passed through the honor-shame . . . filter. And universally that filter was set assiduously to increase honor and decrease shame."[20] Part of the reason for shame was the assumption of criminality; part was the challenge that imprisonment posed to Paul's masculinity in Roman society. True men would never let their "body boundaries" be violated, especially by "agents of the imperial criminal justice system."[21] Paul, then, had a double problem: his own imprisonment *and* his gospel of the crucified Christ.

> Paul is fundamentally redefining for his military community not only honor and shame, but manhood itself.

Paul, in addressing both problems, reimagines for his community the honor-shame filter. The reimagining, for this week's lection, begins in 3:1, when Paul begins to rehearse, and then to dismiss, all of the typical marks of his honor: his birth, education, and zeal. Instead, he holds as a greater honor the power both of Jesus Christ's resurrection *and of his sufferings* (3:10-11). Thus, Paul is fundamentally redefining for his military community not only honor and shame, but manhood itself.

It is this willingness to bear shame and dishonor in this world, in exchange for the glory of the commonwealth (*politeuma*) of heaven (3:20), that Paul calls the Philippians to imitate. Paul is the type, the model, for the community to follow. By contrast, Paul's antitype—which may or may not be a circumcision party—is made of those who are enemies to the cross—that is, to the shame—of Christ (3:18).[22] Paul argues that their enmity, which opposes the community's striving for the gospel, leads to destruction (1:28; 3:19). Thus, their supposed glory, the avoidance of social humiliation on behalf of the gospel—this is their shame (3:19).

By contrast, those who hold to their citizenship in the heavenly *politeuma*, a citizenship in direct challenge to the Roman imperial order, could expect their shamed bodies to be transformed into glorified bodies, not by means of social standing but by the transformative power of the resurrected Christ. It is because of this expectation that Paul is able to call the Philippians, as he does earlier in the epistle, to a military posture in defense of the heavenly *politeuma*: "Stand firm in the Lord, beloved" (1:27; 4:10; my trans.).

Preaching the Reading

At least three homiletic themes emerge from the second reading. First among these is the call away from enmity to the cross of Christ. While it may be tempting to identify various groups as the epitome of the antitype, truthfully, most Western Christians fall into the temptation to privilege social standing over the shame and suffering that mark both the cross of Christ

> What does it mean for twenty-first-century Western Christians to stand firm on the resurrection, the sufferings, and the transformative power of Jesus Christ?

and the citizenship of heaven. A more honest appraisal might consider how the ultimate Western marker of honor and shame—wealth—figures in this equation. It might indeed be a significant Lenten discipline to examine the connection between wealth, honor, shame, and the cross.

A second homiletic theme is that of the importance of role models. Paul holds himself up to the Philippians as a "type," a model for how best to live into the Christian life. But he doesn't hold up himself alone. He calls the Philippians to "pay attention to those who live like this" (*skopeite tous houto peripatountas*; 3:17; my trans.). As part of the Lenten walk, a possible discipline might be "paying attention" to those role models that exemplify living a life that strives to know Christ, crucified and resurrected. The two themes are, of course, linked; for often those who serve as role models also serve as critics of the wider society's marks of honor and shame. And it is often these who, having lived lives for the Christ, have been transformed even in the ways they are remembered, from shame to glory.

A third theme is epitomized by the final charge of today's lection: stand firm, beloved. Of course, the danger in this theme is that Christian people have, in the name of the gospel, stood firm on matters of injustice and brutality, the examples of which are legion. So, in preaching this theme, one must be careful not to concretize matters that are neither central nor crucial to the resurrection and the sufferings of Christ. But, for all of the danger inherent in the theme, it also poses a challenge. What does it mean for twenty-first-century Western Christians to stand firm on the resurrection, the sufferings, and the transformative power of Jesus Christ? What does it mean to relinquish allegiance to this society in favor of a *politeuma* in the heavens? What does it mean to believe and to proclaim the gospel fearlessly, regardless of the consequences, knowing that societal shame may well be heavenly glory? This, above all, is the Lenten challenge of the second reading.

The Gospel
LUKE 13:31–35 (RCL)
LUKE 13:(22–30) 31–35 (BCP)
LUKE 9:28–36 (RCL alt.)
LUKE 9:28b–36 (LFM)

Understanding the Gospels

Three different Gospel readings are proposed for the Second Sunday of Lent. The first of these begins with an odd exchange. In Luke 13:31-32, certain Pharisees approach Jesus, warning him that Herod seeks to kill him. Jesus retorts, "When you go, say this to that fox . . ." (v. 32; my trans.). There is an irony here: Herod Antipas, the king in question, is in violation of Jewish law by his marriage to Herodias, the divorced wife of his brother (3:19). For Pharisees to be Herod's clients and messengers, they would have had to ignore his lawbreaking, a courtesy they never extend to Jesus. Responding, Jesus refers to Herod as "that fox," meaning certainly that sly one, but also possibly meant as a contrast to the lion that is supposed to be on Judah's throne.[23] This retort challenges the legitimacy both of Herod and of the Pharisees who bring his message. Although the threat on Jesus' life is real, his response suggests that it will only happen at the appointed time, on "the third day," that phrase which prefigures his crucifixion and resurrection. Today and tomorrow, however, in the uncertain, ongoing "now," he is casting out demons and healing, fighting forces far greater than Herod.

From the threat of Herod, Jesus turns to the threat of Jerusalem, the city that kills the prophets (13:34). In this lection, Jesus is journeying to Jerusalem, knowing what will happen in Jerusalem. Here, the Gospel writer "emphatically . . . wants the reader to perceive Jesus as 'the Prophet' who must meet his death in that city," as it is necessary for all prophets to do.[24] No threat can keep "the Prophet" from his destined confrontation with either a city or a king that would kill him.

Notably, Jesus does not respond to Jerusalem in anger. Jesus, in the face of a rapacious fox and a homicidal city, takes upon himself the persona of the mother hen, the one who puts her very body between her chicks and the predator that she might save them. This is a striking metaphor of a hen facing down a fox, but the ultimate danger to Jesus' "chicks" is not Herod. Anachronistically, Luke is referring to the impending Roman siege and destruction of the holy city. For Luke, Jerusalem was blameworthy; it would not accept Jesus. Jesus' response is perhaps more compassionate. Jesus laments.

> For Luke, Jerusalem was blameworthy; it would not accept Jesus. Jesus' response is perhaps more compassionate. Jesus laments.

The BCP suggests an extension to the first lection: Luke 13:22-30. As he journeys to Jerusalem, Jesus is confronted by the question, "Will only a few be saved?" (13:23). Mitzi Minor correctly points out that, as in the parable of the Good Samaritan, Jesus does not directly answer the question asked.[25] Rather, he turns his attention to the questioner and, by extension, to us. "Strive to enter through the narrow door," is found only in Luke. Matthew speaks about narrow and wide gates, but these lead to paths, a metaphor of pilgrimage (Matt. 7:13-14). By contrast, Luke proposes a metaphor of entrance and welcome into a house, entrance only achieved through a narrow door.

Jesus' response can seem enigmatic, for the implications of "narrow door" are not necessarily obvious. Robert Shirock proposes a solution. He suggests that we consider a building—in this instance a house—that has grand doors that open for important people and narrow doors that open for those considered to be of an abased status.[26] If his suggestion holds, Jesus' response becomes one that speaks less to orthodoxy than to orthopraxis, and that echoes a Lukan theme of social reversal. Those who enter through the narrow door, then, are not the self-important who expect the door to be opened to them because "we ate before you, and we drank, and in our wide streets, you preached" (v. 26; my trans.). Rather, they are those who, although only able to enter through the narrow door, nevertheless do not qualify as "workers of injustice" (v. 27; my trans.).

Adding 13:22-30 to the set lection for this Sunday injects into the discussion of the fox, the hen, the murderous city, and the chicks a question of status and power. Herod and Jerusalem would be representatives of the "wide door." Between the power of Herod and the Jerusalem religious establishment "that kills the prophets" (v. 34), Luke seems to have clear examples of "workers of injustice" that nevertheless would expect admittance to the commonwealth of God. By contrast, those who enter by the narrow door represent those who accept the protection of the wings of the hen; and, according to Luke, the establishment in Jerusalem is not representative of these persons.

The LFM proposes an alternative lection: the Lukan transfiguration narrative. Although each of the Synoptic Gospels contains this narrative, no two writers tell the story in exactly the same way. As in all of the Synoptics, Jesus' transfiguration takes place on top of a high mountain. Characteristically, Luke begins his narrative with Jesus in prayer (9:28-29). During this prayer, the transfiguration of Jesus begins, complete with the appearance of Moses and Elijah. Here, however, Luke veers from the common narrative, including details not found in Matthew or Mark.

Luke tells us the subject of the conversation between Moses, Elijah, and Jesus. According to Luke, they were "speaking of his exodus, which he was to fulfill in Jerusalem" (v. 31; my trans.). The use of "exodus" here is striking, as are some other parallels to the exodus narrative of Moses on Mount Sinai found in Luke. As David P. Moessner points out, Luke chooses vocabulary that closely parallels the Sinai tale, figuring Jesus as a second Moses.[27] Jesus, like Moses before him, speaks directly to God, deals with a stubborn people, goes to speak to a powerful king, and will lead his people out by means of his own exodus—his crucifixion.[28]

> Luke chooses vocabulary that closely parallels the Sinai tale, figuring Jesus as a second Moses.

Meanwhile, Peter and the other disciples are "weighed down with sleep" (v. 32). They awaken to see the glory of Christ and the presence of the departing Moses and Elijah; however, they miss the discussion of Jesus' "exodus" (v. 31). Instead, they find themselves surrounded by a cloud and commanded to listen to Jesus (v. 35). Perhaps, in light of this, silence is their only viable response (v. 36).

Preaching the Gospels

The shorter RCL/BCP reading suggests two homiletic readings, the first being that of Jesus as a mother hen, who places her body squarely between her chicks and the foxes of this world. Here is a new image of the Lenten call to take up one's cross, an image of the sacrificial love of a mother for her chicks. Jesus, in the face of the threat of Herod the fox, stands his ground and longs to gather together his chicks to protect them. When we as disciples face the threats of life—yes, even with the ultimate threat of death—what shall we do? Might we, as chicks of that mothering hen Jesus, also stand our ground, covering the most vulnerable among us, until that day when we are completed in death? Do we trust Jesus enough to run to him for protection?

This theme of sacrificial love parallels the one-sided covenant in the first reading. Just as YHWH takes on the curse of destruction by singly sealing the covenant with the firepot through the halved animals, so also Jesus takes on the risk to his life, placing himself as mothering hen between the predator and his chicks. As we frequently sing during our Lenten wanderings, "What wondrous love is this, O my soul!"

A second homiletic theme that emerges from the shorter RCL/BCP reading is that of the lament of the Christ. Only rarely do the Gospels give us a glimpse into the emotions of Jesus. What is remarkable about this text is that Christ laments for those he describes as unjust, the prophet killers, the establishment that will have no part of him.

> What might Lent look like if one of our Lenten disciplines was a call to lament on behalf of the unjust?

What might Lent look like if one of our Lenten disciplines were a call to lament on behalf of the unjust? What might a lament look like for U.S.-based and global terrorists? For those who deny resources to the poor and who oppress those with no advocate? And what if we were to lament our own silence and collusion with international crimes of poverty, hunger, and disease? What might it mean to follow this Jesus through Lent? The call goes out from the weeping Messiah: let us weep for the unjust.

This second homiletic theme connects well with the Pauline reminder that our citizenship is not of this world. Indeed, when these two texts are read together, there is both lament and assurance, even as there in Psalm 27. The lament goes up for a people, a city, a nation that does not see the injustice that will be the basis of its undoing. In the case of Jerusalem, the leaders of the city are in league with the very empire that will destroy it. They would rather kill God's prophets than repent. Nevertheless, hope remains, for the citizenship of the exiled one is in a land of promise: not so much a geopolitical one as a heavenly one. Therefore, even through our lamentations, there is hope for the promise of the city of God.

For those preaching the longer BCP passage, the theme is that of choosing the right door. The inclusion of Luke 13:22-30 introduces the "reversal of fortune" motif into this Gospel reading. The key here is the narrow door, which is not the same as the narrow gate. This door is the servant's entrance, the back door. It is not the door of those with prestige or power; it is the door used by the children and poor, the powerless and the voiceless. Nevertheless, it is through that door that we are to enter, says Jesus in Luke's Gospel. The Lenten journey through this Gospel is a journey of humility, one that leaves us dependent upon that self-sacrificial mother hen called Jesus.

As in the RCL/BCP reading, so also this longer BCP lection deepens in meaning when preached alongside Paul's *kerygma* of the shameful cross. Those who are enemies of the cross are usually not fans of the narrow door either. For them, their earthly honor is more important than their heavenly citizenship. Although they have been in the company of the Christ, they cannot find a way in because they must enter by the way of humility, perhaps even of shame. Luke and Paul speak of a reversal of fortune, however, of a shame-filled acceptance of the cross becoming an honorable citizenship in heaven.

For those preaching the LFM passage, the theme of the exodus of the Christ is of primary importance. Here Jesus, like Moses before him, is changed as he communicates with God on top of God's holy mountain. He, too, is given a great exodus mission. Like Moses, he will give up his life while leading his people out to freedom, a freedom characterized by "repentance and forgiveness of sins" (24:47). We stand with the disciples, overcome by weariness yet mesmerized by the transfigured presence of the Christ in the middle of our

> The Lenten journey through this Gospel is a journey of humility, one that leaves us dependent upon that self-sacrificial mother hen called Jesus.

Lenten journey. How shall we react? Shall we try to preserve the moment in booths? Shall we turn in fear from the very powerful presence of God? Or shall we bear witness, in awe and silence—and in obedience to the voice from the cloud, "listen to him"?

The transfiguration narrative connects to both the first and second readings. Once more, Paul's *kerygma* of the cross looms large, the cross that is to be the mark of Jesus' exodus. It is only through this exodus that we gain our *politeuma*, our new place of citizenship in heaven. However, we too must follow our new Moses as he leads us to freedom. While we are yet on the mountain, the first reading echoes. For it reminds us of the dark obscurity of God, an obscurity mirrored by the presence of the cloud upon the mountain, the fear that it invokes in the disciples, and the voice from that cloud that silences us. Even though Jesus, who will do God's actions among us, appears to be as dazzling as lightning, the God of the universe comes to us in the darkness of a cloud. For only in that cloud can we listen, really listen, for the promise and the charge of God.

Notes

1. This has long been noted by scholars. For a full bibliography, see Claus Westermann, *Genesis 12–26: A Continental Commentary* (Minneapolis: Fortress Press, 1995), 214. For the implications of this, see Moshe Anbar, "Genesis 15: A Conflation of Two Deuteronomic Narratives." *JBL* 101, no. 1 (1982): 39–55.

2. See especially Victor Hamilton, *The Book of Genesis: Chapters 1–17,* The New International Commentary on the Old Testament (Grand Rapids: Eerdmans, 1990), 419.

3. Thus Martin Kessler and Karel Deurloo, *A Commentary on Genesis: The Book of Beginnings* (Mahwah, N.J.: Paulist, 2004), 107. As they put it, *mgn* "reminds us of 14:20 where we read that YHWH gave Abram his enemies as a gift (*miggen*)."

4. Richard H. Hiers, "Transfer of Property by Inheritance and Bequest in Biblical Law and Tradition," *Journal of Law and Religion* 10, no. 1 (1993–1994): 127.

5. Ibid.

6. For the dating of these sacrificial animals as First Temple period, see Anbar, "Genesis 15," 54.

7. Ibid., 40.

8. W. Gunther Plaut, ed. *The Torah: A Modern Commentary,* rev. ed., ed. David E. S. Stein (New York: Union for Reform Judaism, 2005), 108.

9. Anbar, "Genesis 15," 55.

10. Daniel A. Klein, "Who Counted Righteousness to Whom: Two Clashing Views by Shadal on Genesis 15:6," *JBL* 36, no. 1 (2008): 29.

11. Ibid.

12. Ibid.

13. For the argument for two psalms, see Arthur Weiser, *The Psalms,* trans. Herbert Hartwell (Louisville: Westminster John Knox, 1962), 245; for the counter-argument, see John Eaton, *The Psalms: A Historical and Spiritual Commentary with an Introduction and New Translation,* rev. ed. (New York: Continuum, 2005), 134.

14. Herbert Levine, "The Symbolic Sukkah in Psalms," *Prooftexts* 7, no. 3 (1987): 262.

15. Shalom Paul argues that, in parallel to the Babylonian theodicy, the abandonment of mother and father is a euphemism for their death (cf. "Psalm XXVII 10 and the Babylonian Theodicy," *VT* 32, no. 4 [1982]: 489–92).

16. Jeffery Niehaus argues convincingly that 15:12b (*ki qamu-vi 'ede-sheqer vifeakh khamas*) is the dependent clause connected to 15:13 (*lule he'emanti lir'oth betuv-YHWH be'erets khayim*) ("The Use of *lûl* in Psalm 27," *JBL* 98, no. 1 [1979]: 88–89).

17. Raymond Brown suggests that this letter was written when Paul and Silas were jailed in the Acts 16 account of Philippi; although Bart Ehrman points out that evidence for this is sketchy. Luke Timothy Johnson proposes at least three sites: Rome, Caesarea, and Ephesus. As the location of Paul's imprisonment is immaterial for the understanding of this letter, readers would probably be wisest to allow the location to be unknown. Raymond Brown, *An Introduction to the New Testament,* Anchor Bible Reference Library (New York: Doubleday, 1996), 484–85; Bart D. Ehrman, *A Historical Introduction to the Early Christian Writings,* 3rd ed. (New York: Oxford University Press, 2004); Luke Timothy Johnson, *The Writings of the New Testament: An Interpretation,* rev. ed. (Minneapolis: Fortress Press, 1999), 369.

18. Paul A. Holloway, *Consolation in Philippians: Philosophical Sources and Rhetorical Strategy* (New York: Cambridge University Press [Virtual Publishing], 2003).

19. Several studies depict Philippi as a Roman military colony. Two of them are Joseph A. Marchal, *Hierarchy, Unity and Imitation: A Feminist Rhetorical Analysis of Power Dynamics in Paul's Letter to the Philippians* (Atlanta: SBL, 2006), 99–112; and Joseph H. Hellerman, *Reconstruction Honor in Roman Philippi* (Cambridge: Cambridge University Press, 2005), 69–79.

20. J. Paul Sampley, ed., *Paul in the Greco-Roman World: A Handbook* (Harrisburg, Pa.: Trinity Press International), 10.

21. Maud Gleason, "By Whose Gender Standards (If Anybody's) Was Jesus a Real Man?" *New Testament Masculinities,* Semeia Studies 45, ed. Stephen D. Moore and Janice Capel Anderson (Atlanta: SBL, 2003), 326.

22. In Galatians 6, those advocating circumcision for Gentiles are considered "enemies of the cross of Christ," so it is possible that the same metaphor holds here; but there is no concrete proof that this is the case.

23. I. Howard Marshall, *The Gospel of Luke*, The New International Greek Testament Commentary (Grand Rapids: Eerdmans, 1978), 571.

24. Luke Timothy Johnson, *The Gospel of Luke,* Sacra Pagina, vol. 3, ed. Daniel J. Harrington (Collegeville, Minn.: Liturgical, 1991), 221.

25. Mitzi Minor, "Luke 13:22-30—The Wrong Question, The Right Door," *Review and Expositor* 91 (1994): 551–54.

26. Robert J. Shirock, "The Growth of the Kingdom in Light of Israel's Rejection of Jesus: Structure and Theology in Luke 13:1-25," *Novum Testamentum* [hereafter *NT*] 35, no. 1 (January 1993): 22–23.

27. David P. Moessner, "Luke 9:1-50: Luke's Preview of the Journey of the Prophet like Moses of Deuteronomy," *JBL* 102, no. 4 (December 1983): 558ff.

28. Ibid.

THIRD SUNDAY IN LENT

MARCH 7, 2010

Revised Common (RCL)	Episcopal (BCP)	Roman Catholic (LFM)
Isa. 55:1-9	Exod. 3:1-15	Exod. 3:1-8a, 13-15
Ps. 63:1-8	Psalm 103 or 103:1-11	Ps. 103: 1-2, 3-4, 6-7, 8, 11
1 Cor. 10:1-13	1 Cor. 10:1-13	1 Cor. 10:1-6, 10-12
Luke 13:1-9	Luke 13:1-9	Luke 13:1-9

FIRST READING

ISAIAH 55:1-9 (RCL)
EXODUS 3:1-15 (BCP)
EXODUS 3:1-8A, 13-15 (LFM)

Understanding the Readings

Isaiah 55:1-9 is both a familiar text and one difficult to interpret. It is an excerpt of Second Isaiah (Isaiah 40–55), written in the sixth century B.C.E. during exile.[1] Primary among the themes of Second Isaiah are the sovereignty and activity of YHWH and the promise of the restoration of Zion, a restoration that will include all nations.[2] Particular to this passage are calls to come and buy, and promises that the nations will in fact come to Zion (55:1-5). But who is calling whom?

Although many interpreters read 55:1-3a as a call from YHWH to the exiles, Simone Paganini suggests that there many be as many as four voices speaking in this exchange: the voice of YHWH, the voice of a narrator, the voice of the people or a chorus, and the voice of Lady Zion.[3] Of these four, Lady Zion is the first voice; she calls to the exiles to come, to buy, and to eat in a market of grace and abundance (vv. 1-3a). The narrator responds directly to her, telling her, in the second person feminine, that YHWH has glorified her (*pearakh*; v. 5b).[4]

The voice of YHWH answers Lady Zion's call by promising to cut an eternal covenant with the future Davidic king.[5] This will be a covenant characterized by the *chesed* or faithfulness of David (v. 3b), faithfulness previously unrealized in the Davidic line.[6] In turn, the *chesed* of the new David will draw nations to Zion.

It is little wonder, at the promise of restoration, that the chorus urges the listeners to repent and to seek YHWH, two themes that play throughout Second Isaiah.[7] However, warns YHWH's voice once more, one must change both lifestyle and mind-set. For, "my thoughts are not your thoughts, nor my ways your ways," is the declaration of YHWH (v. 8).

Both BCP and LFM have the call of Moses in *Exodus 3* as the first reading for the Third Sunday in Lent. The most striking feature about this text is the various names that it uses for the Deity. God is called *Elohim*,

> It is little wonder, at the promise of restoration, that the chorus urges the listeners to repent and to seek YHWH.

YHWH (vv. 2, 4, 15), and *Ehyeh Asher Ehyeh,* which can mean "I am that I am" and "I will be what I will be."[8] This may be intentional, a bridge connecting the postexilic worship of *Elohim* with the prenational worship of YHWH.[9]

Moses learns these names for God through a theophany, an image of an unconsumed, burning bush, an image that may contain a double meaning. Not only is its burning a symbol of the presence of God that Moses sees; it may also be a symbol of the fire of the oppression of the Israelites in Egypt, oppression that God sees. Moses' call emerges from this double vision.

Preaching the Reading

Isaiah 55:1-3a rings with the insistent call, "Come, buy, eat," a call not only to the exiles but, indeed, to the nations. A sermon on this part of the reading might focus on the covenant community's call to the world: come without condition, buy without silver, eat well, and let your soul live. At the heart of this refrain is a challenge to the Lenten community, even in the midst of its sober discipline, to be a place of welcome, of nourishment, and of life, an irresistible source of water and of life for all nations.

The middle of the Isaiah reading hints at the "suffering servant" theme found in Isaiah 53. For this same servant is the inheritor of the Davidic line, the new, faithful David with whom YHWH promises to cut an eternal covenant. A sermon here might focus on what it means to be a leader after God's own heart. Drawing from the earlier chapters of Second Isaiah, a preacher might focus on faithfulness to God, even in the face of suffering, as the true mark of divine kingship. This could illuminate the Lenten journey to the cross in many ways.

The end of the Isaiah reading resonates with the words *thoughts* and *ways*, the thoughts and ways of YHWH. Here is perhaps the most familiar call within this sermon: seek YHWH while it is possible to find YHWH. It is the Lenten call to turn and to return to the holy. At the heart of the holy is not just mercy and pardon, although that is surely good news. At the heart of the holy is a change of mind and a change of direction. This, too, might powerfully shape the Lenten journey.

When preaching the burning bush theophany, one can hardly avoid addressing the names of God. YHWH, the old ancestral God, is revealed as the *Elohim* of Abraham, Isaac, and Jacob, regardless of whether or not they knew the name YHWH. Even more powerfully, YHWH's name is revealed as both "the one who is" and "the one who will be." While Christians often linger on the former, thanks to the Gospel of John, there is an important reminder in the latter message. "The God who will be" is not confined to the past, crystallized in creeds and formulae. Rather, "the God who will be" is always re-creating God's own self. There is a grace in this. For this God precedes us into an uncertain, potentially dangerous future. This God goes ahead of us as we journey to Jerusalem, this Lent. This is God incarnate: "I will be" with you.

> At the heart of the holy is not just mercy and pardon, but also a change of mind and a change of direction.

RESPONSIVE READING
PSALM 63:1-8 (RCL)
PSALM 103 OR 103:1-11 (BCP)
PSALM 103:1-2, 3-4, 6-7, 8, 11 (LFM)

Understanding and Using the Psalms

Psalm 63, attributed to David, is an "anonymous, individual lament" properly understood as a "protective psalm."[9] Much of the plea for protection, however, is omitted from the reading. What remains is a passionate expression of the psalmist's love and longing for *Elohim*, and for the sanctuary in which *Elohim* dwells. The psalm contains striking imagery. Extreme thirst and weakness depicts the longing of the psalmist (vv. 1-2). *Elohim*, in response, is "comfort food": "as if with fatty meat and oil, you will sate my being" (v. 5; my trans.).[10] Further, *Elohim* is the psalmist's *female* helper (*'ezratah*), the same root used to describe the "helper" for the man in Genesis 2.

This psalm resonates well with the assigned readings. To the Isaiah call to "come," the psalm responds, "I long to come." In the face of the exodus theophany, the psalm sounds as a longing for such a vision, and perhaps, as the cry of the "children of Israel" in Egypt. In contrast to the Pauline warning against idolatry, the psalm illustrates the correct orientation of the heart. The Lukan warnings invoke the protective message of the psalm: in the midst of terror and doubt, my soul longs for you.

For a brief discussion of Psalm 103, please see the responsive reading for Ash Wednesday.

SECOND READING

1 CORINTHIANS 10:1-13 (RCL, BCP)
1 CORINTHIANS 10:1-6, 10-12 (LFM)

Understanding the Readings

In the second reading, Paul makes some of his case against eating meat sacrificed to pagan gods. In his first argument, 10:1-5, Paul alludes to many of the great movements of God on behalf of God's people: the pillar of cloud (Exodus 13, 14, 40); the parting of the sea (Exodus 14); the provision of "manna" in the desert (Exodus 16); and the provision of water from the rock (Exodus 17; Numbers 20). These Paul explicitly connects to the sacraments of the early church: baptism and the Lord's Supper. The people were baptized (*ebaptisthesan*) into the cloud and the sea; and they ate and drank spiritual (*pneumatikos*) food (vv. 2-4).

Paul considers these events as types (*tupoi*), models of behavior for the current community of believers (v. 6). And as such, they come with a warning that "*in most of* [the desert wanderers], God was not pleased, for, they were turned away in the desert" (v. 5; my trans.). This, alarmingly, suggests that baptism and participation in the ritual feast of the community are not sufficient means of avoiding God's displeasure.

In the second part of his argument, Paul proceeds to remind the Corinthians of five incidents, all of which have food somewhere at the heart of them, in which the wrath of God raged against the "baptized" community. The "lust after evil" may refer to Numbers 11, the complaint about lack of food that brought quails but also a plague. "The people rose up to play" recalls the feast connected with the golden calf in Exodus 32. The charge of prostitution (*porneia*), a double entendre for sexually illicit behavior and for worship of other gods, reminds the listeners of the great plague that erupted when the wilderness wanderers feasted with Moabite women and their gods in Numbers 25. The curse of the snakes in Numbers 21 begins with a complaint about the lack of food. And the destroyer, possibly a reference to Korah's rebellion in Numbers 16, moves against the people in response to the charge, "Is it too little that you have brought us up out of a land flowing with milk and honey to kill us in the wilderness, that you must also lord it over us? It is clear that you have not brought us into a land flowing with milk and honey" (Num. 16:13-14; my trans.).

> Even in the face of warning, Paul provides hope: God will not let you be tested without a means of escape.

In light of these reminders, Paul's warning is to be expected. "You, who seem to stand, watch that you do not fall" (v. 12; my trans.). Paul is warning those for whom eating sacrificed foods is unproblematic that such behavior could invoke divine wrath upon the community. Even in the face of warning, however, Paul provides hope: God will not let you be tested without a means of escape (v. 13).[11]

Preaching the Reading

Lent is often a time of fasting for Christians, and three weeks into a six-week fast, themes of renunciation of food may be quite timely. However, this passage is not really about fasting as a discipline. It cautions of the dangers of conceding too easily to the "gods" of this world. It is possible, following Paul, to make the Corinthian controversy a type, a model for our postmodern engagement with twenty-first-century "idols."

This reading, then, invites the preacher and the congregation to ask three probing questions, the answers to which may also have a profound effect on the Lenten disciplines of the congregation. The first is this: What are the "other gods" that surround us? It would probably be wise not to turn this into a referendum on ecumenism. Certainly, wealth, oil, media, and other twenty-first-century phenomena can serve as objects of worship. For the Corinthian congregation, meat sacrificed to pagan gods would have been a ubiquitous temptation, as it would have been the standard fare at the market. For twenty-first-century Christians, what might this be?

The second question that Paul invites is this: What does it mean to eat food dedicated to these "gods"? Is drive-up fast food eaten in the car, or food delivered by car to your home, food dedicated to the automobile? Are noodles, microwaveable popcorn, and other such dormitory foods dedicated to the computer? To the TV? What, besides food, might be dedicated to our "idols," and what might this look like? Part of the ritual of Lenten confession might be to name these ubiquitous forms of sustenance that we justify to ourselves.

> What kind of Lenten discipline could call the baptized, spiritually fed members of the congregation to abstain from feasting with other gods?

The third question for the community is the corollary: What does it mean to abstain from foods dedicated to these gods? For oil, could it mean engaging the congregation in growing and purchasing local foods to cut back on oil expenditure? For media, could the congregation be called to a six-week media fast, perhaps modified for those who work with media for a living? What might it mean to live more simply, rather than to feast with the gods of wealth; and to use one's extra income to tend to those without enough? What kind of Lenten discipline, individual or corporate, could call the baptized, spiritually fed members of the congregation to abstain from feasting with other gods?

Such a discipline may well be a hard sell—and harder yet to do for oneself. Yet, Paul gives us assurance that the way is not impossible. "God," he reminds us, "is faithful." God "will not let you be tested beyond your strength, but with the testing . . . will also provide the way out so that you may be able to endure it" (10:13).

The Gospel
LUKE 13:1-9 (RCL, BCP, LFM)

Understanding the Gospel

The Gospel reading for the Third Sunday of Lent contains two separate but related pericopes. Together, they paint a picture of impending destruction. However, the response to disaster seems to be a change of mind-set, one more concerned with preparing for the in-breaking of the kingdom of God than with placing blame.

In the first pericope, certain people report to Jesus about one of Pilate's atrocities: the murder of Galileans and the comingling of their blood with the blood of the sacrifices that they had brought. Although there is no other historical evidence for this event, such actions would not have been out of character for Pilate. Luke crafts Jesus' response to this report, and to a parallel report of the disastrous collapse of a tower in Siloam that killed eighteen persons, in two strophes.

In the first, Jesus asks the question, "Do you believe [*dokeite*] that these persons were worse sinners [*hamartoloi*] or debtors [*opheiletai*] than all others like them?" (vv. 2, 4; my trans.). Jesus, here, is challenging a standard first-century perspective on the world. Bruce Malina calls it "the perception of limited good."[12] As Malina notes, from the first-century perspective, "every effect that counts in life is caused by a person."[13] The answer to Jesus' question, then, would have been "yes." For, by first-century cultural understanding, such disasters came because of one's own sinfulness.[14]

Jesus, in both cases, denounces that perspective of disaster and oppression. Those affected were no worse than were their peers. However, the denunciation is accompanied by a warning: "If you do not change your mind [*ean me metanoete*], you will perish just as they did" (vv. 3, 5; my trans.). Most translators render the Greek verb *metanoeo* as "repent" in this passage. However, translating it as "change your mind" preserves the balance between "do you think" (*dokeite*) and "change your mind" (*metanoete*). It also raises a more pointed set of questions than the more traditional translation. About what is Jesus warning his listeners to change their mind? Is it only about the cause of disasters?

Reading this passage in light of what immediately precedes it can help us to discern an answer to that question. Luke 12 contains a lot of counsel about one's mind-set. It is to be fearless (12:1-12), unconcerned with earthly treasure (12:13-34), and prepared for the in-breaking kingdom of God, knowing that the kingdom will bring division. Such a mind-set would have little time to consider, unduly, whether persons involved in disaster were to blame for their own demise.

The second pericope in today's Gospel is an incomplete story about a fig tree, a landowner, and a vintner. The story is a particularly difficult one to interpret because of its unknown variables. For example, we know that the landowner has been looking for figs on the fig tree for three years. What is unclear is whether the fig tree was planted three years ago, in which case the landowner is acting foolishly because it takes three years for newly planted fig trees to bear, or whether the tree has simply been barren for three years.[15] Further, the offer of the vintner to dig around the tree and fertilize it begs the question why this has not been done before.[16]

> One's mind-set is to be fearless, unconcerned with earthly treasure, and prepared for the in-breaking kingdom of God, knowing that the kingdom will bring division.

The conflict in the story lies between the will of the landowner and the will of the vintner. The former desires to chop the tree down, because of its barrenness. The latter argues to preserve it, for unknown reasons. Complicating matters, Jesus does not tell us what the landowner decides. There is, perhaps, a clue in the ellipsis in 13:9: "If it bears fruit in the future . . . ." No "then" (apodasis) accompanies this "if" (protasis), leading commentator Charles Hedrick to suppose a negative response from the landowner.[17]

Determining how to interpret this story, then, is a challenge. It is too facile to see this as a conflict between two parts of the Trinity. Not only does such a reading preserve the Marcionite heresy of the judgmental God and the merciful Christ, but it is not necessarily supported by the text, especially when read together with Luke 13:1-5. After having just said that one's sinfulness is not the cause of one's demise, it would seem an odd reversal for Jesus to argue just the opposite in the next breath.

A possible reading, in light of 13:1-5, might well be that this parable illustrates the position that the Galileans and those killed at Siloam were in. They were the fig tree, caught between destruction (Pilate) and neglect (the collapse of a tower). In that case, it would be foolish to blame the fig tree; rather, the blame rests with those responsible for tending to the fig tree well. The change of mind advocated in 13:3, 5, then, might include how one hears the story of this fig tree, and thus of every victim caught in such a bind.

To read in this way, one must be willing to stand with the fig tree, fearlessly, to be unconcerned with the fig tree's produce or any other earthly wealth, and to be prepared to take a position that will cause conflict, both with the landowners and the vintners. If one reads this way, however, then the rest of Luke 13 begins to cohere. The woman in Luke 13:10-17 is the untended fig tree, and Jesus' rebuke of the religious officials, a call to a change of mind. The growth of mustard and yeast reflects that change of mind—as does one's view of the narrow door. And perhaps Jerusalem, at the very end of the chapter, represents another fig tree, fought over by a landowner (Rome) and neglectful vintners (those who kill the prophets). Jesus, ultimately, is unable to change the mind of Jerusalem; but perhaps Luke, in telling the story, is able to change the mind of his audience.

Preaching the Gospel

The Gospel for the Third Sunday of Lent raises at least three homiletic themes. In the first, Jesus challenges the perception that bad things happen to those who are more sinful than are their neighbors. This is a particularly important message to preach during times of economic uncertainty and natural disaster. Notably, Jesus makes the same claim for those undergoing political repression by the government of his own land. His argument does not address the perennial question, "Why do bad things happen to good people?" However, it does address the ongoing misconception that those who die in disaster or attack, those who are infected by disease, and those who face political repression are more sinful than the general population. A Lenten sermon on this theme might call a congregation to an awareness of its participation in human mortality, regardless of personal piety; and of the words of the equally mortal Jesus, "Do you believe that bad things happen only to the sinful? By no means."

A related homiletic theme is Jesus' call to "change your mind," often translated "repent." This theme is an opportunity to challenge the faith community to change its mind, not just about natural disasters, but about the way in which it approaches the world as it journeys to the cross. What might it mean to change your mind so that you are fearless about life, generous with treasure, and expectant about the coming reign of God? What might it mean to live a Lenten discipline that spent less time judging others' culpability and more time reordering one's own mind-set? At this, the midpoint of the Lenten journey, what might it mean to reissue the call to repentance, to the changing of one's mind?

> What might it mean to change your mind so that you are fearless about life, generous with treasure, and expectant about the coming reign of God?

The third theme is the call to stand with the fig tree. Here, a careful reading of the second part of the Gospel may be helpful. It may even be an interesting challenge to preach on behalf of the fig tree, both oppressed and neglected. Who are the fig trees in your community, and in the planet? Who are they who suffer both from oppression and neglect? Here a Lenten discipline emerges: standing with the fig tree. It is a prophetic discipline: the role of the church to call for justice from the oppressors, and for care from those who neglect their chargers. What might it mean to reject all suggestions that those facing neglect and oppression somehow brought it upon themselves? What might it mean to call the congregation to stand with the fig tree?

The Gospel resonates with both of the set lections for the first reading. With the Isaiah passage, the Gospel calls for a change of mind and of action. "Seek the LORD," says Second Isaiah. Turn from your old ways and return to God, for human thoughts are not God's thoughts. Here, Jesus' question resonates. What is it that you believe? Do you believe that evil only happens to bad people? Do you believe that, if you go along to get along, you will somehow be safe? Do you believe that the coming of the Christ brings nothing but tranquility? By no means. Seek the Lord. Change your mind.

For those reading the Exodus 3 passage, the Gospel resonates with what God sees. God sees the oppression of the children of Israel in Egypt. It is in response to this sight that God appears to Moses and reveals his name, a name that contains a promise that God will be in the future even as in the present. Exodus 3 presents a God who intervenes on behalf of a people oppressed by their captors, and neglected by those whose parents' lives they saved. This is a God who stands with the fig tree; a God who understands that sometimes people are in a difficult place through no fault of their own. In response to the privilege of hearing the name of the Holy One, an appropriate Lenten prayer might be, "Help us to see what you see." Help us to see those who stand like a bush aflame, oppressed but not destroyed. Send us to set them free. Help us, God who is and God who will be, to stand with the fig tree.

> This is a God who stands with the fig tree; a God who understands that sometimes people are in a difficult place through no fault of their own.

The Gospel for this Sunday also resonates with the second reading, although this might not be readily apparent. In many ways, the second reading contradicts Jesus' assertion, for, in every instance that Paul cites, God kills the wilderness wanderers for their sinfulness, their disobedience. In the midst of contradiction, however, two themes emerge in common between these two readings. The first is that call, again, to repentance, to a change of mind. To a community too certain about their uprightness before God because they share a common baptism and the Lord's Supper, Paul calls for a change of mind. For, he reminds them, the wilderness wanderers also shared a common "baptism" and common "spiritual food," but God was not pleased with them. Paul's warning, then, becomes the counterpoint to Jesus' rebuke. The latter calls the community of faith away from smug self-righteousness; the former challenges the community of faith on its complacency. Both are necessary correctives, in any season but particularly on the journey of faith that Christians take in Lent.

Second, Paul's longer argument against eating meat sacrificed to idols, 1 Corinthians 8–11, is a way to stand with the fig tree. For the decision not to eat meat sacrificed to other gods, the meat readily available at the market and in people's homes, would have come with a price. The price may have been relatively small: questions or ridicule. For the new convert, however, the price might have been confusion, even rejection of the new faith. And for the Christian woman trying to cook for her pagan family and for the Christian slave trying to find something to eat in her master's kitchen, the price may have been very high indeed. It would have been tempting for the richer, more sophisticated Corinthians to rely on the grace of their baptism, but Paul calls them to a more just stance. Stand against Korah and all those who would rebel on behalf of their own comfort. Stand with those who are struggling to be faithful, in the face of oppression and neglect. Stand with the fig tree.

Notes

1. Bruce Birch, Walter Brueggeman, Terrence E. Fretheim, and David L. Petersen, *A Theological Introduction to the Old Testament,* 2nd ed. (Nashville: Abingdon, 2005), 372; Lawrence Boadt, *Reading the Old Testament: An Introduction* (Mahwah, N.J.: Paulist, 1984), 417; Norman K. Gottwald, *The Hebrew Bible: A Socio-Literary Introduction* (Philadelphia: Fortress Press, 1987), 426.

2. Boadt, *Reading the Old Testament,* 423–27.

3. Simone Paganini, "Who Speaks in Isaiah 55.1? Notes on the Communication Structure in Isaiah 55," *Journal for the Study of the Old Testament* 30, no. 1 (2005): 92.

4. For the argument that this verb is a feminine rather than a masculine second person singular, see ibid., 86–88.

5. Ibid., 91.

6. Peter J. Gentry, "Rethinking the 'Sure Mercies of David' in Isaiah 55:3," *Westminster Theological Journal* 69 (2007): 292–98. Gentry's argument rests on the translation of the construct chain *chesedey David* in 55:3. He argues for the more straightforward rendering of it as the *chesed* of David, with David as the subject of the *chesed.* His argument is too long to reproduce here, but it is entirely convincing.

7. Boadt, *Reading the Old Testament,* 423.

8. *Ehyeh* means both "I am" and "I will be," allowing for at least four variations on the name: "I am who I am," "I will be who I will be," "I am who I will be,"

or "I will be who I am." Further, *Asher* is not only "who" but also "what," adding to the complication.

9. For one version of this argument, see Thomas L. Thompson, "How Yahweh became God: Exodus 3 and 6 and the Heart of the Pentateuch," *Journal for the Study of the Old Testament* 68 (1995): 57–74.

10. Gottwald, *The Hebrew Bible*, 527–28.

11. J. Smit offers a helpful reading of this passage that places it in parallel with the rest of 1 Corinthians 10 ("'Do Not Be Idolaters': Paul's Rhetoric in First Corinthians 10:1-22," *NT* 39, no. 1 [1997]: 40–53.

12. Bruce Malina, *The New Testament World: Insights from Cultural Anthropology*, 3rd ed. (Louisville: Westminster John Knox, 2001), 81–106.

13. Ibid., 102.

14. When the disciples ask, "Who sinned, this man or his parents, that he was born blind?" in John 9, the same perspective of the world applies.

15. Charles W. Hedrick, "An Unfinished Story about a Fig Tree in a Vineyard (Luke 13:6-9)," *Perspectives in Religious Studies* 26, no. 2 (Summer 1999): 179–81.

16. Ibid., 182–83.

17. Ibid., 189.

FOURTH SUNDAY IN LENT

Revised Common (RCL)	Episcopal (BCP)	Roman Catholic (LFM)
Josh. 5:9-12	Josh. (4:19-24) 5:9-12	Josh. 5:9a, 10-12
Psalm 32	Psalm 34 or 34:1-8	Ps. 34:2-3, 4-5, 6-7
2 Cor. 5:16-21	2 Cor. 5:17-21	2 Cor. 5:17-21
Luke 15:1-3, 11b-32	Luke 15:1-3, 11-32	Luke 15:1-3, 11-32

FIRST READING

JOSHUA 5:9-12 (RCL)
JOSHUA (4:19-24) 5:9-12 (BCP)
JOSHUA 5:9A, 10-12 (LFM)

Understanding the Reading

The story of Gilgal, the first reading for the Fourth Sunday of Lent, is a welcome respite before the bloody conquests of Joshua begin. It is set in the middle of Joshua 3–5, a description of the longed-for ending of the wilderness wanderings of the children of Israel, signified by their crossing of the Jordan River and entrance into Canaan. As part of that crossing, Joshua instructs twelve men, one from each tribe, to remove a boulder from the river bottom of the Jordan. These twelve stones, according to the suggested additional reading for BCP, are set up in Gilgal, on the west bank of the Jordan, as a reminder to the generations to follow what God had done.

The etiological saga for Gilgal, however, is in Joshua 5.[1] The very end of that saga is 5:9, the starting verse for the first reading. In wordplay with *gll*—"to roll away"—the root of the word *Gilgal*, YHWH proclaims to Joshua, "This day have I rolled the disgrace of Egypt from you." The "disgrace" may refer to one of two realities. It could mean the shame of slavery, the dishonor of having no control over one's body or life. At Gilgal, the people are finally free. No longer are they escaped slaves running from a cruel master, or wandering through an unknown wilderness. This newfound freedom undergirds the Gilgal Passover, the first community ritual on free soil.

However, Joshua 5 also refers to a more immediate "disgrace"—the uncircumcised condition of those entering Canaan. The disgrace "rolled away," in this case, would have been the foreskins of the Israelite men, or more broadly, the way in which the uncircumcised status of the Israelite men violated the covenant relationship with YHWH.

Only after this "rolling away" had occurred could the celebration of the first Passover meal in Canaan have begun; for only after this "rolling away" were the people once more in covenant community with YHWH. There is a sense of completion in this telling of the Gilgal Passover. As in the original Passover, it takes place on the fourteenth day of the first month (Exod. 12:1-11; Josh. 4:19; 5:10). But, unlike the first Passover, which was eaten in a hurry before leaving the land of slavery, this meal is eaten in celebration for entering the land of freedom.

Unlike the first Passover, which was eaten in a hurry before leaving the land of slavery, this meal is eaten in celebration for entering the land of freedom.

As if to punctuate the change in status of the children of Israel, the day after Passover they eat from the food of Canaan; and the manna that had marked and sustained their wilderness journeys stopped. From now on, there will be no need for a supernatural provision of food. They have arrived in a fertile land, and they are free.

Preaching the Reading

When preaching the first reading, one might choose from at least three homiletic themes. The first of these has to do with naming. The early stories of Abraham's descendants are replete with stories of naming. More than convenient monikers, names told a story about places and people. Names, and the stories that went with them, were a way to remind God's people of the good things that God had done for them. An interesting Lenten discipline, two weeks from Holy Week, might be to look back over the first full month of Lent and to name the places to which God has brought your congregation. Is there, on your journey, an Ebenezer—a stone of help—or a Gilgal—a place in which God "rolled" something away? When we name things, we help ourselves to remember the presence of God with us, in all parts of the journey.

Second, the text speaks eloquently about God's removal of disgrace from God's people. As the people move through the Jordan, they move from slavery to freedom. And earlier in chapter 5, they move from uncircumcision to circumcision, from violating the covenant to keeping the Passover. The grand narrative behind Lent, Holy Week, and Easter is ultimately that of a people, God's people, moving from slavery to freedom, with Christ as the one who parts the waters, the one who, as Paul notes in the second reading, reconciles us to God. This reading, then, calls the people of God to focus on the ways in which, during this season, God is rolling away their disgrace, just as God did for the people of Israel at Gilgal.

On the Tuesday of Holy Week, Jewish people around the world will celebrate Passover, and many of them will sing "Dayenu," which means "Enough!" The song rehearses all of the ways in which God blessed the Israelites on their journey—and it proclaims that even if God had not done some of these things, it would have been enough for us. The third theme of this first reading is "Enough"—the realization that those who have crossed the Jordan now have everything they need. The Passover meal, this time, is followed not by a hurried departure from Egypt but by un- | An important discipline, not only for Lent, is the fettered access to the produce of Canaan. Even | discipline of knowing when there is enough. the heavens seem to recognize that the people now have enough, for the manna ceases, the food that had sustained them when they had nothing else. An important discipline, not only for Lent, is the discipline of knowing when there is enough. What might it mean this Lenten season to practice celebration of a God who can provide both plenty and relinquishment of all that we no longer really need?

RESPONSIVE READING

PSALM 32 (RCL)
PSALM 34 OR 34:1-8 (BCP)
PSALM 34:2-3, 4-5, 6-7 (LFM)

Understanding and Using the Psalms

Both Psalm 32 and Psalm 34 are part of the first book of Psalms, which is also the first Davidic collection.[2] Although most of the psalms surrounding them are psalms of lament, neither of these psalms is. Psalm 32 is, as its title says, "a *maskil*," a psalm of wisdom or good counsel.[3] Thus, in Psalm 32, YHWH promises the psalmist: "I will instruct you" (*askiylekah*). Psalm 34 is a hymn of thanksgiving that, according to the superscription, David wrote after escaping from Abimelech. Repeatedly, the psalm extols YHWH as the one who delivers in a time of trouble.

Psalm 32 highlights two themes from this week's readings. The psalmist's certainty that "the rush of mighty waters shall not reach them" (v. 6; this passage is particularly difficult to translate) echoes the crossing of the Jordan. "Happy, the one whose rebellion is forgiven" (v. 1; my trans.) calls to mind both the second reading and the Gospel. Psalm 34 serves as a response of praise and thanksgiving for the gifts of God, gifts of safe passage and of the removal of shame, gifts of reconciliation and celebration. Lent can be a solemn time. However, each Sunday of Lent is a celebration of resurrection. Psalm 34 in its exuberance reminds us of this.

SECOND READING

2 CORINTHIANS 5:16-21 (RCL)
2 CORINTHIANS 5:17-21 (BCP, LFM)

Understanding the Reading

The second reading catches Paul at the climax of an argument, signaled to the reader by the presence of "therefore" or one of its synonyms. Whether one begins in 5:16 or 5:17, the opening adverb refers one back to the creedal statement in 5:14-15: "We are convinced that one has died for all . . . so that all who live might live no longer for themselves but for him who died and was raised for them." Paul's two opening statements rest on this credo.

The first of these (v. 16) refers to how Paul understands people, and even Christ. The confession that Paul once understood the crucifixion "from a human point of view" explains some of his earlier hostility to the Christian church. From a human point of view, the crucifixion would have been devastatingly shameful, and that in a world where honor is carefully guarded. However, Paul now understands the crucifixion as a source of life and justification, rather than of death and shame. As a result, his understanding of people has changed also. For if Christ died "for all," then how could Paul see any other person except as one who might live for Christ?

The first "therefore" of 5:16 leads to the second "therefore" of 5:17. Here Paul argues that the result of Christ's death and resurrection is nothing short of the establishment of a new creation in each Christian. This is not something that will be accomplished in the future. Paul argues that the new has already come, for God has made it so. Indeed, God is the principle actor in all of this, stepping in to reestablish the broken relationship with humanity, and indeed with the entire cosmos through Christ. Just as God creates the cosmos, in the beginning, God also re-creates the cosmos, and as such, every person who is in Christ.[4]

> Just as God creates the cosmos, in the beginning, God also re-creates the cosmos, and as such, every person who is in Christ.

All this, Paul argues, is the effect of the cross. Through "the one who did not know sin, God made sin on our behalf" (v. 21; my trans.). The interpretation of this verse is tricky. Raymond Brown suggests three possible solutions. First, as the words *sin* and *sin offering* are identical in Hebrew (*hatta't*), Paul could be playing a word game here: "God made him *hatta't* [a sin offering] who did not know *hatta't* [sin]."[5] A second option emerges from Paul's theology, that "God allowed Jesus to be *considered* a sinner"; a parallel assertion is in Galatians 3:13.[6] Or one could read this, within the context of 2 Corinthians itself, as kind of trading places. Christ became sin *so that we might become* God's justice or God's righteousness.[7] Whichever is the case, the result is the same: we become ambassadors of the gospel, given a ministry of reconciliation.

Preaching the Reading

This reading challenges the church to Lenten disciplines that affect our relationships with God and our neighbors. First, we are challenged to trust that God is able to create all things new. In this liturgical season when we are acutely aware of our shortcomings, Paul's "therefore" becomes, first, a call to trust. This can be difficult if we believe in our own immutability or that of our neighbors or our world. However, Paul asserts that anyone who is in Christ is a new creation, and that God, through Christ, has renewed the divine relationship with the entire cosmos. One of the hardest Lenten disciplines may well be to trust and to act on that message, an assertion not only that God *will* renew us but that God *already has* made us and all things new.

One way to act on that truth constitutes a second Lenten homiletic theme. Paul confesses that although he used to see Christ and others through a human lens, now he sees everyone through the lens of the crucifixion and resurrection of Christ. What might it mean for us to do the same? What might it be, as a Lenten discipline, for us to try to see every person we meet through the lens of the reconciling death and resurrection of Christ rather than through the lens provided to us by our culture? Changing the way we see others might require us to sit down face-to-face, rather than framed by a computer screen. It might require us to see the person we ignore in passing, to acknowledge that one against whom we are holding a grudge. And, in the face of international war and climate change, such a perspective might push us beyond despair to hope, and beyond hope to action.

> We may call for reconciliation, but we do not cause it. Instead, we have the responsibility to be ambassadors, encouraging others.

That action is the basis of the third Lenten homiletic theme: a Lenten discipline of reconciliation. Paul claims that one of the impacts of Christ's death is that we have been given the responsibility of being ambassadors for the reconciliation to God offered through the cross and resurrection of Christ. There is danger in that claim, as it is tempting to think that we, somehow, effect the reconciliation.

However, Paul makes it clear that God has already done the work of reconciliation through Jesus Christ. We may call for reconciliation, but we do not cause it. Instead, we have the responsibility to be ambassadors, encouraging others. In a nation in which the people of God often are seen as mean-spirited or oppressive, we are to call people to a self-understanding that they, like we, are already new, already reconciled. This is the implication of Paul's "therefore," the consequence of the crucifixion and resurrection of the Christ.

THE GOSPEL
LUKE 15:1-3, 11B-32 (RCL)
LUKE 15:1-3, 11-32 (BCP, LFM)

Understanding the Gospel

Sometimes the best-loved biblical stories are the hardest to approach because we assume there can only be one meaning for them. Such is the case with Luke's misnamed parable of the "Prodigal Son." In fact, the most prodigal person in this family is the father, for he is the one who spends both his money and his honor without counting any of the cost.

The parable begins with a remarkable scandal. Never in a good first-century Middle Eastern family would a son dare to request his portion of the inheritance from his father. And no sensible father would ever have acquiesced to such a demand. Yet both of these scandalous events are the premise of Luke's great parable. To make matters worse, not even the elder son objects. Rather, without comment, this older one also takes his share of the family fortune, making him no better than his brother.[8] The father, in splitting his property, has put himself at the mercy of his two sons, whose character we have every reason to suspect. His livelihood and his ability to care for himself and his wife, as a man in his society, are in jeopardy. To complicate matters, by giving away property on which an entire village may have depended for support, the father would have lost face with his neighbors as well.[9]

> The father, in splitting his property, has put himself at the mercy of his two sons, whose character we have every reason to suspect.

As if this were not bad enough, the younger son sells the father's property, takes the proceeds from the sale, and leaves the village. Richard Rohrbaugh cautions us not to read this through the lens of medieval Europe, when younger sons benefited from having adventurous spirits. Instead, he argues, we should consider the blow that such a sale was to a village, likely made of extended family members, connected deeply to the land as a family inheritance.[10] Now, not only was the father missing likely one-third of his original property, it was also unavailable to the village, which would have increased his dishonor among his neighbors. The son, meanwhile, would have suffered a kind of social death; he would have cost both his father and his neighbors dearly. Surely he would never be welcomed home again.

Once out of the house, the narrator tells us that the younger son spent his money wastefully. The narrator does not tell us how the son spends his money. Although it is often tempting to believe the elder son's assertion that prostitution was involved, this need not have been the case. Like many peasants before him, he may not have known how to manage his money in the city, thus finding himself penniless just when a famine is beginning in the land.[11]

With no source of income, the son takes the only recourse for many peasants: he indentures himself to a citizen of the town. J. Albert Harrill suggests that the relationship into which the son enters is one of *paramone*, or bound labor.[12] "Willing to do whatever was necessary or required, the son indentured himself to a servant in a non-specific way: the degradation of the task eventually received demonstrates the youth's obligation to do anything."[13] From master of his own inheritance, the younger son falls to the status of all but a slave.

In this precarious position, the narrator gives us an unusual glimpse into the mind of the younger son. As the narrator puts it, "he came to himself." Often this is understood as the son's repentance, although the word *metanoia* appears nowhere in this story. Instead, his stomach drives him to his senses: "How many of the hired hands of my father are abounding in bread, and I am perishing here in hunger?" This, rather than a true change of heart, drives him to make a plan for return to his village, complete with a rehearsed speech. He cannot hope to be welcomed, but at least he can hope that he will not starve.[14]

> The younger son cannot hope to be welcomed, but at least he can hope that he will not starve.

The son's return would have been even more bizarre to the villagers than the son's departure. For the father's reaction to the return of the son is neither to beat him nor to shun him. Rather, he runs to him, a very unusual display for a Middle Eastern man, kisses him, and immediately has him dressed in the appropriate clothing worthy of a son of the house: a robe, shoes, and a ring.[15] Such a welcome also would have signaled his protection of his son from irate neighbors.[16] To celebrate his son's return to life, and in order to mend fences with the neighbors, the father sacrifices the fatted calf and throws a party for the neighbors.[17]

The older son, however—technically the sole owner of all of the property including his brother's newly acquired robe, ring, and shoes—knows nothing of the party, the fatted calf, or the return of his sibling. His reaction to his father's decision is pure fury. His refusal to come in was an insult to his father, for it would have taken him away from his rightful place at the door of the party welcoming guests.[18] Once more, the father reacts uncharacteristically. He could order his son's compliance, but instead he comes out to reason with this second dishonorable son of his.

Even then, the elder son cannot help but to insult his father. After insinuating that his brother has thrown away the family money on prostitutes, he completes the insult by referring to his sibling as "*this your son*" (v. 30; my trans.). The father, a third time, reacts uncharacteristically. Rather than to challenge his son, the father pleads once more with him. Everything, he reminds the elder, belongs to him. However—and here he turns the tables—"*this your brother*, was dead and is alive; he was lost and is found" (v. 32; my trans.). The reader is left to wonder what the son's reaction will be.

There are others whose reaction is equally important. For, as 15:1-3 reminds us, Jesus is telling this parable to scribes and Pharisees. Like the elder son, they are displeased with Jesus' associations and with Jesus' seeming unwillingness to defend his own honor. The reader is also left to wonder what their reaction will be to the hearing of this parable.

Preaching the Gospel

Each of the three men in the parable can stand as his own homiletic theme. First, there is the theme of prodigality: the unthinking expenditure of money regardless of what it ultimately costs. The prodigal in this story is the father, who allows for the splitting of his estate during his lifetime; the father who, without considering the fiscal injury to the elder son, gives the village the fatted calf and gives the younger son a robe, a ring, and shoes when he returns to the village. This father is foolish. What parent today would act as he does? Yet, like the foolish shepherd and the careless woman in the parables that precede this, the father is willing to do anything, to give anything, and to endure anything to make sure that neither son is lost.

The father is a problematic metaphor for God. He does not seek the lost son, as the shepherd and woman do. He never offers the son wisdom or counsel, reproof or instruction, as YHWH does in the *maskil* above. If he is like God, it is only in the generosity of his love. But what if the father is not intended as a metaphor for God? God, after all, is not the one in violation of all honor and decency, as the scribes and Pharisees point out in 15:1-3: Jesus is, precisely because he associates with "younger sons," "tax collectors and sinners."

Perhaps, then, the father is to be a metaphor for the faith community. For surely the two sons of the story live together in the Christian church: the younger who comes out of hunger and desperation, and the elder who disdains the welcome given to the younger. It may be that the parable is not speaking about how God *will* act but about how we *should* act to the one who was dead but is now alive, the one who was lost but is now found. For, surely that one is our kin.

The hungry son stands as a challenge to people of faith, as we consider how we treat the hungry. The citizen of the faraway country treats him justly but not warmly. He is welcome to work, but is given nothing else: neither food nor the emotional sustenance of a hug, a kiss, or a welcome. Sent to do the dirtiest and most menial task, he is all but forgotten as one of the mass of the homeless poor, nameless and alone. By contrast, when he returns to the home he rejected, and to the father he dishonored, he is welcomed as a son of the house. He is given all of the emotional and physical sustenance he might need; and his return becomes a gift to the whole community.

> It may be that the parable is not speaking about how God *will* act but about how we *should* act to the one who was dead but is now alive.

This parable asks of us hard questions. How do we treat those who come to our doors hungry and homeless? Do we provide the basics, as though we were citizens of a faraway country who cared not for the welfare of this child of God? In the parable, Jesus paints a picture of what the faith community could be: a community that celebrates the return of every hungry child, not asking how or why that child was hungry, but welcoming that child as part of the family of God. Such a move is prodigal. The challenge is this: What might it mean, this Lent, to be the prodigal church?

The elder son may well be a bigger challenge to the church. As dishonorable, arrogant, and greedy as this son is, he is also right. If the father has not celebrated his work and his faithfulness, surely the father has been remiss. For all of his justified rage, however, he errs the minute he says "this your son" instead of "this my brother." For even as he charges the father with accepting his brother's shameful behavior, he cannot see the shamefulness of his own behavior. Out of his anger, he cannot fathom the gentleness of his father, both toward his brother *and toward him*. Whether he ever will understand this gentleness is left to the imagination of the hearer.

The elder son poses this difficult Lenten question: Whom are we unwilling to forgive? To whom are we unwilling to offer the father's prodigal welcome? Whom are we unwilling to accept, because we know that we are right? What would it cost to lay down our righteous indignation

> The parable of the Prodigal challenges us again: stop being right and come, join the party.

and come into the house? The scribes and Pharisees are often painted as cruel, but they are no different from many good, churchgoing Christians in their objection to Jesus' associations. The parable of the Prodigal challenges us again: stop being right and come, join the party.

This parable and the first reading share a theme of deliverance. In each case, a person or a people in need is rescued from wandering and brought to a place of safety and plenty, not on their own merits but out of the prodigality of someone else: God or the foolish father. In each case, the response is to celebrate deliverance, from death in the case of the younger son and from slavery in the case of the Israelites. Juxtaposing these two readings might encourage a Lenten discipline of celebration for the gift of deliverance, not just on Easter but every day.

This parable and the second reading share a theme of reconciliation. Here the foolish father proves wise: as prodigal as he is with his resources, he is a master of reconciliation. He reconciles his younger son to the village, and they to him. And he tries to urge his older son to be reconciled also, not to God but to his family and village. For this father, reconciliation is a mandate that far outweighs all cost to himself in wealth or dishonor. What might it mean for us, as a Lenten discipline, to work for that kind of reconciliation, the reconciliation ultimately afforded us by the cross and resurrection of Christ?

Notes

1. Norman K. Gottwald, *The Hebrew Bible: A Socio-Literary Introduction* (Philadelphia: Fortress Press, 1987), 234.

2. Nancy L. deClaissé-Walford. *Introduction to the Psalms: A Song from Ancient Israel* (St. Louis: Chalice, 2004), 64.

3. Ibid., 151.

4. *katallassw,* in Frederick William Danker, A Greek-English Lexicon of the New Testament and other Early Christian Literature, 3rd ed. (Chicago: University of Chicago Press, 2000), 521.

5. Raymond E. Brown, *An Introduction to the New Testament* (New York: Doubleday, 1996), 556–57. For the use of *hatta't* both as sin and sin offering, see Lev. 4:22-31.

6. Ibid., 556.

7. Ibid., 557.

8. I am largely summarizing a far more detailed study by Richard Rohrbaugh that takes seriously the cultural anthropology of the first century Mediterranean ("A Dysfunctional Family and its Neighbors: The Parable of the Prodigal Son [Luke 15:11b-32]," in *Jesus and His Parables: Interpreting the Parables of Jesus Today*, ed. V. George Shillington (Edinburgh: T&T Clark, 2000), 150–51.

9. Ibid.

10. Ibid, 151–52.

11. Ibid., 152–53.

12. J. Albert Harrill, "The Indentured Labor of the Prodigal Son," *Journal of Biblical Studies* 115, no. 4 (1996): 714–17.

13. Ibid., 715.

14. Many commentators note that the son's internal dialogue, in itself, does not constitute an act of repentance. Clearest among them is Phillip Sewell, "Interior Monologue as a Narrative Device in the Parables of Luke," *JBL* 112, no. 2 (1992): 239–53.

15. Rohrbaugh, "A Dysfunctional Family and its Neighbors," 155–57.

16. Ibid.

17. Ibid, 157–58.

18. Ibid., 158–60.

FIFTH SUNDAY IN LENT

MARCH 21, 2010

Revised Common (RCL)	Episcopal (BCP)	Roman Catholic (LFM)
Isa. 43:16-21	Isa. 43:16-21	Isa. 43:16-21
Psalm 126	Psalm 126	Ps. 126:1-2a, 2b-3, 4-5, 6
Phil. 3:4b-14	Phil. 3:8-14	Phil. 3:8-14
John 12:1-8	Luke 20:9-19	John 8:1-11

FIRST READING

ISAIAH 43:16-21 (RCL, BCP, LFM)

Understanding the Reading

Isaiah 43:16-21 is part of what scholars now call Second Isaiah, or Isaiah of the exile.[1] Written during the middle of the sixth century B.C.E., Second Isaiah rings with promises of Israel's restoration to Jerusalem.[2] Second Isaiah is written in particularly high and stylistic poetry, characterized by several recognizable forms.[3] Today's text exemplifies one of those forms: the "proclamation of salvation."[4]

The "proclamation of salvation" form is made of three distinct sections. First is the introduction of the proclamation (43:16-17).[5] Second Isaiah introduces the proclamation as the declaration of YHWH (v. 16). The prophet then reminds the exiles that YHWH is "the one who gives a way in the sea, and a path in the mighty waters; who brings forth chariot and horse, army and strong person together" (vv. 16-17a; my trans.). The prophet underscores further the power of YHWH, for despite the power of armies, "they lie down; they will not get up; they are extinguished like a flaxen wick goes out" (v. 17b; my trans.).

To the exilic community, this introduction would have called to mind the songs of Miriam and Moses on the far shore of the Red Sea celebrating the triumph of YHWH over the chariots and horses of Egypt. However, such a recollection might quickly have soured. Where was YHWH when Babylon destroyed Jerusalem? Where was the mighty God of heaven and earth when our grandparents were taken into captivity, never to see their homeland again? The second section of a "proclamation of salvation" addresses this anger. It is called the "community's complaint."[6]

Interestingly, in today's passage we can only intuit the community's complaint. But we do know that the complaint addresses "the former things," that which has happened to the community in the past. For an exilic community, this complaint about the past must have begun and ended with their forced exile and YHWH's seeming absence. The prophet does not attempt to address the sticky matters of theodicy brought up by the complaint. Instead, the community is charged to forget the past, and not to dwell on what went before this proclamation.

For, declares the prophet, YHWH is about to do a new thing. This is the heart of the proclamation: the promise that YHWH will intervene in the lives of the exiles in a new and unexpected way. The new way sounds remarkably like the old way: the creation of desert paths and water for wilderness wanderers. In this new way, however, even creation is redeemed; and the scavengers of the desert, ostriches and jackals, will glorify YHWH.[7] For the promise is not one of wandering, but ultimately is one of return. YHWH will ensure that the return is smooth, even by providing water in the desert.

> This is the heart of the proclamation: the promise that YHWH will intervene in the lives of the exiles in a new and unexpected way.

Preaching the Reading

In this last week before Holy Week, today's readings evoke three homiletic themes. The first of these is a reminder of who God is. The prophet reminds us that God is the "way-maker," in the colloquialism of the black church. God is the one who creates ways through the sea and paths of dry land through mighty waters. This declaration the prophet makes not to those in comfort and contentment, but to those in exile, those who have lost home, language, and possibly even family. The prophet declares who God is to those who may have forgotten, for life has been so hard for so long. So, too, we, as we walk the last few days to the great feast of Easter, may take our cue from the prophet. We can make it our Lenten discipline to rehearse the truth about who God has been and continues to be. Further, in a world full of those who feel lost and alone, particularly as holidays approach, we can reach out to others to declare the good news of who God is to a world that may have forgotten.

But, while we are to remember who God is, a second Lenten homiletic theme is that we are to forget the past. There is an irony in this theme, for the prophet starts with an illustration from the glorious past of the children of Israel. It is not, however, this past that we are to forget. The prophet calls us to forget past traumas, past hurts, past pains, both individually and as a people. For us as individuals, this is a call past

> The prophet calls us to forget past traumas, past hurts, past pains, both individually and as a people.

forgiveness to the yet-harder discipline of letting go. However, there are also national implications. What might it mean for us to turn our attention away from our national pain on September 11, 2001? What might it mean for us not to dwell on the southeastern floods caused by Hurricanes Katrina and Rita? The call here is not to stop helping those affected. The call is to a vision for the future, to live a Lenten discipline characterized by a relinquishment of past pain.

These two themes build to the ultimate prophetic assertion: God is doing something new. Here the prophet affirms that God renews all of creation, even the beasts of the field and the desert land. God's promise of newness calls us, as a Lenten people, to walk forward in faith and in trust. Looming ahead of us is the awful cross; but the promise of God is this: not exile, not even crucifixion shall have the last word. The God of Lent is also the God of re-creation, always making things new.

RESPONSIVE READING

PSALM 126 (RCL, BCP)
PSALM 126:1-2A, 2B-3, 4-5, 6 (LFM)

Understanding and Using the Psalms

The psalm for the Fifth Sunday of Lent is part of the fifth book of the Psalms, a book that celebrates the rule of YHWH.[8] In the midst of this book of celebration is a collection called the Songs of Ascents. Liturgically, this collection was central to the festival of Sukkoth (or Booths), a celebration of God's provision for Israel in the wilderness.[9] Psalm 126 stands in the midst of this celebration as one of the few laments in the entire fifth book of the Psalms. Yet it is an abbreviated lament, invoking God's presence by remembering God's past salvific acts (vv. 1-3); petitioning YHWH for help (v. 4a); and expressing deep trust in the goodness of YHWH (vv. 4b-6).[10]

Psalm 126 resonates with the promise in Isaiah of God's "new thing." Further, there are similarities between Paul's knowledge of Christ's suffering and the one who sows with tears. So, too, in John 12 and in Luke 20 can Mary of Bethany and the landowner be seen as sowing in tears, anointing for burial or retaking the vineyard after the death of his son. And, in John 8, the woman caught in adultery was surely like one who was dreaming, when her fortunes were restored by Jesus' well-placed challenge.

PHILIPPIANS 3:4B-14 (RCL)
PHILIPPIANS 3:8-14 (BCP, LFM)

Understanding the Reading

In my commentary for the Second Sunday of Lent, I explained the way in which honor and shame would have informed Paul's letter to the church of Philippi. In this section of Philippians, the theme continues, as Paul redefines honor.

In 3:4b-7, Paul begins by giving a highly idealistic assessment of his status as a Jew. His heritage is unquestioned, born of the right nation and of a recognized tribe and circumcised on the eighth day as the law required. His actions, he claims, were above reproach. Not only did he follow the law; he taught the law as a Pharisee. Not only was he zealous on behalf of the law, he also pursued those whom he saw as heretical: members of the church. Not only did he hold to the tenets of the law; by his own account, he was "becoming blameless" (v. 6b; my trans.). With such status, Paul was unassailable, an ideal "type." His pedigree is a challenge to those who would question his piety because of his stance on Gentile circumcision (v. 2).

Just as Paul reaches the pinnacle of accomplishment, however, he reverses course, claiming to count all of his pedigrees a net loss (vv. 7-8). As Joseph Marchal points out, this rhetorical reversal echoes one found earlier in Philippians: "It is in giving up this status that Paul attempts to parallel his own life with the arc of the hymn he presented a chapter earlier."[11] In the Christ hymn, Jesus gives up his status of "being in the form of God" to take the form of a slave (2:6-7). Earlier in Philippians, Paul challenges his community to have the same mind as was in Christ; in his dismissal of his pedigree, Paul demonstrates what this means.

Just as God exalts Christ, Paul's hope, in the relinquishment of his status, is to gain Christ (2:9-11; 3:8-9). His ideas follow a curious progression: from power, to suffering, to death, to resurrection (3:10-11). Paul Holloway notes that Paul uses a similar progression in 2 Corinthians 4:7-11, suggesting a pattern of thought.[12] Further, he suggests that

> Paul makes it clear that his purpose is to seize upon Christ, for Christ has already seized upon him.

Paul's tentative hope for resurrection is not an eschatological hope, but a hope for an experience of the resurrection in the midst of his pursuit of Christ.[13]

Given Paul's earlier self-assessment, Philippians 3:12 is ironic. Paul claims no mastery of the pursuit of Christ. Rather, he makes it clear that his purpose is to seize upon Christ, for, as he says poetically, Christ has already seized upon him.[14]

Paul has yet to reach his goal, and so he pushes toward it. For this new goal constitutes a different kind of honor, not status in the community but "the calling of God in Christ Jesus" (v. 14).

Preaching the Reading

The second reading for the Fifth Sunday of Lent issues a challenge to lifelong, faithful Christians who come from the right families, have always gone to the right churches, and have done the best they can to live upright, Christian lives. None of that matters. This is an uncomfortable—but perhaps a necessary—sermon for communities of faith that take their pedigree more seriously than they take the cross. As Paul points out, even he, with an unattainable pedigree, had to count that a net loss in his pursuit of Christ. In so doing, Paul patterns himself after Christ, our ultimate pattern, who left his pedigree behind in obedience to God. Paul's challenge causes the community of faith to hear the prophet's challenge differently: do not remember the former things. The former things, in this instance, are not the traumas of exile but the comforts of status. As we journey steadily to the cross, in pursuit of the call of God in Christ Jesus, Paul challenges us to examine what we might need to leave behind.

The obverse of this homiletic theme is a call to pursue "the prize of the calling of God in Christ Jesus" (v. 14; my trans.). If the former theme focuses, once more, on what the faith community should be "giving up for Lent" and beyond, this one focuses on what the faith community should be "taking up."

> Paul challenges us to respond to this grace of being "seized" by pursuing true honor.

As Christians, we claim to be seized by Christ at baptism, claimed as one of Christ's own people. Paul challenges us to respond to this grace of being "seized" by pursuing true honor. This honor is not easily or quickly attainable; it requires effort on our part and a relinquishment of "what lies behind." Here again, the words of the prophet echo. Paul does not tell us concretely what such a pursuit might entail. This much we can surmise: it will consume our very lives, as we live out the faith of the church that we are baptized into Christ's death and raised to new life in him.

Finally, Paul's curious progression from power, to suffering, to death, and to resurrection reminds us of the Lenten journey itself. In Lent, the community of faith moves from the power of resurrection, celebrated every Lord's day, to the suffering, death, and resurrection of Christ. But the purpose of this familiar movement is not just cyclical. The purpose is that we come to know Christ better, to live better into the faithfulness that he personified, to stand more fully as people made just by God. So, the final homiletic theme might be: Why are you going? For if the only reason for the Lenten journey is the ritual of Lenten journeys, we have perhaps missed the whole point.

JOHN 12:1-8 (RCL)
LUKE 20:9-19 (BCP)
JOHN 8:1-11 (LFM)

Understanding the Gospel

John 12:1-8 begins with a threefold repetition of the Greek adverb "therefore" (*oun*), a word that, as in English, ties together two parts of a narrative in a causative relationship. The Gospel writer states, "Jesus, *therefore,* came to Bethany before the days of Passover" (v. 1; my trans.) This first "therefore" refers to the order to arrest Jesus issued by the Jerusalem hierarchy (11:57). *Therefore,* says the Gospel writer, Jesus goes to Bethany.

Bethany had been the site of Lazarus's resurrection. Jesus' return is, *therefore* (*oun*), cause for a meal, at which are Martha, Lazarus, and Mary. The posture of the three siblings is telling. Martha is serving; the word here is *diakoneo,* from which we get the title "deacon."[15] Lazarus has joined the rest of the male disciples, reclining at table.

In response to these two postures of discipleship, the author writes: "*therefore,* [*oun*] Mary took a pound of pure nard, anointed Jesus' feet, and wiped them with her hair" (v. 3; my trans.). Mary's act was not an act of penitence, as is that of the unknown woman in Luke's Gospel (7:37-38). Rather, as Helen Orchard points out, Mary's act is an act of profound discipleship, parallel to but far greater than those of Martha and Lazarus.[16] Disciples were known to render such a service to their teachers; even though the act was seen as a profound self-abasement.[17] Mary's actions thus make her the symbol of the ultimate disciple. She puts her wealth (a year's wage worth of pure nard) and her honor (bathing his feet and wiping it with her unbound hair) at the disposal of her teacher and master.

Judas's response stands in stark contrast. His concern for the cost of the nard—or more accurately, as the narrator tells us, for what he could have stolen of that money—stands in juxtaposition to Mary's humble posture. While he has given himself to the riches of the community, she has given herself completely to Jesus. It is not for her benefit that Jesus explains her action—a preparation for his burial—but for Judas. Judas will not, finally, understand; it will not come as a surprise when he, not she, betrays Jesus.

> While Judas has given himself to the riches of the community, Mary has given herself completely to Jesus.

Jesus responds twice to Mary of Bethany. First, he praises her. We must be careful here, for it is easy to misinterpret Jesus' quip, "The poor you have with you always." Jesus is balancing one truth, the command to care for the poor in

Deuteronomy 15:11, with an even more urgent truth, his imminent death and burial. It is to this need that Mary's act responds.

Jesus' second response is often missed, because it takes place in John 13. Just as Mary "anointed Jesus' feet [*tous podas*] and wiped them with her hair [*ekmassō*]," so also Jesus, in imitation of Mary, will wash the disciples' feet [*tous podas*] and wipe them with a towel [*ekmasso*] (12:3; 13:5).[18] The author's repetition is likely intentional. Just as Mary has humbled, perhaps humiliated, herself in an act of pure discipleship, Jesus will follow her lead and humble, perhaps humiliate, himself to show true service to those at his last supper.

The narrative of the woman caught in adultery, John 8:1-11, the LFM lection for the Fifth Sunday of Lent, is widely accepted to be a later addition to the Gospel of John, with some manuscripts placing it after John 21:38.[19] Further, its language is uncharacteristic of the Gospel of John, notably in its mention of "scribes," who do not occur elsewhere in this Gospel.[20] Still, the narrative remains scripture in much of the Christian church.

According to the narrative, Jesus is teaching in the Jerusalem Temple when a woman caught "in the act" of adultery is brought to him. This was likely a trap intended for the woman, as no man is accused.[21] The woman presents a real problem for her society. Such an act, unresolved, could lead to a blood feud between kin groups over the dishonor to the woman's husband. The decision to kill the woman would restore peace, as the dishonor would be removed.[22]

Jesus thus faces a classic "challenge and riposte" situation, for which his honor as a teacher is at stake.[23] Should he not respond to the question, or respond incorrectly, he would lose face before those whom he was teaching. In addition, the life of another human being depended on his decision. Cleverly, Jesus responds to the challenge with another challenge. Without arguing the point of law, Jesus issues a ruling that "dishonors his challengers."[24] Since none of them can throw a stone without losing face, they all leave, Jesus' honor remains intact, and the woman's life is spared.

The BCP sets the Lukan parable of the vineyard (Luke 20:9-19) as its Gospel reading for this Sunday. This parable is meant as a further response to the challenge of Jesus' authority in 20:1-8. It opens with a rich, absentee landlord, leaving tenant farmers in charge of his property and going away for a long time (v. 9). Tenant farming was an oppressive practice in which poor farmers had their family lands taken from them and then were hired back to work their own lands. Such practices led to high amounts of resentment.[25] In light of this resentment, it is not surprising that the tenants act violently against the representatives of the landowner. The crowd would have sympathized, becoming more enthusiastic with each new beating. The murder of the son would have been the ultimate victory. If the owner were dead, the tenant farmers could then regain control over their ancestral properties.[26]

But the owner is still alive, and he responds in righteous anger toward those who have killed his son. This sparks the crowd's reaction: "May it never be so!" (*me genoito*), an exclamation only seen here and in the writings of Paul. But what the people don't understand, the dénouement of this parable clarifies. With its veiled reference to God and to God's appointed king as stones that flesh cannot withstand, the parable becomes a humiliating challenge to the Jerusalem hierarchy, making them the tenant farmers, those who "kill the prophets and stone those who are sent to them."[27]

Preaching the Readings

In light of the variety of Gospel passages assigned, I can only address a few homiletic themes. For those preaching the RCL text, two possible themes emerge. The first is the role of Mary as model disciple. Mary's discipleship is full-body service. No part of her person, her status, or her livelihood is withheld from Jesus. For Christians this poses a challenge: Are we really willing to put our whole

> Are we really willing to put our whole being at the service of this Jesus of Nazareth, even in the face of his death?

being at the service of this Jesus of Nazareth, even in the face of his death? Are we willing to discard all propriety to proclaim that he is our teacher, our Savior, our Lord? What might such a declaration look like today? What implications would that have for our economics? Our dignity? Our hermetically sealed, dirt-free lives? Whose feet are we, the church, willing to anoint in memory of her?

The second theme emerges from the meal at Bethany, a meal that prefigures Jesus' last meal. The poignancy of this meal, in the shadow of Jesus' arrest and death, raises another challenge. What does it mean to celebrate the feast in the face of mortality? Many churches celebrate communion regularly, some every week. But the question emerges: Are these just ritual acts or is this really a meal of the people of God? The Bethany dinner is striking for three elements: the presence of siblings, the practice of ministry by all of them, and the acknowledgment—in the midst of the feast—of impending, unavoidable mortality. The same elements are present in the Eucharist meal, and in all of our meals, when we sit long enough to eat together. In a society marked by a lack of community and conversation, what might it mean for the church to witness prophetically to the importance of meals, family and ecclesial, as a locus of membership, ministry, and mortality?

For those preaching from the LFM, the clearest theme emerging from this passage is Jesus' challenge: "Let the one without sin cast the first stone." Jesus' retort to the Jerusalem hierarchy neither denied nor excused the fault of the woman caught in adultery. To the contrary, Jesus charges the woman to "sin no more." However, Jesus' strongest challenge is issued to the Jerusalem hierarchy, and it is a challenge to which, upon reflection, they cannot respond. This narrative issues a challenge to the Christian church also. When have we been so focused on another's sin that we have blissfully forgotten our own? Who are we so eager to stone that we have conveniently ignored the directive of Jesus? Is there ever a time when we are not called to put the stones down and find another way? Jesus' challenge speaks to us also: unless you are sinless, put the stones down.

The Gospel set by the BCP issues a warning: the owner will return. This assertion is at the heart of the parable of the vineyard and its tenants. The warning speaks to the Jerusalem hierarchy of Jesus' day; but it speaks to the church as well. By this text we are warned to be careful if we get to thinking that the Christian church somehow "belongs" to us, and that we can control who has access to it. The text cautions us not to act too swiftly

> Is there ever a time when we are not called to put the stones down, and find another way?

against those who claim to come in the name of the owner of the vineyard. They may be telling the truth. We, as the church, are merely tenant farmers tending a vineyard. We must be vigilant, then, lest we forget to whom the vineyard belongs and attempt, intentionally or not, to wrest it, by force, from the owner. That is a stone over which we dare not stumble. For though he tarry long, the owner of this vineyard will return.

Both the first and second readings resonate with the three Gospel selections for the Fifth Sunday of Lent. For those using RCL, one finds that Mary, like YHWH, is opening the door to a new thing. She is demonstrating what it means to leave all of the former things behind, and not to recall them. Instead, even in the face of Jesus' impending death, Mary claims a "new thing," a model of discipleship and of service so radical that Jesus himself imitates it. Mary, too, resonates with Paul's honor reversal. She, like he, could fairly claim to count her status and her financial wealth as rubbish, in order to claim the prize of the call of God in Christ. In her example, the echoes of Second Isaiah and of Paul ring true.

> Mary is demonstrating what it means to leave all of the former things behind, and not to recall them.

If Mary is evidence of YHWH in action, doing a new thing, for those preaching the LFM the woman caught in adultery is representative of the exilic community looking for that "new thing" to emerge. Jesus' counsel to her not to sin anymore resonates with Isaiah's call to forget the former things and Paul's challenge to count all former things as rubbish. With her, Jesus Christ demonstrates a "new thing," a second chance to live.

For those preaching from the BCP, the warning of the owner's eventual return connects first with Isaiah's counsel to forget the former things. When the owner returns, he, like YHWH, will set things right. He will not create springs in the desert, but he will remove the unfaithful from their places of power. And he will take pleasure in his vineyard, just as YHWH's people and all of creation will take pleasure in desert springs. Paul's counsel sounds even more urgent then. For when the owner does return, we need to be pressing forward to that which lies ahead, rather than repeating the violent acts of the past, the rejection of the prophets of God. Next week, the Lenten journey enters Jerusalem; the son of the owner returns to his father's vineyard. Will we welcome him this time?

Notes

1. Norman K. Gottwald, *The Hebrew Bible: A Socio-Literary Introduction* (Philadelphia: Fortress Press, 1987), 492.

2. Lawrence Boadt. *Reading the Old Testament: An Introduction* (Mahwah, N.J.: Paulist, 1984), 416.

3. Gottwald, *The Hebrew Bible,* 492.

4. Ibid. 493.

5. Boadt, *Reading the Old Testament,* 421.

6. Ibid.

7. These animals are seen in a much less pleasant light wandering through the ruins of Edom, just south of Jerusalem, in Isaiah 34. Paul D. Hanson, *Isaiah 40–66*, Interpretation: A Bible Commentary for Teaching and Preaching (Louisville: Westminster John Knox, 1995), 75.

8. Nancy deClaissé-Walford, *Introduction to the Psalms: A Song from Ancient Israel* (St. Louis: Chalice, 2004), 113.

9. Ibid., 120.

10. A lament psalm also typically includes a complaint and an "expression of praise and adoration." Ibid., 24.

11. Joseph A. Marchal, *Hierarchy, Unity and Imitation: A Feminist Rhetorical Analysis of Power Dynamics in Paul's Letter to the Philippians* (Atlanta: SBL, 2006), 142.

12. Paul A. Holloway, *Consolation in Philippians: Philosophical Sources and Rhetorical Strategy* (New York: Cambridge University Press [Virtual Publishing], 2003), 139.

13. Ibid.

14. Marchal, *Hierarchy, Unity and Imitation,* 143. In a marvelous irony, the one who pursued Christians has been caught by Christ.

15. One should not assume this posture as typical for Martha, in John's Gospel. While Luke characterizes Martha in this way (Luke 10:38-42), in John, she is nothing short of a theologian and only secondarily a hostess (John 11:21-27). In John's Gospel, Martha is the only one of Jesus' disciples that recognizes him as the Christ.

16. Helen C. Orchard, *Courting Betrayal: Jesus as Victim in the Gospel of John,* Journal for the Study of the New Testament Supplemental Series 161; Gender, Culture, Theory 5 (Sheffield: Sheffield Academic Press, 1998), 151.

17. Ibid., 152.

18. Ibid.

19. Bruce Malina and Richard Rohrbaugh, *Social-Science Commentary on the Gospel of John* (Minneapolis: Fortress Press, 1998), 293.

20. Leon Morris, *The Gospel According to John*, rev. ed., The New International Commentary on the New Testament (Grand Rapids: Eerdmans, 1995), 780.

21. Ibid., 781.

22. Malina and Rohrbaugh, *Social-Science Commentary on the Gospel of John,* 292–93.

23. Ibid., 293, cf. 174.

24. Ibid., 293.

25. Bruce Malina and Richard Rohrbaugh, *Social-Science Commentary on the Synoptic Gospels* (Minneapolis: Fortress Press, 2003), 308.

26. Ibid.

27. Luke 13:34 (see the Second Sunday of Lent); Joel B. Green, *The Gospel of Luke,* The New International Commentary on the New Testament (Grand Rapids: Eerdmans, 1998), 709. The references are to Isa. 8:14, in which YHWH is described as a stone of stumbling; and to Psalm 118, one of the enthronement psalms of the king, in which the anointed one is the rejected stone. Psalm 118, in particular, would have called to mind the triumphal entry, with its cry, "Blessed is the one who comes in the name of the LORD," and "Save us, we beseech you, O LORD" (*hosiy'a na*). Both of these references would suggest not only that the hierarchy were the tenants, but that Jesus himself was the son of the owner.

HOLY WEEK

CHARLES L. RICE

The great Lutheran theologian and preacher Joseph Sittler described preaching as organic to a time, a place, and to particular personalities.[1] He was assuming, of course, a fourth organic source of Christian proclamation, the Scriptures. Each sermon springs not only from the sacred text but also from essential connection to the moment, the particular situation in which preacher and hearers find themselves. Where and when and among whom the words are spoken gives them their life and power. As Robert Raines once put it, "The text is just so much wind until I put up my life as a sail."[2]

Given such an understanding of preaching, Holy Week provides an unparalleled hermeneutical matrix. No day or season in the church calendar can match these seven days for their drama, sense of place, and movement in time. From Palm Sunday to Holy Saturday each day presents its unique story, a narrative unfolding at a particular time and place. It is as if the preacher, like those early bishops, were walking around Jerusalem recalling and interpreting the events tied to those sites.

"Concreteness," Paul Hoon once said, is the essence of Christian worship. Christianity has earthy beginnings, its origins with persons, places, discrete moments. Our liturgy, accordingly, springs from connection to these material, historical, and geographic sources, and our worship at its best maintains this specificity and concreteness.[3] This would be a corollary of the incarnation: the word become flesh in a particular person at a particular time and place. In our liturgical life, this takes the form of a "repetitious uniqueness." For example, once a year we kneel down and wash each other's feet, an act for which there is no parallel and no substitution: washing hands or laying a towel on the altar falls short. The action of the liturgy is tied to the story we read and tell every year on a certain Thursday.

The Christian year comprises a whole series of unique events that show this concreteness: Annunciation, Nativity, Baptism of Jesus, Triduum, Pentecost. To these great christological liturgies, the church has added its own, such as Ash Wednesday and All Saints. On each of these occasions, text, the action of a community in time and space, and interpretive words merge in the people's greatest work, the worship and service of God. This is, obviously, a description of the church's constantly repeated but unique event, the Eucharist, in which memory and action join with the spoken word in life-giving celebration.

So, as we approach once more the task of preaching in Holy Week, we will do well to keep in mind its concreteness, the uniqueness of this annual pilgrimage through time and space. It goes beyond mere sentiment to consider that we are walking where Jesus walked, putting ourselves by imagination and devotion in the places where he and his first followers found themselves, and right there attempting to say something to our companions on the way. Holy Week reminds us of something that is true of all preaching: it always addresses actual persons at a moment in history and a locatable place on earth. At the same time, among the seasons of the Christian year, it presents seven days like no other for doing that.

This week, in fact, by its drama and movement, can empower the preacher. That would be true of all the great liturgical days, so long as the preacher is ready to go with the occasion. At Easter it is the preacher who is ready to celebrate—more than to, say, prove or explain—the resurrection, who will be most up to the day. The same can be said of Christmas Eve or Pentecost or All Saints: joining in with what is happening would be the best possible homiletic.

Holy Week is itself an innovation of the church working out its ways of worship. When Etheria made her pilgrimage to Jerusalem in the late fourth century, she found the church there observing an expanded version of the "Great Week." The community in Jerusalem occupied the ground on which the great events leading up to Easter had occurred. Consequently, they developed a weeklong liturgy tied to the sacred sites.[4] This caught on in the Christian world and persists to this day, in places far from Pilate's pavement, Olivet, and Calvary. Christian imagination throughout the world finds its way to those times and places. There lies the beginning of the Christian year itself and the power of the liturgy of Word and Sacrament.

There is a particular stake in this for people today, in the peculiarity and integrity of the church's times and seasons. The more experience is homogenized, with a paved-over landscape and fast food to match, the more acute grows the need for times and seasons that stand out. To put it one way, *kairos* can enliven *chronos,* saving us from life as "one damn thing after another." The philosopher Josiah Royce opposed the idea of America as a "melting pot," a popular idea in his day. Royce believed that following that road would lead to "a harassed dead level of mediocrity."[5] The recurrence of the Christian year and the concreteness of its liturgies provide relief from what Royce regarded as the tedium of sameness.

Marianne Micks has written about this from her perspective as a liturgical scholar. Many people, she acknowledges, have no connection to the Christian year. Modern life provides its own rhythms: "Separated from any real dependence upon seedtime and harvest, many workers in an industrial society tune their lives to the recurring cycles of weekends and annual vacations—two bright times to count on in the progress toward age sixty-five and retirement."[6]

Remnants of the Christian marking of time remain—Sundays, Christmas, Halloween, Easter—but, for many, the narratives related to these days are lost or obscured by secular overlays. Today, for many, the stories and images that accompany our public rituals come from sports, entertainment, commercial interests, and connection to the Internet. The connection to religious tradition and shared history is minimal. Just ask any young person what Halloween *means.*

But secular observances of times and seasons reveal the need for a ritualized common life. Halloween is now the second largest holiday in the United States, measured by commercial activity. Super Bowl Sunday generates enormous, if temporary, community spirit, pulling people together for celebration and common cause. Even news of an approaching hurricane or blizzard is seized upon as an opportunity for joining together. Finding the stories we share and devising ways to tell them to each other and to act them out together remains, even in a culture of "bowling alone," a constant need.

I grew up in Southern California, where the weather varied only moderately from day to day, season to season. College years and graduate studies brought me to the East, to spring and summer, fall and winter. Those distinct seasons—really hot and truly cold, the newness of spring, the melancholy of fall—somehow fed my spirit, and have continued to do so. That has seemed to me analogous to the liturgical seasons: the story of Christ told by the calendar, the unique days and seasons, the ritual action—all conspire to take us more deeply into the mystery and to keep us on our spiritual toes.

Do we not need more than ever these set-apart days and weeks? Can we be content with the passage of time as mere *chronos,* the days going by as a kind of ticking it off? Nelson Thayer, teacher of psychology and religion, observed that the secular year begins on January 1 with a hangover and ends with overindulgence. What is more needed, he thought, is the Christian year that begins with the hope of Advent and that ends with the fulfillment of Christ the King.[7] Marianne Micks puts it this way:

> At least since the fourth century, the Church Year has invited men to think about the past and about the future. And at least since the fourth century some Christians have dissolved the tension by choosing what might be called a tourist's view of time, while others have elected to affirm it through their understanding of mystery in holidays.[8]

Micks's point is that we do not simply make the Christian festivals and seasons one more stop along the way as we go from this to that. Rather, by letting each day and season be what it is, we enter into the depth and breadth and mystery of the gospel. The pilgrim is different from the tourist: on a pilgrimage there is an *embodiment* of knowledge. We come to know by walking a road with others—those gone before and those walking with us now.

Holy Week calls us loud and clear to this, to walk a road once more, stopping at important places to hear the stories connected with that terrain and to add our own words to the occasion. In this pilgrimage the word can be embodied and a community newly formed in its own time and place. That way of seeing it provides a paradigm for all our preaching, and it opens opportunities for imaginative and transforming biblical proclamation on the way from Bethpage to the garden tomb.

The Homiletics of Holy Week

We are aiming for *liturgical* preaching, tuning the sermon to the liturgy by attention to the movement of the week and to the mood, tone, and language of each occasion. Each day, from the Liturgy of the Palms to the new fire of Easter, has its own texture and color, grounded in the christological drama and refined by catholic tradition and local custom. Preaching in Holy Week should remind us that we would do well always to take our cues from the liturgical occasion. In this dramatic week that is inevitable.

Palm/Passion Sunday places the preacher in the middle of the action, especially if the homily is given in the procession. In one way of doing it, "All Glory, Laud, and Honor" stops halfway, the preacher gives the homily, then the singing and the procession resume. Placed here among the people beginning their walk through Holy Week, the homily becomes one step on the way. Placing the homily here subordinates the preacher to the later reading of the Passion—on which it often seems barely possible to preach anyway. Standing there in the midst of the procession preaching, as it were, on the way to the cross, the preacher participates in the first steps of the Holy Week journey and joins in the ironic confession of the day: we are not able to say unambiguously what we mean by the kingship of Jesus. So we will, preacher and congregation waving our palms with the children, follow him toward that most ambiguous place where his true royalty will be revealed. On this day, amid the music and hosannas and a very well-worn story—the preacher does best who takes her or his place in that long line of pilgrims.

Monday, Tuesday, and Wednesday have their own cast of characters, their poignant stories of love and betrayal. It is as if these men and women themselves come out once more to walk through Holy Week, asking to be remembered, to be given a second hearing, to find the way to greater love, more devotion, forgiveness, their own place in the procession at last. Can we see them trying to find their places there in Jesus' unfolding story? Are we able, given all the glosses of piety, caricature, and bias, to see them as grateful, puzzled, frightened, hoping-against-hope men and women? Are they worth a second look? Could we try to listen to their stories as if hearing them for the first time? With which of them do we identify this year? These three days, the story is the thing: to listen, to put ourselves into it, to question our usual interpretations, to walk with these men and women on the way to the cross. This goes for the preacher as much as for the listeners.

Then we come to Holy Thursday, the Thursday of the New Commandment, Maundy Thursday. We could even call this Family Night, and many of our churches now observe it that way, with a meal together and an informal atmosphere. That last supper was a family affair, Jesus gathered around the table with those he loved. In the simple actions of the evening—washing their feet, breaking bread, and drinking wine—he draws them close, and he prepares them both for his departure and for their continuing life together. All the marks of a family are there: intimacy, service, eating and drinking, looking to the future, facing separation and death. The sermon that takes the form of table talk is not inappropriate to this occasion.

For some congregations this will be a more ceremonious occasion, marking the founding of the Holy Eucharist. Even the ritual of foot washing will be observed with as much liturgical dignity as baring one's feet and being washed in public will allow. The Holy Meal that has come down to us through many refinements from that night when Jesus took bread, blessed and broke it, will be a far cry from its prototype, though the words at the heart of both will be there. But whether it is over the leftovers and dishes from the supper of soup and bread, or in view of a glowing altar, the preacher's role this evening is to point to the host and servant of all, the one who washes their feet and feeds them. These actions, now deeply embedded in our common stories and liturgical life, are the essentials of the journey through Holy Week and beyond. "Wash one another's feet," "Take and eat," "Love one another," Jesus commands. Inseparable, all three of these words lead us to the possibility of living by a new commandment. The preacher begins and ends here, at the table with Christ and each other. This night, perhaps above all others, tells us what and how to preach.

At the old Good Friday service, usually from noon until three P.M., the preacher was often given seven texts, the collage of short words from the cross. Here is an obvious example of liturgy choosing texts and shaping the content, length, and mood of preaching. Anyone who has preached all of the Seven Words on that Friday afternoon will tell you how quickly it goes, as the preacher is both tethered and pulled along by those terse texts. Liturgical wisdom recognizes the preacher's limits, hems him or her in, and makes up in music and drama, silence and starkness, for the preacher's inadequacy to tell the meaning of this day.

At the end of the Good Friday service it is the custom in some places for a wooden cross to be carried into the church, in silence, and placed in the sight of the people. It is as if to say, when all has been said and done: you must fall silent, look upon the cross for yourself, and seek its meaning for you. There is about this day that which is beyond words. In considering how to preach, the preacher will want to keep that in mind. Would a sermon explaining the doctrine of the atonement be the thing for Good Friday?

One resource for preaching on this day is the rite itself. The preacher can read through the prayers, the rubrics, and the hymns for the day. What do the people do today, and how can the preacher mirror as well as complement their work? Someone has said that the American Thanksgiving is the ideal holiday, because it is so unambiguous. Everyone knows exactly what to do: just cook the turkey, be sure there is plenty of stuffing and cranberry sauce, and keep to the usual ritual of the day. Preachers could learn from that. On these big days, just enter into what is happening—its shape, color, and movement—and contribute your part with skill and grace. A rule of thumb follows from that: the bigger the occasion, the smaller the sermon.

The Great Vigil of Easter, its roots in the earliest practice of the church, has two big themes: light shining in darkness and Holy Baptism. A new fire may be kindled at the entrance to the church, from which the paschal candle is lighted. This candle—that in some times and places burns for the whole fifty days of Easter—is carried into the darkened church to the chanting of the *Exsultet*, a song of rejoicing in the coming of the light of Christ, with its repeated litany, "This is the night . . . . This is the night . . . ." This dramatic action, which often includes every person lighting a candle from the paschal candle, and the *Exsultet*'s chanted recollection of God's mighty deeds, tells the preacher how to preach. The sermon will, in its own way, echo "The light of Christ" and "This is the night . . . ."

The other great theme is Christian initiation. The Vigil recalls the night when the catechumens, after years of preparation and the final discipline of Lent, come for baptism and reception into the church. The preacher might give the homily at the baptistery, connecting going down into the water and rising to new life to this night, when the light overcomes darkness and Christ is risen among his people. On this night, as on all the occasions of Holy Week, the preacher is instructed and empowered by organic connection to the people and their holy work.

Notes

1. Joseph Sittler, *The Anguish of Preaching* (Philadelphia: Fortress Press, 1966), 8–11.

2. Robert Raines, unpublished lecture, delivered at a conference on "Training in the Art of Preaching," Kirkridge Retreat and Study Center, Bangor, Penn., June 1988.

3. Paul Hoon, *The Integrity of Worship* (Nashville: Abingdon, 1971), 156–61, 287–91.

4. J. G. Davies, *Holy Week: A Short History* (Richmond, Va.: John Knox, 1963).

5. Stuart G. Brown, *The Social Philosophy of Josiah Royce* (Syracuse: Syracuse University Press, 1950), 56.

6. Marianne Micks, *The Future Present: The Phenomenon of Christian Worship* (New York: Seabury, 1970), 6.

7. Nelson Thayer, lecture on "The Church Year and Pastoral Care," Drew University Theological School, Madison, N.J., c. 1980.

8. Micks, *The Future Present,* 45.

SUNDAY OF THE PASSION/ PALM SUNDAY

MARCH 28, 2010

Revised Common (RCL)	Episcopal (BCP)	Roman Catholic (LFM)
Liturgy of the Palms	*Liturgy of the Palms*	*Processional Gospel*
Ps. 118:1-2, 19-29	Ps. 118:19-29	
Luke 19:28-40	Luke 19:29-40	Luke 19:28-40
Liturgy of the Passion	*Liturgy of the Word*	*Palm Sunday: At the Mass*
Isa. 50:4-9a	Isa. 45:21-25 or	Isa. 50:4-7
	Isa. 52:13—53:12	
Ps. 31:9-16	Ps. 22:1-21 or 22:1-11	Ps. 22:8-9, 17-18, 19-20, 23-24
Phil. 2:5-11	Phil. 2:5-11	Phil. 2:6-11
Luke 22:14—23:56 or	Luke (22:39-71) 23:1-49	Luke 22:14—23:56 or
Luke 23:1-49	(50-56)	23:1-49

LITURGY OF THE PALMS / PROCESSIONAL GOSPEL

RESPONSIVE READING
PSALM 118:1-2, 19-29 (RCL)
PSALM 118:19-29 (BCP)

Despite all, the psalmist can declare: "I shall not die, but I shall live, and recount the works of the LORD" (v. 17). The celebration that unfolds in verses 19 and following. is a festal procession, perhaps describing the parade of a triumphant military force. As the celebrants approach the gates of the temple, the accoutrements of the feast of Tabernacles (Sukkoth) appear. They enter the temple court and even process around the altar carrying bouquets of palm, myrtle, and willow, singing a song of thanksgiving.

The psalm takes a theme from the temple. The cornerstone—a bondstone at the corner of the building—had been rejected, but now it occupies the crucial place in the edifice. This, sings the psalmist, is the Lord's doing: "It is marvelous in our eyes" (v. 23b). What we could not have expected, and what at times seemed impossible, the Lord has accomplished. The conclusion, then, is "Blessed is the one who comes in the name of the LORD" (v. 26).

Samuel Terrien tells us that verse 24 has been a song of martyrs: "On the scaffold or at the stake they met their death singing: 'This is the day which the Lord hath made; we will rejoice and be glad in it.'"[1] Jesus riding into Jerusalem on the way to his death would inevitably lead the church to this psalm that combines lament and victory.

THE GOSPEL
LUKE 19:28-40 (RCL, LFM)
LUKE 19:29-40 (BCP)

The emphasis as this story is told in Luke's Gospel is upon the role of Jesus' followers. It is they who set him on the colt and who, as his disciples, emerge from this event praising God in his name. Luke tells of no "Hosannas"—which would connect the entry to Zechariah's royal procession—and he has no interest in the waving of leafy branches with their evoking of Judas Maccabeus and his revolution. In the third Gospel, Jesus' entry into the Holy City is not so triumphal and not so much a public event. This is more private, closer to one of those chilly Palm Sunday mornings in the local parish when a handful of hardy souls put on their little procession around the churchyard.

> In the third Gospel, Jesus' entry into the Holy City is not so triumphal and not so much a public event.

Whatever messianic expectations they may have pinned on Jesus, the Davidic figure who rides into Jerusalem on a lowly animal comes as a man of peace, not as a heroic captain of war. This motif would have been particularly important to Luke, a theme that we hear as the disciples shout, "Peace in heaven, and glory in the highest heaven!" (v. 38b), echoing the angelic choir of Luke 2:14. These early followers may be no more sure of the precise identity or the ultimate intentions of the man on the donkey than they are of themselves. But even amid the uncertainty, they seem to be clear at two points: he is going somewhere important, and they intend to follow him. He will do what was promised to Mary—he will change the world (Luke 1:46-55)—and to Joseph—he will save his people (Matt. 1:21).

Jesus approaches Jerusalem—city of peace—as the peaceable king. There is no war horse, only an untried colt. The palm branches with the nationalistic overtones, Luke omits. Jesus, in Luke's account, plays a passive role: he is "set on" the donkey, and he does not speak until the end of the narrative. Since it is the band of disciples who are lauding Jesus, the ovation is quite small. In Charles

Talbert's summary, "The ride on the colt in the third gospel sets Jesus forth as the peaceable king who is recognized as such by his disciples (cf. 20:21-26; 23:2-4)."[2] This view of Luke's account in no way diminishes the significance of the story. "In Jesus God had come calling on Jerusalem" (19:44), says Talbert, and though the event remained ambiguous it was undeniably consequential. Talbert sees this as content-laden time.

> We may think of time either in terms of duration or of content: for example (a) duration—chronological time that can be measured on a clock or a calendar; (b) content—the character of time, that which fills the moment, so the time of planting or meal time. The latter kind of time confronts us with an opportunity and demands of us a response. In 19:44 Jesus speaks of "the time of your visitation." He means that in his ministry God had come calling, had visited his people (cf. 7:16). . . . The visit of God in the ministry of Jesus was recognized by his disciples who set him on the colt (v. 35).[3]

The acclamation of Jesus by the disciples reiterates his ministry; it is praise for all the mighty works that they had seen from the beginning of his ministry in Galilee. This, says C. F. Evans, "makes the entry into the city a climax and continuation of that ministry, and defines the nature of Jesus' kingship."[4] That this takes place on the Mount of Olives, with its eschatological associations, provides the stage for announcing and redefining the messianic identity of Jesus.[5]

This sets the spreading of the garments and the placing of Jesus on the colt in the context of Jesus' entire ministry and ultimate mission. Evans sees the details of the entrance narrative as acts of enthronement in verses 35-36. When they throw their garments under the animal as it proceeds, they are probably acting out Zechariah 9:9 (cf. 2 Kgs. 9:13), "where the garments represent the men themselves, and the piling of them to form a throne indicates submission to Jehu's authority." As the animal walks over the garments, the scene is set for the disciples' acclamation of Jesus as king.[6]

So we see the disciples seating Jesus on the animal with its royal associations while proclaiming his ministry of preaching, teaching, and healing. The pre-Easter Jesus merging with the exalted Christ of the emerging church comes into view. Here the disciples begin to take on a corporate entity in what is "almost a designation of the church."[7] Be that as it may, we can see here a glimmer of what will happen, as the young man from Nazareth, teacher and healer, rises in the events of that week in Jerusalem to be the exalted Christ the King and Lord of the church.

ISAIAH 45:21-25 (BCP)

Here we have three strophes of prophetic poetry that celebrate the saving sovereignty of God. The fall of the great Babylonian Empire is imminent; the gods of the Babylonians are being carried out of the city like so much baggage. God will liberate the exiles, using even such an unexpected means as Cyrus of Persia. Whatever may be the means of their deliverance, the exiles can rely on the unseen but ever-provident one who has seen them through exiles and threat before. A central theme of Deutero-Isaiah is the contrast between the powerlessness of idols and the power of God.

Therefore, the absolute claim is made: "There is no other god besides me . . ." (v. 21). The invitation springs from that assertion, and the invitation becomes a command: "Turn to me and be saved, all the ends of the earth! For I am God, and there is no other" (v. 22). The very being of the one true God stands behind the word of promise: "By myself have I sworn . . ." (v. 23). Echoing the assurance of Isaiah 55:11—"my word . . . shall not return to me empty"—and the universal worship of the true God of Philippians 2—". . . every knee shall bow and every tongue confess"—the prophet/poet calls the people to trust and hope.

ISAIAH 50:4-9a (RCL)
ISAIAH 50:4-7 (LFM)
ISAIAH 52:13—53:12 (BCP ALT.)

These Servant Songs are set amid the threat and uncertainty of exile. Here is the lament of Jeremiah, but at bottom is a confident, even defiant hope. The writer, who himself identifies closely with the figure of the servant—most likely the ideal Israel, the chosen and suffering people—expresses discouragement along with faithful determination: "I have set my face like flint . . ." (50:7). We hear a parallel to this unflinching spirit in 53:7, repeated twice, ". . . yet he did not open his mouth."

The source of this faithfulness is an intimate relationship with God. Like a loving parent waking a child, "Morning by morning he wakens . . . my ear" (50:4). It is this awakening that enables the servant to listen, even to the complaining and rebellious exiles, and to be their teacher. In close relationship to the Lord God, the servant is able to endure giving his back to be whipped, his beard to be plucked out, trusting in

> It is God's awakening him that enables the servant to listen, even to the complaining and rebellious exiles, and to be their teacher.

God to help him. He does not hide his face from insult and spitting, believing that through him "the will of the LORD shall prosper" and that he shall "see his offspring" (53:10).

This intimacy sustains the servant: "He who vindicates me is near" (50:7). Upheld by God, he is able to encourage the weary exiles, people who have lost their homes and face an uncertain future. Worn down as they are, what they must not lose is hope.

THE GOSPEL
LUKE 22:14—23:56 (RCL, LFM)
LUKE 23:1-49 (RCL ALT., LFM ALT.)
LUKE (22:39-71) 23:1-49 (50-56) (BCP)

Jesus dies not because the Romans convict him of a seditious act. The third Gospel tells the story in such a way as to show that Jesus was found innocent of conspiring against Rome. Rather, this Gospel tells us that Jesus dies as the rejected Christ, God's Chosen One who is distinct from the Jewish messiah-king. Luke includes in his Gospel four trials—before the Sanhedrin, Herod, and two before Pilate. The conclusion is that Jesus was innocent, but that the Jewish leaders plot the death of Jesus because he is the Chosen One.[8] Also, Luke's particular treatment of the inscription over Jesus' head, "This is the King of the Jews," does not follow the usual form of the Roman *titulus*. By omitting the definite article—he writes of *an* inscription—Luke suggests that this was not an official act of the Romans.[9]

The exegete/preacher will want to choose a pericope or motif within the long narrative of the Passion. Given Luke's interest in the question of Jesus' kingship, the preacher might focus on the trial before Herod (23:6-16) and/or the inscription and mocking (23:36-43).

Talbert says that Jesus, though submissive to the Father's will, does not seek martyrdom.[10] All four of the trials make this clear. Even before Herod, where Jesus does not speak to refute the charges, his demeanor is such that Herod pronounces him innocent and—in one way of seeing the outcome—treats the whole thing as a joke.[11] Who Jesus was must have mystified Pilate and Herod, even as his teaching and manner of life offended the Jewish leaders. The ambiguity of Palm Sunday springs from what we see at the trials: as they accuse and probe, Jesus stands mostly silent, unable to tell them in so many words the dawning truth of who he is.

Jesus, in Luke's account, appears before two powerful earthly rulers, Pilate and Herod, evoking Psalm 2:2: "The kings of the earth set themselves, and the rulers take counsel together, against the LORD and his anointed . . . ." The Lukan book of Acts (4:26ff.) makes it clear that the "holy servant" of Isaiah 53 is Jesus, who has suffered at the hands of the rulers and people of Israel, with the compliance of the "Gentiles," the Romans. The true King, the Anointed One, is declared innocent by the rulers but not recognized as the Christ. Only the faithful can see who he is and raise their hosannas.

In a chapter titled "Innocent and Obedient," Talbert goes to considerable lengths in stressing that Jesus gave up his life willingly. When Jesus faces death, he does so not as one seeking martyrdom but as one seeking to do the will of God. What we see in the week of his Passion is Jesus acting out the whole meaning of his life: "Thy will be done." The taunting words flung at him on the cross—"If you are the Christ, save yourself . . ."—take us back to the beginning of his career. He goes directly from his baptism to the temptations in the wilderness, where we hear the same words: "If you are . . . ."

> The true King is declared innocent by the rulers but not recognized as the Christ. Only the faithful can see who he is and raise their hosannas.

> Since then Jesus has been walking the way of rejection, suffering, and now death. It is a way that perfects his obedience to God by stripping him of every possible idolatrous attachment. Now, at the end, hanging on the cross, his life ebbing away, the same question is raised again: Will you use the divine power with which you are endowed for self-preservation? The final attachment to this world to which one is tempted to cling in an idolatrous way is life itself, mere continuance of physical existence.[12]

To the end, Jesus commits himself to the Father. In Luke, Jesus' last words from the cross show us his trusting obedience, "Into thy hands . . . ."

SECOND READING
PHILIPPIANS 2:5-11 (RCL, BCP)
PHILIPPIANS 2:6-11 (LFM)

It may help to keep in mind as we approach this lofty christological text that it was prompted by the inability of a Christian congregation to live in harmony. Paul appeals to a church divided by jealousy and a petty spirit. He calls Christians to be more like Christ, to let his mind be theirs.

J. Hugh Michael translates verse 5: "Treat one another with the same spirit as you experience in Christ Jesus."[13] Members of the church are to treat one another with the same deference and humility that we see in Jesus, who, not only in his earthly life but in his preincarnate life with the Father, gives up his prerogatives and "pours himself out."[14]

Like the servant of Isaiah 53:12, Jesus is obedient even to death—and that the most humiliating death imaginable—death on a cross. Michael quotes Cicero:

> To bind a Roman citizen is an outrage; to scourge him a crime. It almost amounts to parricide to put him to death; how shall I describe crucifixion? No adequate word can be found to represent so execrable an enormity. . . . Far be the very name of a cross not only from the body, but even from the thought, the eyes, the ears of Roman citizens.[15]

How could members of the body of Christ divide the church by asserting their rights or demanding special consideration?

Rather, says Paul, followers of Jesus are called to what Robert Wicks calls "Not creeds, sacraments, rites, or correct morals, and certainly not any beliefs in economic or political systems, but a disposition of mind."[16] Such a disposition of the mind springs from the awareness of grace and mercy that come from knowing Christ. In Jesus' parable of the unforgiving servant, the action of the man forgiven so much who is unrelenting toward his fellow servant reveals unawareness of the mercy by which he lives. The parable ends with the admonition: "[You must] forgive your brother or sister *from your heart*" (Matt. 18:35).

> It is the link between the self-giving Christ and his disciple that ensures a gracious community.

It is the link between the self-giving Christ and his disciple that ensures a gracious community. Jesus, who humbles himself, is exalted to be the Lord. Those who acknowledge his lordship become one with him, in heart and mind. Just as a Roman soldier swore allegiance to Caesar—the oath was the Roman sacramentary, a binding oath of loyalty—so Holy Baptism and Holy Communion bind the believer to Jesus the Lord. In this relationship, Jesus' disciples get a new mind, a new heart, the heart and mind of Christ who pours himself out for the life of the world (2 Cor. 8:9).

RESPONSIVE READING
PSALM 31:9–16 (RCL)

"Be *gracious* to me, O LORD . . . ." The psalmist opens himself to the merciful one; in deep distress he begins on a note of hope. He is in the depths: the weakness and anxiety of illness; the loneliness of grief; the unspeakable suffering of rejection and, worse, being forgotten like a broken pot that has been thrown away as useless. "*But,*" he says, "I trust in you, O LORD . . . ." Everything is in that word *but*. This enables the sufferer to speak his woe frankly to God. Terrien writes:

> These psalmists did not attempt to repress or suppress their feelings and desires, because they found in the presence of God a complete freedom of expression. . . . In God's presence these men "poured out their heart" without shame; they showed themselves as they were, outraged by the injustice of society, baffled by the remoteness of healing or restoration; but they did not silence the moans of their aching flesh or the anguish of their distraught minds. They found an outlet for their inward storms. They prayed and they persisted in prayer, even when submission or resignation lay beyond the reach of their will.[17]

Terrien reminds us that John Hus, Jerome of Prague, and the great preacher Savonarola all recited Psalm 31 on their way to the stake. *"But* I trust in you, O LORD; I say, 'You are my God.'"

PSALM 22:1–21 OR 22:1–11 (BCP)
PSALM 22:8–9, 17–18, 19–20, 23–24 (LFM)

Beginning with "My God," the psalmist pours out an account of rejection and hostility: curling lips and wagging heads, a circle of wild young Syrian bulls, ravening lions, and packs of dogs. His body aches, his heart is weak; he is parched and at the same time "poured out like water." He cries out day and night, but gets no answer and finds no rest. Here is the faithful servant of God—Jeremiah, Job, Jesus—who speaks his complaint, the believer's anguished *Why?*

The psalmist acknowledges his forebears and their continuing worship of the Holy One, "enthroned on the praises of Israel" (v. 3), but he finds himself standing outside this community of faith, unable to reconcile his personal experience with their confident praise. "A worm, and not human" (v. 6), he is isolated from Israel's prayers and from common humanity, but he tries to keep on trusting while suffering without apparent cause.

He manages a kind of prayer: *knowing what I know of the faith of Israel, and still aware of God, I cry out for God to come closer.* In the midst of suffering he asks for the presence of God.

The psalmist emerges from his suffering confident that those yet to come will share in his experience, sustained by the story of Israel's deliverance: "All the ends of the earth shall remember and turn to the LORD, and all the families of the nations shall bow before him" (22:27).[18]

On this Sunday we see to what extent the preacher's theme may be determined as much by occasion as by text. *Palm* and *Passion*: the multiple texts for this complex day are chosen by the liturgical occasion. The preacher may be swamped by the sweep and force of the rites of this morning. The best approach is to join in, walking with the congregation into Jerusalem today, and then on to its sacred sites, each calling for its own texts and its own words from the preacher.

Luke presents an overarching theme: The Ironic King. *Irony* is not a word that ordinarily works well in the pulpit, but if we move beyond simply employing the word itself and apply it to images and stories of the one who is much more than he appears to be, then we come close to Luke's presentation. The one who comes riding into Jerusalem is much closer, let us say, to that ironic figure Charlie Chaplin than to Donald Duck: the reticent little guy with a big heart as opposed to the loud-quacking cartoon character.

> The one who comes riding into Jerusalem is much closer to that ironic figure Charlie Chaplin than to Donald Duck.

The theme of royalty is right up front, in the paraphernalia and acclamation of the parade: the virgin colt, the spreading of the garments, their cries, "Blessed is the king who comes . . . ." The first words of the day connect Palm Sunday to Luke's narrative of the nativity: "Blessed is the king who comes in the name of the Lord! Peace in heaven, and glory in the highest heaven." The Gospel is read and then comes the announcement: "On this day he entered the holy city of Jerusalem in triumph, and was proclaimed King of kings . . . ." The blessing of the palms asks that "we who bear them in his name may ever hail him as our King . . . ." Then this royal procession comes to a halt and the collect intones:

> Almighty God, whose most dear Son went not up to joy but first he suffered pain, and entered not into glory before he was crucified: Mercifully grant that we, walking in the way of the cross, may find it none other than the way of life and peace; through Jesus Christ our Lord.[19]

This is where the preacher stands today, in the procession proclaiming the strange kingship of Jesus.

This homily can be given right there, in the procession. Most likely the children will be leading the way. About halfway through the hymn, the procession stops, the children sit down on the floor, the adults are seated in the nearest pews, and the preacher, standing among the children, gives a shorter-than-usual homily: this is a day for understatement.

The adults are listening in—and by eavesdropping, as Søren Kierkegaard and Fred Craddock have said, are hearing clearly what is said—as the preacher talks with the children about Jesus as King.[20]

How to do that? Irony is lost on some adults, and it is not readily available to children. Using a childlike mode of communication, here are two possibilities. Using the garb of royalty—a paper crown, a scepter, and the like—dress one of the children as a king or queen. Mention what is missing, such as a golden coach, beautiful jewels, a castle, and so forth. Then, contrast this with Jesus, by drawing the children into the story: Who can tell us what happened on that first Palm Sunday? What was Jesus riding as he entered Jerusalem? What do you guess he was wearing? Lead the children—and the adults—to see that Jesus is a different kind of king, without trying too much to explain exactly *how* he is different. Leave something to imagination and questioning.

Or simply use the action of the day. What we are doing right now is like being in a play. We have a story, stage directions, props, and our lines, all right there in Luke's Gospel—with the palms coming from Mark and Matthew. So, we are putting on a play today: saying our lines, taking our places, waving and walking and singing. Why are we doing this? Are we, like those people, walking down a road with Jesus? Where is he leading us? Why would we follow him? This hymn we are singing—"All Glory, Laud, and Honor"—What is it about? (Maybe read hymn verse 3, "The people of the Hebrews with palms before him went . . . ," and link that to what we are doing today.) The simple idea to get across is that we are joining a long procession of people following Jesus as our king. That is what the church is.

> We are putting on a play today: saying our lines, taking our places, waving and walking and singing.

Remember: The bigger the occasion, the smaller the sermon. The Sunday of the Passion is about as big as they get. The liturgy becomes the chief medium, enabling the preacher to find the words and images, while inviting imagination and engaged participation.

In many congregations the proclamation of the Gospel on this Sunday is the reading of the Passion narrative. Read well, this Gospel coming from the people, including young and old and drawing in the whole congregation, is perhaps the most effective means of interpreting this story and launching Holy Week. It provides contrapuntal balance over against the Liturgy of the Palms, even as by its dramatic action involving the whole congregation it mirrors that earlier liturgy. Simply reading the story of the cross deepens the irony of Palm Sunday. The voices and personalities of the readers bring the congregation into the story. Their "Crucify him, Crucify him" leads them to confront the question: "Crucify your *king*?"

If, for one reason or another, the preacher feels called upon to give a sermon, the theme of the ironic king serves Luke's Gospel well. As noted above, the accounts of Jesus' trial before Herod (23:6-16) and of the mocking soldiers and the inscription (23:36-38) are manageable pericopes. Either of these texts takes us to the question raised by Palm Sunday—What do you mean, *King?*

Or the preacher might want to choose one of the three words from the cross given to us by Luke: "Father, forgive them" (23:34), "Today . . . in Paradise" (23:43), or "Father, into your hands . . ." (23:45). In these small episodes—singly or all together—as Jesus hangs powerless on the cross, where do we see his royalty?

The Psalms. The psalms for today provide sharp contrast, *hallel* (118) and lament (22, 31). This juxtaposition serves the dramatic movement of the day and its ironic power. It is a long way from the sweet voices of children to the crowd crying, "Crucify him." The preacher could place two of these psalms together—Psalm 118 and either 31 or 22—glad praise and thanksgiving alongside the near despair of the lament, to capture the light and darkness of the coming week.

Psalm 118 comprises much of the language by which the church lives, the language of prayer and celebration. This has been called "Luther's psalm," because of its exuberant expression of gratitude, its frank acknowledgment of the goodness and presence of God, and its call for congregational worship.[21] Here is faith that wants to stand up and sing praise to God, unabashed and joyous.

The liturgy today begins with a celebrative parade—often on a fine spring day—and moves toward the darkness of Calvary. The preacher might look for images that capture the stark contrast. For example, the prosperous church I was attending in those days, in its beautiful old building with people and music to match, had just made the switch from Palm Sunday to the Sunday of the Passion.

> It is the contrast, the tension, so much that is un-re-solved on this day, that gives the pairing of Palm and Passion its power.

It was a fine morning in that leafy New Jersey town. There had been the usual procession of the palms, and the first two lessons had been read. Then came the Passion narrative, most of two chapters read by one of the ministers. As it went on and on, I could see that the two elegant ladies sitting in front of me were showing signs of puzzlement, little sideways glances, restlessness. You could see that my two neighbors were not a little relieved when the reading finally ended. One leaned toward the other and whispered with a not inaudible sign of relief: "Well, *that* wasn't very pleasant." It was a good guess that they would be off soon to a nice place for lunch.

Psalms 22 and 31 mute whatever festive atmosphere might linger from the parade of children and palms. Our hosannas still echoing and palms still in our hands, we are called upon to share the loneliness and anguished questioning of an afflicted soul. Right there we begin the journey into the saving mystery of Holy Week, at the point where the beauty of the day, the loveliness of the music and the beauty of children, the glad hosannas and festive royal psalm, come up against the cry of the psalmist that will become the cry from the cross. What preacher could improve upon the clashing wisdom of the liturgy?

The procession of the palms soon becomes, as the liturgy proceeds, the *via dolorosa*. The preacher can enter into this—is it too much to say *wild ride?*—and there find the words for the day. These words should not resolve the tension, but heighten it in a way that starts us down the road, singing Hosanna to the King, not quite sure where the road will lead him or us. It is the contrast, the tension, so much that is un-re-solved on this day, that gives the pairing of Palm and Passion its power. This is no more a day for oversimplification than for overstatement. Better on this day to join the procession and to make ourselves vulnerable to the mystery unfolding.

> Assist us mercifully with your help, O Lord God of our salvation, that we may enter with joy upon the contemplation of those mighty acts, whereby you have given us life and immortality; through Jesus Christ our Lord. Amen.[22]

The preacher does best for now—on this day of parades and passion—to give way to the unresolved questions put by the strange little royal procession.

If we think of Holy Week as a walk-about, then another motif emerges: we discover in a *community* what it means to proclaim Jesus King. Walking together, *we* enter and contemplate these "mighty acts." Palm Sunday is a good time to remind the congregation of the meaning of those simple acts of every Sunday: getting out of bed, getting dressed, going to the church, greeting one another, joining symbolically—all of us in the procession—as we stand together singing. This is the church *following* Jesus, walking together in the way of the cross. In its early days Christianity was called the Way. We see that acted out on Palm Sunday.

The ritual actions of Palm Sunday remind us also that our faith is, to one degree or another, inherited. Most of us belong to a congregation and worship in a certain way as a heritage from families and communities. We are told religious affiliation is similar to political alignment: if patterns in which we were brought up survive college we are likely to stick with that—Democrat or Republican, this denomination or that—all our lives. This does not always hold true, and some think this more a detriment to personal growth and spiritual development than something to be valued. Nonetheless, much of what turns out to be most precious to us is a gift from the past. So, in one way of seeing it, "just going through the motions" is not altogether bad, especially when it comes to religious ritual acted out together. We do that on Palm Sunday.

Isaiah 45:21-25. The visible gods of the empire are loaded on the backs of animals and carried out of the city. The prophet mocks the idols and the arrogance of human regimes they represent. Today's preacher should have no difficulty in pointing to the tangible idols that make their promises but in the time of trouble fail and crumble. The collect suggests that it is in loving "things heavenly" that we will be able live rightly among "earthly things."[23]

> Not only is it the invisible God who is there for those who call, but it is the *suffering* God.

It is the unseen one who saves: "Truly, you are a God who hides himself, O God of Israel, the Savior" (45:15). Holy Week deepens this mystery. Not only is it the invisible God who is there for those who call, but it is the *suffering* God. As we see Jesus silent before accusers and torturers, and as we stand before the cross of his suffering, we are as far as we could go from the blatant idols and boisterous religion that the prophet mocks. Here we see overturned every idolatrous claim, and we hear with new ears the prophet's words: "Turn to me and be saved, all the ends of the earth!" (45:22). Over the main door of Holy Cross Monastery up on the Hudson River are the words: *Mundi Medcina*—medicine of the world. What heals and gives us new life?

Isaiah 50:4-9a; 52:13—53:12. Whether we think of the servant as the whole people of Israel, some particular figure, or even Jesus—to whom these images of patient and hopeful suffering inevitably adhered—we have here a profile of courage and faith. The suffering servant in Isaiah 50 somehow finds the words for discouraged, even disconsolate people. Morning by morning—like the gift of manna or daily bread—it is the Lord who wakes him up. What is more, he has been given the great gift of open ears and a mind ready to receive from the teacher (50:4). These gifts—the presence of God and an attentive and expectant attitude—enable him to find the right words, to sustain the weary in a difficult time.

> Prophetic and transforming speech is a gift, and it is inseparable from the gift of listening "as one who is taught."

Father Michael Lapsley, a determined opponent of apartheid, was the target of South African operatives in 1990. A car bomb took both of his hands and one eye. He writes of "the irony . . . that the only automatic weapon I have ever used is my tongue. They eventually took away my hands and left my weapon reasonably intact."[24] He continues his ministry of reconciliation and healing, especially to veterans who have suffered their own severe losses and deep psychic wounds.

Where do we get the words? What is an encouraging word, a truly helpful and life-giving word? This is always a question facing the prophet, and it is a question for every preacher every week. Prophetic and transforming speech is a gift, and it is inseparable from the gift of listening "as one who is taught." Where does wisdom come from? How does one find the arresting word, the healing and helpful, the true word that can also win over?

Nelson Mandela comes to mind. Somehow, after twenty-five years of unjust imprisonment on Robbin Island, missing the growing up of his children and the freedom to enjoy his beautiful country while in the prime of his life, Mandela came out with the right words to heal and bless his people. His autobiography, *Long Walk to Freedom,* is the story of a man whose time of silence and suffering has given him the voice of a reconciler and the words of a wise teacher.[25] He has also emerged from all of this as a joyful man, deeply grateful for life and hopeful for his people. This Holy Week we could reflect on how this particular road—this way of walking—has led in troubled South Africa to a measure of joy and peace.

Philippians 2:5-11 (6-11). Imagine an adult group in your congregation, discussing a difficult text or a controversial subject. They listen carefully, leave some open spaces, try to find the right words and to speak them in the right tone. Would that be an example of Paul's hope for the church at Philippi: "sharing in the Spirit," "having the same mind," in "full accord," "looking to the interest of the other"? The apostle

> The gracious community, with common purpose and civil conversation, flows from the deep spring of grace.

calls us to have a disposition of mind that reflects the mind of Christ, to be to one another as Christ is to us.

How could we get such an attitude? Paul tells us that it is a gift: What else could it be? Even as he calls on the community to work out its salvation with "fear and trembling," he assures them that "it is God who is at work in you, enabling you . . ." (2:13). The source of such a disposition of mind is the unaccountable gift of grace. The gracious community, with common purpose and civil conversation, flows from the deep spring of grace.

These themes are all there in the Shaker song, "Simple Gifts": "'Tis the gift to be simple, 'tis the gift to be free / 'tis the gift to come round where we ought to be / And when we find ourselves in the place just right / 'twill be in the valley of love and delight." Then there is that line that comes close to Paul's vision of the humility of Christ present in us: ". . . to bow and to bend, we shan't be ashamed."

This possibility comes, as Paul sees it, from being *in Christ.* It is not first of all a matter of being *like* Christ. Having the mind of Christ depends upon our living in him and he living in us. A sacramental way of putting this is that we receive his body and blood and then live out that gift in the world. You can hear it in the old liturgy, Rite I in the *Book of Common Prayer*. The prayer is that we might "worthily receive the most precious body and blood of thy Son Jesus Christ, be filled with thy grace and heavenly benediction, and made one body with him, that he may dwell in us and we in him."[26] Here lies the possibility of our following his example, offering "our selves, our souls and bodies," just as he "poured himself out."

Luke 22:14—23:56. This long reading does not lend itself to a single sermon. If the preacher decides to preach on the Passion narrative, focusing on a smaller portion will be necessary. Here are two possibilities, both coming from Luke's telling of the story.

As previously noted, the preacher can treat one or more of Luke's three regal words from the cross: "Father, forgive them"; "Today . . . in Paradise"; and "Father . . . into thy hands." One of Luke's great themes is the mercy of God. Where Matthew calls for being perfect in imitation of the perfection of God (Matt. 5:48), Luke says, "Be merciful, even as your Father is merciful" (6:36). The mercy of God is revealed even at the cross, where brutality seems to win the day. Jesus' attitude toward those who mock and kill, and his kindness to the criminals on either side, reveals who he is, the beloved Son of God the All Merciful. It is to this one that he trusts himself absolutely and finally, "Father, into thy hands . . . ."

> The mercy of God is revealed even at the cross, where brutality seems to win the day.

Charles Williams is buried in the cemetery of Christ Church, Oxford. At the end of his creative and sometimes troubled life, he chose his epitaph. Williams's gravestone reads simply: "Under the Mercy." Luke's Gospel gives us one parable after another telling us that this is how God reigns, in mercy and unaccountable lovingkindness. With his last breath, Jesus reveals that it is by this mercy that he lives and dies, and even on the cross he extends this mercy to the most unworthy.

A second possibility is to combine in the sermon the narratives of the entry into Jerusalem and of the journey to the cross. Luke's portrayal of the Palm Sunday procession shows Jesus being lifted up onto the donkey and proclaimed king by his followers. Then, in the Passion narrative, he reaches the place of crucifixion utterly humiliated—mocked, scorned, beaten, spat upon—then once more *lifted up.* The ambiguity of the first procession is intensified in the second, as the lowly king riding on the beast of burden is nailed to the cross with the mocking sign over his head. In both cases it is the eyes of faith that see who he is, the very embodiment of the mercy of God poured out in his ministry of teaching and healing and finally in his life-giving death.

One of the bright students around the table at one of our best prep schools asked the question: "What is the difference between Jesus of Nazareth and the post-Easter Christ of faith?" The class had been reading a book by Marcus Borg, who roused such a surprising question to come from such a young person. One way to answer such a question is to point to these two narratives, the entry and the crucifixion. We see the beginnings of the early church's elevation of Jesus when the disciples that Palm Sunday—those who have heard Jesus' teaching and experienced his gracious ways—place him on the donkey and hail him as king. And we see it at the crucifixion, as Luke—looking back with his community from the other side of the resurrection—tells this story to present the astounding truth: it is in the suffering and merciful Jesus that God is accomplishing the salvation of the world. This is the mystery of redemption as Luke sees it: perfect love and mercy revealed in the humility and suffering of Jesus. Lifted up—on lowly donkey and cruel cross—Jesus is revealed at the anointed King, the Christ of God.

> This is the mystery of redemption as Luke sees it: perfect love and mercy revealed in the humility and suffering of Jesus.

Two contemporary processions, both in the context of tragedy, connect with the Palm/Passion stories. In the declining center of Worcester, Massachusetts, a young man was killed, the victim of gang violence. All Saints' Church, itself going through difficult adjustments to a changing neighborhood, found a way to respond. On several Sunday afternoons, members of the congregation, led by their pastor, The Rt. Rev. Mark Beckwith (now bishop of the Episcopal Diocese of Newark), simply walked quietly through the sorrowing neighborhood. This ministry of presence somehow spoke to their neighbors of the presence of God to human suffering and loss.

In Allentown, Pennsylvania, in a similar downtown neighborhood, a twenty-year-old man was killed by an eighteen-year-old gang member. The murder took place early on Sunday morning in the parking lot of Grace Episcopal Church. The people of Grace Church, with the paschal candle and the church's banner, processed to the spot where it happened, "to recommit themselves to holding out a corner of grace in a troubled neighborhood."[27] In Worcester and Allentown, in ravaged and brutal places, followers of Jesus once more lift up for all to see the signs of mercy and grace and proclaim the crucified teacher and healer as Savior and King.

Notes

1. Samuel Terrien, *The Psalms and Their Meaning for Today* (New York: Bobbs-Merrill, 1952), x.

2. Charles H. Talbert, *Reading Luke: A Literary and Theological Commentary on the Third Gospel* (New York: Crossroad, 1989), 179.

3. Ibid., 179–80.

4. C. F. Evans, *Saint Luke* (London: SCM, 1990), 680.

5. Ibid., 678.

6. Ibid., 679.

7. Ibid., 680.

8. Ibid., 870.

9. Ibid., 871.

10. Talbert, *Reading Luke,* 215.

11. G. B. Caird, *St. Luke* (Philadelphia: Westminster, 1963), 247.

12. Talbert, *Reading Luke,* 220.

13. J. Hugh Michael, *The Epistle of Paul to the Philippians* (New York: Harper, 1927), 84.

14. Ibid., 90.

15. Ibid., 93.

16. Robert R. Wicks, "Exposition of Philippians," in *The Interpreter's Bible*, ed. George A. Buttrick (New York: Abingdon, 1955), 11:43.

17. Terrien, *The Psalms,* 159.

18. William R. Taylor, "Exegesis of the Psalms," in *The Interpreter's Bible,* 4:116.

19. "The Sunday of the Passion: Palm Sunday," in *The Book of Common Prayer* (New York: The Church Hymnal Corp., 1979), 270–72.

20. Fred B. Craddock, *Overhearing the Gospel* (St. Louis: Chalice Press, 2002), 93–94.

21. Frank H. Ballard, "Exposition of Psalms 90–150," in *The Interpreter's Bible,* 4:618.

22. "The Sunday of the Passion: Palm Sunday," in *The Book of Common Prayer,* 270.

23. Ibid., 234.

24. Citation for the Annual Diakonia Award, Cape Town, South Africa, August 14, 2008.

25. Nelson Mandela, *Long Walk to Freedom* (Boston: Little, Brown: 1994).

26. "Holy Eucharist I," in *The Book of Common Prayer,* 336.

27. Bethlehem *Diocesan* 19, no. 10 (October 2008): A8.

MONDAY IN HOLY WEEK

MARCH 29, 2010

Revised Common	Episcopal (BCP)	Roman Catholic (LFM)
Isa. 42:1-9	Isa. 42:1-9	Isa. 42:1-7
Ps. 36:5-11	Ps. 36:5-10	Ps. 27:1, 2, 3, 13-14
Heb. 9:11-15	Heb. 11:39—12:3	
John 12:1-11	John 12:1-11 or	John 12:1-11
	Mark 14:3-9	

FIRST READING

ISAIAH 42:1-9 (RCL, BCP)
ISAIAH 42:1-7 (LFM)

Here, says the poet, is a world conqueror, but of a quite different kind. He does not broadcast his station or use aggressive tactics, finish off a bruised plant or a flickering candle. But he is strong, does not tire, or grow discouraged (Isa. 40:31). Like yeast, he works silently and unobtrusively to save God's people.

This servant—probably in the mind of Isaiah it is Israel—is presented as the world's savior by the Creator of all, who "spread out the world," gives breath to every living creature, and whose purpose is life, light, justice, and freedom. The one who takes Israel by the hand intends to lead the people not just to a new land but to a new purpose for all lands and all people (vv. 5-7). Eventually, those who came to know Jesus of Nazareth saw in him the fulfillment of this promise.

RESPONSIVE READING

PSALM 27:1, 2, 3, 13-14 (LFM)

As we hear the psalmist sing, "The LORD is my light and my salvation; whom shall I fear?" we could imagine a dire diagnosis, an enemy, financial disaster. The psalmist hopes to see the goodness of God even in this life (v. 13). But when life disappoints and the lovingkindness of the Lord is obscured, the psalmist waits in hope. Did Jesus have this psalm close at hand as he began this week's journey?

PSALM 36:5-11 (RCL)
PSALM 36:5-10 (BCP)

By contrast to those who do not fear God, "who plot mischief while on their beds," the psalmist sings of beauty and abundance: the heavens and the clouds, mountains and sea, a well-provided house, a delightful river, fountains, and light itself, all reflecting the goodness of God. By contrast to those who lie awake at night plotting, the psalmist meditates on the wonder of creation and divine providence. He prays that continued awareness of this goodness will keep him from the "foot of the arrogant" and the hands of the wicked (vv. 10-11). As the story of Holy Week is told once more, these contrasts between light and darkness, trust and trickery, become sharp.

SECOND READING
HEBREWS 9:11-15 (RCL)

The writer of Hebrews operates entirely within the sphere of the Jewish sacrificial system, and takes for granted the commonly held view of the blood as the "seat and mysterious essence of life itself."[1] In that context, he shows the vast superiority of Christ to ordinary priests who offer the blood of animals. Here, Jesus the Great High Priest brings into the Holy of Holies the sacrifice of his own body.

The result of this is a new covenant and the purifying of the inner person. This high priest, whose sacrifice exceeds the usual ritual offering, frees us from dead works and makes a wholly new person. This is the consistent theme of Hebrews: by contrast to the system of sacrifices, *how much more* has been accomplished in the work of Jesus Christ?

HEBREWS 11:39—12:3 (BCP)

The writer issues a clarion call. He calls the roll of those from Abraham forward "who died in faith without having received the promises," but who nonetheless "from a distance saw and greeted them" (11:13). Then he calls us to consider Jesus, "who endured such hostility against himself . . . so that you may not grow weary or lose heart" (12:3).

The call to "lay aside" every weight has resonance with the Passion narrative. Jesus lays aside his divine prerogatives (Philippians 2). He lays aside his garments and bows to wash their feet. He lays aside even defensive speech, falls silent before his accusers. To run his race, he empties himself. With so many looking on—a cloud of witnesses—and with such a race before us, we, too, are called to slough off what holds us back.

THE GOSPEL
JOHN 12:1-11 (RCL, BCP, LFM)
MARK 14:3-9 (BCP ALT.)

John and Mark tell essentially the same story, though John has incorporated some elements of Luke's separate account. Raymond Brown believes that John retained Luke's details of the anointing of the feet in keeping with his understanding of this story as a preparation of Jesus' body for burial. Brown says that this is the theological import of the story and that it has never been told in Christian circles without that understanding.[2]

In John's account, and in Mark's, the scandal here is not that she is a sinful woman. It was the Syrian church father Ephraem who in the fourth century identified Mary of Bethany with Mary Magdalene and with Luke's sinful woman, leading to continuing confusion that persists.[3] The twofold scandal was that she, a woman, barged in on a men's gathering, and that she was extravagantly wasteful. In response to their objection on the latter matter, Jesus implies not indifference to the poor but that there is always that obligation and opportunity to be generous to those in need.

> The twofold scandal was that she, a woman, barged in on a men's gathering, and that she was extravagantly wasteful.

In Mark's account, the woman remains anonymous, and it is Mark who tells us that this story will be told in the whole world. It is not her name that matters, but that the body of Jesus has been anointed as he makes his way toward the cross. John may have incorporated Luke's details concerning the feet of Jesus for this reason: anointing for burial would have included the feet.

HOMILETICAL INTERPRETATION

Isaiah 42:1-9 (1-7). One image for meekness is a bridled horse: the bit in the horse's mouth, the side blinders, and the reins keep the horse steady in its task. God's servant is meek in this sense, intent upon fulfilling the divine purpose. "Behold, my Servant," the humble one whose purpose is to bless the nations. For him "the coastlands"—the farthest reaches of the earth—wait.

Many drifting, distracted, and bored people have found in Rick Warren's *The Purpose Driven Life*, the most popular religious book of this decade, something they need, the sense of purpose.[4] This we see in Israel at the nation's best, in her prophets consumed with a passion for justice, and in the one who steadily walks this week's hard road. Walking this road with him, sharing his suffering and death, we find new purpose and new life.

Psalm 27:1, 2, 3, 13-14. The framed motto in one of the seminary's offices—"God Is Good All the Time"—may have had its place, but to some it seemed a little glib, to most not quite what was needed on some days. Psalm 27 is better beside a sickbed or on a Monday morning with a depressed or lonely person. The words of this confident poetry are spoken in the face of threat and into the teeth of anxiety. The key word is *yet* (v. 3).[5] The psalmist acknowledges that the constant goodness of God is not always so evident: fear, evil, adversaries, and war fill the background of the psalmist's call: "Wait for the LORD . . . ." The best that the most faithful person can do sometimes is to wait *for the Lord*.[6] There we learn what it means to say, "The LORD is my light and my salvation."

Psalm 36:5-11 (5-10). The wicked, says the psalmist, are very far gone; even as they go to bed they are plotting mischief. They have given up any pretense of goodness and are "set on a way that is not good." Consistently self-absorbed and flattering themselves, they are unmindful of the consequences of their actions.

But God, the psalmist sings, is as consistently steadfast in love. The words of the gospel song, "The love of God is greater far, than tongue or pen can ever tell . . . ," could be based on the psalmist's images: faithfulness that reaches to heavens and is stretched out like the clouds; righteousness like the mountains; judgments profound as the sea; care that reaches even to the animals. God's love is like sheltering wings, an abundantly provided house, the life-giving river, a fountain of life.

> God's love is like sheltering wings, an abundantly provided house, the life-giving river, a fountain of life.

The gardens of Spain are often centered around water. Garden fountains are sometimes large urns, with a hidden source of water that fills the vessel to the brim. The water quietly overflows, not gushing or playing upward, simply flowing into a surrounding pool or out into the garden. The psalmist's images suggest this, the goodness and righteousness of God as an overflowing fountain, like Jesus' living water welling up (John 4).

Hebrews 9:11-15. In the eucharistic prayer the presider says:

> After supper he took the cup of wine; and when he had given thanks, he gave it to them, and said, "Drink this, all of you: This is my blood of the new Covenant, which is shed for you and for many for the forgiveness of sins. Whenever you drink it, do this for the remembrance of me."[7]

Jesus Christ, "as a high priest of the good things that have come," through the "greater and perfect tent," surpasses the temple, offering himself and so bringing his people to a new and greater covenant. In the Spirit, we are freed from "dead works" to live purified lives of worship and service to God. *How much more*, the writer of Hebrews wants us to see, is this new life given to us by Jesus' priesthood.

Hebrews 11:39—12:3. Asked which part of the Sunday service she liked best, an elderly woman answered: "I like the go-forth part." Asked what that meant, she went on to say that, now in her eighties, she doesn't get out a lot. "My friend Betsy still drives, so we go out on Tuesday to shop and have lunch. But mostly I don't. So I like it when the pastor ends up with 'Let us go forth.'" That is the call of this text: to keep running the race, getting out there, keeping at it, not pooping out.

As Jesus journeys toward the place where he will pour out his life fully, the woman pours out the expensive perfume. The writer of Hebrews calls on the runners of the race to lay aside everything that might hold us back, and to give it all we have. Empty yourself; pour it all out; get rid of what is weighing you down: those are the words of Holy Week, and they suggest its disciplines or fasting and almsgiving. We are able to do this by looking to Jesus, both to his endurance and his joy.

John 12:1-11/Mark 14:3-9. Mary of Bethany would never have to say those regretful words: "If only . . . ," "I wish I had . . . ," "Why didn't I . . . ?" Forgetful of prudence, practicality, even the pressing needs of the world, she simply let it be known that she loved and did not hold back in saying so. Krister Stendahl said of this story: "[She] stakes out a place at the center of Christianity for a celebrative devotion which does not count the cost."[8] There is something about this profligacy, Jesus says (in Mark's account), that will be remembered and told to the ends of the earth, something that is quite simply *beautiful*. Whoever this woman is, her outlandish gift comes from the heart, from profound gratitude, like that of Jesus' parable of the man in deep debt (Luke 7:40-43).

> The writer of Hebrews calls on the runners of the race to lay aside everything that might hold us back, and to give it all we have.

When she learned that her son had AIDS, Barbara couldn't handle it. A fundamentalist reading of the Bible, a rural community that never understood why the boy would want to go live in New York, simple lack of experience with these things: so many things made it hard for her to accept this, and for several years she kept her distance. Then, there came the invitation to dinner, at the big barn where Jack and his friend Archie lived. Barbara had come to stay with them for what turned out to be the last months of Jack's life. That Monday, and for every Monday that followed, she cooked dinner for a dozen or more. We gathered around a long table of the most delicious food that this hearty woman could make. On one of those evenings I sat with Barbara on the back step. "There is a lot about all of this that I don't understand, and some of it I probably can never accept, but I have finally got one thing straight. Jack is my son, and I love him. So please, you and Bob come and have dinner every Monday that you can." How grateful she must have been the afternoon when Jack died in peace while taking a nap after one of her good lunches, that she had not held back.

> Forgetful of prudence, practicality, even the pressing needs of the world, Mary of Bethany simply let it be known that she loved and did not hold back in saying so.

Tom was our parish priest, diagnosed with cancer with not long to live. He had lost a lot of weight, and even though he was still able to be at the church, there was sadness and apprehension in the air. Then came the invitation from Hattie. She was a New Yorker, now living in the South. "Come to dinner at the rectory, with Tom and me." Hattie was known more for her stylish clothes than her cooking, but she laid it on that evening: wonderful food, good wine, laughter around a festive table. She cleared the plates and disappeared into the kitchen. We could hear pots and pans clanging, a mixer going, stove and refrigerator doors opening and closing. Finally she emerged, her apron still on, glasses down on the end of her nose, hairdo a little tussled, presenting a melting baked Alaska. As she put it down on the table in front of Tom, she took us all in with a glance and said, "Well, you should see the kitchen!" A never-to-be-forgotten moment of love poured out, nothing held back.

The story of Mary of Bethany, the anointing of Jesus for his death and burial, is a eucharistic story, of people who are so grateful that they look for anything that is beautiful and true, to pour it out in remembrance, thanksgiving, and unabashed love. Mahler's Second Symphony, "The Resurrection," was composed as if he were standing by the coffin of someone he loved, asking the ultimate questions. The piece reaches its climax as the alto sings, *Hor auf ze beben! Bereite dich zu leben!*—"Cease from trembling! Prepare thyself to live!"

Notes

1. Alexander C. Purdy, "Exegesis of Hebrews," in *The Interpreter's Bible*, ed. George A. Buttrick (New York: Abingdon, 1955), 11:691.

2. Raymond Brown, *The Gospel According to John I–XII*, Anchor Bible 29 (Garden City, N.Y.: Doubleday, 1955), 454.

3. Eduard Schweizer, *The Good News According to Mark* (Atlanta: John Knox, 1977), 290.

4. Rick Warren, *The Purpose Driven Life* (Grand Rapids: Zondervan, 2002).

5. See Karl Barth's sermon "Nevertheless I Am Continually with Thee," in *Deliverance to the Captives* (New York: Harper, 1961), 13–19.

6. See Edmund Steimle's sermon "Wait," in *From Death to Birth* (Philadelphia: Fortress Press, 1973), 19–28.

7. "Holy Eucharist II," in *The Book of Common Prayer* (New York: The Church Hymnal Corp., 1979), 363.

8. See the commentary for Monday in Holy Week in Krister Stendahl, *Proclamation 1: Preaching in Holy Week* (Philadelphia: Fortress Press, 1985).

TUESDAY IN HOLY WEEK

MARCH 30, 2010

Revised Common (RCL)	Episcopal (BCP)	Roman Catholic (LFM)
Isa. 49:1-7	Isa. 49:1-6	Isa. 49:1-6
Ps. 71:1-14	Ps. 71:1-12	Ps. 71:1-2, 3-4a, 5ab-6ab, 15 + 17
1 Cor. 1:18-31	1 Cor. 1:18-31	
John 12:20-36	John 12:37-38, 42-50 or Mark 11:15-19	John 13:21-33, 36-38

FIRST READING

ISAIAH 49:1-7 (RCL)
ISAIAH 49:1-6 (BCP, LFM)

Jeremiah's call comes to mind: "Before I formed you in the womb . . . I appointed you a prophet to the nations" (Jer. 1:5). The chosen servant will serve God's purpose, not just to Israel but to all the nations. "The coastlands"—across the seas, as far as imagination can reach—await him (v. 6).

Whoever this is—Israel, an individual who comes to embody Israel's saving mission, or both—the servant will not fail. His speech will be a "sharp sword"; it will be like a polished arrow in the bowman's quiver. Despite discouragement, the servant will not fail, but will finally come to honor. Even his arrogant despisers—kings and princes—will acknowledge him.

RESPONSIVE READING

PSALM 71:1-14 (RCL)
PSALM 71:1-12 (BCP)
PSALM 71:1-2, 3-4A, 5AB-6AB, 15 + 17 (LFM)

An aged person, keenly aware of waning strength, is nonetheless mindful of God's continuous help in years past: "Upon you I have leaned from my birth";

"It was you who took me from my mother's womb." Now, as a declining old man feeling his frailty, the psalmist continues to praise God (v. 6).

He apparently sees himself as unattractive, even frightening, a "portent" (v. 7). Marginalized, with strength and time running out, he prays: "O, God, do not be far from me; O my God, make haste to help me!" (v. 12). At the end of his life, a man looks back with gratitude and forward with faith: "But I will hope continually, and will praise you yet more and more" (v. 14).

SECOND READING
1 CORINTHIANS 1:18-31 (RCL, BCP)

Among the problems that Paul confronts in the church at Corinth is the disdain of some for others: condescension, boasting, being "puffed up." Most of the Corinthian Christians would not have been learned, powerful, or of noble birth. In this context Paul speaks of the wisdom and power of God. He asserts a simple creed: Christ died and rose again, "the word of the cross" (1:18). This word, the "preaching of the cross," is, in the wisdom of the world, foolishness.

It is not that preaching in general is foolish: it is preaching of the cross as the means of God's salvation that is foolish. Hans Conzelmann writes: "Preaching is not merely *considered* to be foolish. It *is* foolish, by God's resolve. . . . 'God's folly' denotes . . . not an 'attribute' but God's free dealings with the world."[1] Paul is in no way exalting ignorance or asserting that the "lowly will be exalted." Rather, he teaches that in God's act of salvation all human barriers are swept away and only faith is required.[2]

> It is not that preaching in general is foolish: it is preaching of the cross as the means of God's salvation that is foolish.

THE GOSPEL
MARK 11:15-19 (BCP ALT.)

Ancient temples functioned to some degree as banks do today, exchanging currency and holding funds and family treasures. This would have been the case in such a large national temple as that in Jerusalem. Jesus' objection to what he found in the temple that day may have been to the excessive fees charged by the money changers. Or, as others have suggested, he is holding the customary commercialism up against an idealized view of the temple as a place of prayer.[3]

It is not clear just what sort of demonstration this was. The temple was a vast area of activity, so it is not likely that Jesus drove out all the money changers and vendors. Most likely, this was a small-scale affair, along the lines of the dramatic actions of such prophets as Jeremiah, Ezekiel, and Amos, "a prophetic gesture, witnessed by a few, and no more than a minor disturbance in the turbulence of the pilgrim crowds."[4] In this way Jesus got the attention of both the people and the authorities, calling attention to the obscured meaning of the temple and its worship.

JOHN 12:20-36 (RCL)
JOHN 12:37-38, 42-50 (BCP)

In answer to the Greeks' request, coming by way of Philip and Andrew, Jesus points them toward the *hour that has come,* the hour to which Jesus has been pointing his disciples, an hour that no vision of the expected Messiah could have accommodated. Telling them of that hour now fast approaching, Jesus introduced images of falling and burial, loss and death: "a grain of wheat falls into the earth and dies . . . ." Raymond Brown calls this a Johannine parable, paralleling the various parables of seeds that we find in the Synoptics.[5]

The coming day of darkness is an hour of *glory.*

> If you wish to see Jesus truly, you must look to the cross where he is lifted up from the earth.

If you wish to see Jesus truly, you must look to the cross where he is lifted up from the earth. Not only will you see him there for who he is, you and the whole world will be drawn to him and to the Father at this dark place. Paul, in 1 Corinthians 1, calls this the "word of the cross," the "foolishness of God." The hour of Jesus' crucifixion is the hour of his glorification.

Even the authorities are drawn to Jesus (vv. 41-43). Members of the Sanhedrin come to believe in him, fine teacher and able healer that he is. But valuing their position, they do not speak out, " . . . for they loved human glory more than the glory that comes from God" (v. 43). It is only after the hour of his true glory that Nicodemus and Joseph of Arimathea go public.

Jesus calls his hearers to embrace the light and to walk in it while they can. Then, ironically, he goes into hiding (12:36b). John 1 comes to mind: he is in the world that was made by him, and his glory is shining before their eyes, but they do not see him. He is Isaiah's polished arrow hidden in the quiver, soon to be drawn forth and flown to the mark, accomplishing God's salvation and revealing the true glory of Christ.

The death of Jesus will have fruitful results. In Mark's parable, "the tree that grows from the little grain of mustard seed is so great that the birds of the air can nest in it" (Mark 4:30-32). Before his crucifixion, Jesus declares that the glory revealed in that hour will draw together Jews and Greeks—the world—into the church.

Verses 44-50 are a separate, summary proclamation added in the Gospel's last redaction. Modeled on a farewell discourse of Moses (Deut. 32:45-47), it is a call to recognize Jesus, to see who he truly is, and to follow him as a matter of life and death.[6]

JOHN 13:21-33, 36-38 (LFM)

For comments on this text, see the Gospel for Wednesday in Holy Week, below.

HOMILETICAL INTERPRETATION

Isaiah 49:1-7 (1-6). In Isaiah's servant we have the ultimate "purpose-driven life." The servant is called from his birth not just to his own people but to "the coastlands." "From the Womb to the World" might be the title of this sermon. If the servant is an individual, then his vocation is calling Israel to be a light to the nations; if the servant is Israel, then from the beginning with Moses at the burning bush the nation is called to bless the world.

Up front in my boyhood church was the mission board, a map of the world with shiny markers showing all the mission stations supported by our congregation. We were constantly reminded of what we were for: to be a lighthouse in our town and to spread the light to the far coasts of the whole world.

Psalm 71. The man in his eighties was in and out of clarity, still functioning in mind and body but showing signs of Alzheimer's. His wife now had to drive him to the Y, ever since the day he forgot the way home. The important things were, however, still intact: trust, gratitude, a continuing sense of direction in his life. He was still serving on the board of an organization he loved and staying active in the men's group at his church. As a businessman he had suffered some severe financial losses, so they had downsized to a small house. But he was still figuring out how to give as much as they could to good causes. And still the two of them would show up on Sunday mornings, as she in characteristic humor once said, "fully clothed and more or less in our right minds." "The worst thing we could do," she says, "is to poop out."

The old man who composed this psalm is aware of his decline, but equally cognizant of where he has been and how he will live into the future. He does not gloss over the trials of his life, or its present uncertainties. He faces the future as one who prays, "Make haste to help me, O LORD," and persists in faith: "But I will hope continually, and will praise you yet more and more" (v. 14).

1 Corinthians 1:18-31. "God's Folly" would be a good title. Who could ever come up with anything like the humiliation and death of Jesus as the means of saving the world? The Via Dolorosa and Calvary would be exhibit A of Isaiah 55: ". . . my thoughts are not your thoughts, nor are your ways my ways, says the LORD." God's hidden, polished arrow is unsheathed and flies to the heart of sin and death, just at that place where evil seems to triumph.

"Whatever else you do in a sermon, you must finally 'fling them at the foot of the cross,'" advised an old preacher. Is that where we are left, after all our struggling with theology and anguishing over the state of the world—at the place of God's incredible folly? There will be a moment in the Good Friday liturgy when we stop talking and simply look upon a wooden cross.[7] At Taizé the late-night prayers are called "meditation around the cross," as small circles sit on the floor of the twelfth-century church, trying in silence to take in what it means.

> God's hidden, polished arrow is unsheathed and flies to the heart of sin and death, just at that place where evil seems to triumph.

Mark 11:15-19. Since the beginning of the war in Iraq the elderly priest—in his eighties—has taken his stand every Friday on a street corner in Allentown, hoisting his sign—*Stop the War*—ready to talk peace with anyone. This could be something like the prophetic action of Jesus in the temple, not so much a big demonstration as one man making his voice heard.

A little farther north, on an October afternoon in a provincial county-seat town, a small group of teenagers gathers on Main Street to make their political views known. Their homemade signs show their candidate's name and face—both unusual for a presidential candidate. Boisterous adolescents, they call to people in their cars, and stop as many pedestrians as will take their pamphlets. They are a surprising, joyous mixture of girls and boys: black, Asian, and white, laughing and yelling, looking for a better country.

Mark sets his story of Jesus' prophetic demonstration alongside the barren fig tree (11:12-14). Like the temple, it seems to have lost its way: no figs, no prayer. The prophet is always the one who calls the people to remember who they are—you are the ones that God delivered from slavery—and what they are for: you will bless the nations. Like an old priest or a loud group of teenagers on their street corners, Jesus upsets things to get our attention for God who calls us all to be who we truly are.

> Like an old priest or a loud group of teenagers on their street corners, Jesus upsets things to get our attention for God who calls us all to be who we truly are.

John 12:20-36/12:37-38, 42-50. Come Holy Saturday, Joseph of Arimathea will "take courage" and, with Nicodemus bearing his spices, take the body of

Jesus to his own new tomb. In the Gospel for this Tuesday these two members of the Sanhedrin are not so bold. Even though they have come to believe Jesus, they are afraid of the religious zealots. But after the crucifixion, they "come out" and make their first acts of allegiance to the teacher who will be their Lord. Like a seed fallen into the ground, the death of Jesus begins to bear fruit in these two new disciples. The one who is lifted up, lifts them up from fear and timidity to open devotion. Jesus says: "I have come as light into the world, so that everyone who believes in me should not remain in darkness" (12:46). Joseph and Nicodemus know what that means.

The preacher could emphasize the fruitfulness of the cross. From the least promising scene for producing life and love—three forsaken men dying in a barren and despised place, surrounded by mockery and indifference to suffering—springs new life. The Lenten hymn puts it in poetry:

> *Faithful cross! above all other,*
> *one and only noble tree!*
> *None in foliage, none in blossom,*
> *none in fruit thy peer may be:*
> *sweetest wood and sweetest iron!*
> *sweetest weight is hung on thee.*[8]

The cross sprouts fresh branches and new leaves, bursts into bloom and bows with abundant fruit. Who could have imagined?

The Isenheim altarpiece was painted by Matthias Grunewald for the chapel of a hostel for lepers and others with disfiguring diseases of the skin. As those ostracized and suffering men and women gathered for the liturgies of Holy Week, before their eyes was the scene Grunewald painted for this season: Jesus hanging on the cross is a leper, disfigured with the boils and lesions of their various afflictions.

> It is not *uplift,* but the one who is lifted up who draws us to himself, and in the unaccountable mystery of the cross heals us in mind, body, and soul.

Another artist might have painted something more "uplifting," but it is the man on the cross who bears his fruit. Those sufferers saw before their eyes what the eucharistic prayer confesses: ". . . you in your mercy sent Jesus Christ . . . to share our human nature, to live and die as one of us . . . ."[9] It is not *uplift,* but the one who is lifted up who draws us to himself, and in the unaccountable mystery of the cross heals us in mind, body, and soul.

Notes

1. Hans Conzelmann, *1 Corinthians*, Hermeneia, trans. James W. Leitch (Philadelphia: Fortress Press, 1975), 46.

2. Ibid, 51.

3. *Interpreter's Dictionary of the Bible,* ed. George A. Buttrick, vol 4: K-Q (New York: Abingdon, 1962), 435; *The New Interpreter's Study Bible* (Nashville: Abingdon, 2003), 1831–32.

4. C. S. Mann, *Mark: A New Translation with Introduction and Commentary,* Anchor Bible 27 (New York: Doubleday, 1986), 446–47.

5. Raymond Brown, *The Gospel According to John I–XII,* Anchor Bible 29 (Garden City, N.Y.: Doubleday, 1955), 472.

6. Ibid., 490–91.

7. "Good Friday," in *The Book of Common Prayer* (New York: The Church Hymnal Corp., 1979), 281–82.

8. John M. Neale, trans., from "Sing My Tongue," in *The Hymnal* (New York: The Church Hymnal Corp., 1982), #166.

9. "Holy Eucharist II," in *The Book of Common Prayer,* 362.

WEDNESDAY IN HOLY WEEK

MARCH 31, 2010

Revised Common (RCL)	Episcopal (BCP)	Roman Catholic (LFM)
Isa. 50:4-9a	Isa. 50:4-9a	Isa. 50:4-9a
Psalm 70	Ps. 69:7-15, 22-23	Ps. 69:8-10, 21-22, 31 + 33-34
Heb. 12:1-3	Heb. 9:11-15, 24-28	
John 13:21-32	John 13:21-35 or Matt. 26:1-5, 14-25	Matt. 26:14-25

FIRST READING
ISAIAH 50:4-9A (RCL, BCP, LFM)

For comment on this text, see the first reading for Palm Sunday/Passion Sunday.

RESPONSIVE READING
PSALM 69:7-15, 22-23 (BCP)
PSALM 69:8-10, 21-22, 31 + 33-34 (LFM)

This is one of those psalms that makes us uncomfortable; it contains verses that we might want to omit. The writer prays for God's avenging of his enemies in the most violent terms: "Let their eyes be darkened so that they cannot see . . . ." (v. 23). Because they have given him "poison for food" he prays that they will die eating their own feast (vv. 21-22).

But the psalm has a place in our worship, perhaps especially on this day when the dark forces of hostility are gathering around Jesus. Samuel Terrien places Psalm 69 among the "Songs of Ascent," alongside such cries de profundis as Psalm 130: "Out of the depths I cry to you, O LORD."[1] In Psalm 69 we find a man sinking in the mire, unable to find a foothold in the muck.

Even in such distress he confesses both his sins and his faith. Mocked for his love of God's house and his acts of devotion, he continues to pray. The psalm ascends from the depths to a *Te Deum* to God who "hears the needy, and does not despise his own that are in bonds": "Let heaven and earth praise him, the sea and everything that moves in them" (vv. 33-34). Even the threatening waters are now called upon to praise God.

PSALM 70 (RCL)

The contrast here is between those who seek God and those who actively pursue evil. The psalmist hears the malicious motives of those who persecute him in their hostile "Aha, Aha!" (v. 3). Let them be publicly disgraced, is his prayer, like a defeated army or an exposed criminal.

But those who seek God, let them rejoice and be glad, the people who love the things of God. This psalm is the same as a portion of Psalm 40 (vv. 13-17), in which the psalmist gives thanks in the "great congregation" for recovery from illness. In Psalm 70, the writer does what he is calling on all the faithful to do: he rejoices and give thanks in the midst of hostility, as confident as Psalm 23, that a table will be prepared even in the presence of his enemies.

Second Reading
HEBREWS 12:1-3 (RCL)

The great gallery of faith in chapter 11 leads to "Therefore . . . ." The "cloud of witnesses" that have gone ahead of us inspire us like spectators at a race. Better, as one commentator sees it, they are themselves "athletes of faith" who have run the race and are watching and waiting for us. For us, it might be our fellow skiers on a long downhill run who have made it to the bottom and are waiting to see if and when we will make it.

The one they look to is Jesus, who for the promised joy "bravely accepted the cross."[2] Those who follow these athletes of faith discard everything that holds them back, like Paul throwing away whatever impeded his progress (Philippians 3). Not even the "hostility of sinners," bystanders who neither understand nor support their efforts, will keep them from giving it all they've got.

HEBREWS 9:11-15, 24-28 (BCP)

For comments on this text, see the second reading for Monday of Holy Week, above.

JOHN 13:21-32 (RCL)
JOHN 13:21-35 (BCP)

All of the Gospel writers tell the story of the traitor, and we have set aside a day for Judas. As Jesus sets his face toward that hour and, as John tells the story, is in lordly command, Judas plays his part. At the same time, the one he betrays seems to reach out to him in sympathetic understanding.

There is terrible irony in the story: the foot washing, eating from the same dish, Judas described as "one of them." There is even the suggestion that in his role as treasurer Judas is an especially trusted member of the circle; at the table he sits close to Jesus. By oriental custom, the host would find for an honored guest some choice morsel and actually feed it to him. Though the threat of impending doom looms over them as over the Jews that terrifying Passover night in Egypt, there is about this story the aura of that best of all things, a loving community gathered around a supper table.

Here Satan appears: it is the only mention of Satan in the Fourth Gospel (v. 27). The beloved disciple leans on Jesus' breast, as if dreading the wrenching separation this night will bring. Jesus washes their feet, and they break bread. As far as the Gospel goes in probing Judas' motive is that "Satan entered into him." It is not just thirty pieces of silver that leads Judas to plot with the authorities. Who can believe that? What Jesus will confront, and conquer, this night stares us in the face when Judas leaves that circle and goes out into the dark night: the mystery of evil.

> The beloved disciple leans on Jesus' breast, as if dreading the wrenching separation this night will bring.

Raymond Brown comments on the three words: "It was night."

> John's "It was night" is the equivalent of the words of Jesus reported in Gethsemane by Luke 23:53: "This is your hour and the power of darkness." Yet even at this tragic moment in Jesus' life as the darkness envelops him, there is the assurance of the Prologue: "The light shines on in the darkness, for the darkness did not overcome it" (1:5). . . . The long night that now descended upon the earth would have its dawn when "early on the first day of the week, while it was still dark, Mary Magdalene came to the tomb (20:1)."[3]

MATTHEW 26:1–5, 14–25 (BCP ALT.)
MATTHEW 26:14–25 (LFM)

In Matthew we meet the betrayer in the story of Mary of Bethany. As the woman anoints Jesus with the precious perfume, she reveals that she understands what is happening this week. She is pouring out love for him, and anointing him for his burial. On the heels of that we hear of betrayal by one as close to him as those friends in Bethany; Judas who sits at table with him is an instrument of his death.

Matthew stresses the agency of Jesus. To Mark's account Matthew adds the words "My hour is near" (v. 18). Judas must play his role, and it is nonetheless betrayal. But the point of the story and the way it is told is that this is God's doing. The Greek word translated "hour" means "the appointed time." As Eduard Schweizer writes, ". . . appointed by God . . . Jesus' death and resurrection are interpreted as a single eschatological event, precisely determined in advance by God."[4] In his words, "The Son of Man will die as it is written; but how terrible it will be for that man who will betray [him], Jesus is portrayed as not only master of it all, but as friend of sinners, including Judas (v. 24)."

HOMILETICAL INTERPRETATION

Psalm 69:7–15, 22–23/69:8–10, 21–22, 31 + 33–34. The psalm ascends from the depths to the heights. It is the small orchestra on the sinking Titanic, Job who has lost all declaring his faith, the young and frightened but obedient Mary, Christians singing in their prison cells, every song in the night or at a graveside.

True, the psalmist sinks not only into near despair, but down to the level of vengeance. He is as far as one can get from loving his enemies, those he sees as also the enemies of God.

But he comes finally to a *Te Deum*: "Let heaven and earth praise him, the seas and everything that moves in them" (v. 34). The psalmist sees a new day coming, when people will build houses and live in them, cultivate the land and pass it on to their children. Somehow, even from the depths, the psalmist envisions a good future for the faithful (vv. 9, 36). Here is a picture of faithful people who, at the end of a hard week, hear the invitation, "Lift up your hearts," and somehow answer, "We lift them to the Lord."

> Somehow, even from the depths, the psalmist envisions a good future for the faithful.

Psalm 70. During the days of apartheid, the heinous policy of segregation enforced by the government of South Africa and legitimized by a misguided church, a common toast at meals among those seeking a better day was

"Confusion to the Enemy!" It was a kind of prayer that those who were deliberately supporting oppression and exploitation would be frustrated, or, in the words of the psalmist, "put to shame and confusion" (v. 2).

The psalmist is also in a hurry. Evening Prayer begins with one of his lines: "O God make speed to save us . . . ."[5] Another day has passed, hostility to the good is all around, and the good suffer at the hands of the malicious. But we keep on praying, "O Lord, make haste . . . ." Nelson Mandela had to wait for twenty-five years on Robbin Island, hoping and praying, and waiting.

A great hymn, not found in many hymnals, sings the psalmist's hope:

> *Though the cause of evil prosper,*
> *Yet, 'tis truth alone is strong;*
> *Though her portion be the scaffold,*
> *And upon the throne be wrong.*
> *Yet that scaffold sways the future,*
> *And behind the dim unknown,*
> *Standeth God within the shadow*
> *Keeping watch above his own.*[6]

Hebrews 12:1-3. The marathon races of today provide a good image. Along the way supporters are waiting with bottles of water and encouraging words. Picture those runners at the eighteenth mile, drinking and then pouring the cooling water over their heads! That image connects not only with the saints gone before, but with those women and men, boys and girls around us right now, in flesh-and-blood congregations, who cheer and refresh us.

We are called to run this race as Jesus did, not so much with gritted teeth as with exuberant joy. Now, many of us may not have run just for the joy of it in some time. It is, for sure, most often to keep in shape or just to keep our cardiovascular systems going. But it is not all grunt and strain, but also the reward of just doing it, getting out there and finishing the run. As Hebrews suggests, there is anticipation of what lies at the end of the race.

> We are called to run this race as Jesus did, not so much with gritted teeth as with exuberant joy.

That laying aside, what would that be? What is it that drags us down, holds us back from giving all we have to what truly gives us joy? What is that "sin that clings so closely"? Ironically, it could even be a kind of running: the preoccupied and driven life that turns our effort into a rat race. Or it could be that disabling sin of *acedia*, just giving up, pooping out, lacking the courage to take those first hard steps that could loosen our muscles and get our blood going.

Matthew 26:1-5, 14-25. The preacher could recall the story of Monday's Gospel. A woman whose identity remains uncertain barges in and showers Jesus with affectionate devotion. By contrast, Judas is part of the inner circle as he begins the deceitful conspiracy that will end in a kiss of death.

John 13:21-32 (21-35). Just about the best thing most of us can imagine is sitting at table, sharing food with the people we love. Memories are often made and usually kept alive around a table: Thanksgiving, Christmas, birthdays, anniversaries, the evening of the funeral. A meal can be a time of reconciliation, gift giving, healing laughter, and prayer.

The false kiss in the garden would be bad enough, but Judas's betrayal begins as they break bread together. To the question—Why did Judas do this?—there must be many possible answers. But *that* he did it when and where he did it, that gets to us. Those small details: Jesus has washed their feet; Judas sits close to Jesus and eats from his hand; Jesus shows, even as his words and searching eyes pierce the deceit, that he feels for Judas. It is a betrayal indeed. Perhaps "Satan entered" is the best we can do.

> As Judas goes out into the night the compassion of Jesus follows him.

Even here the love of Christ shines through. As Judas goes out into the night the compassion of Jesus follows him. We gather around our own table, seeking forgiveness, reconciliation, and the presence of Christ. No less than the beloved disciple, we lean on Jesus and pray for grace to stay close and remain loyal to those who dine with him. We sometimes sing this hymn at the end of the Eucharist.

> *Savior, again to thy dear name we raise*
> *With one accord our parting hymn of praise; . . .*
> *Guard thou the lips from sin, the hearts from shame,*
> *That in this house have called upon thy Name.*[7]

We hardly need to be reminded that there are many opportunities for betraying this table. Much that is occurring today within the church—as self-righteous moralism, exclusivism, division—wounds the body of Christ. Those of us who dine regularly with Jesus and his disciples need this story of Judas on the eve of Holy Thursday.

Notes

1. Samuel Terrien, *The Psalms and Their Meaning for Today* (New York: Bobbs-Merrill, 1952), 181–82.

2. William Manson, *The Epistle to the Hebrews* (London: Hodder and Stoughton, 1951), 81.

3. Raymond Brown, *The Gospel According to John I–XII*, Anchor Bible 29 (Garden City, N.Y.: Doubleday, 1955), 579.

4. Eduard Schweizer, *The Good News According to Mark* (Atlanta: John Knox, 1970), 489.

5. "Daily Evening Prayer: Rite II," in *The Book of Common Prayer* (New York: The Church Hymnal Corp., 1979), 117.

6. James Russell Lowell, from "Once to Every Man and Nation" (1845), in *The Baptist Hymnal* (Nashville: Convention Press, 1991), #470.

7. John Ellerton (1826–1893), "Savior, Again to Your Dear Name," in *Lutheran Book of Worship* (Minneapolis: Augsburg/Philadelphia: Lutheran Board of Publication, 1977), #262.

MAUNDY THURSDAY / HOLY THURSDAY

APRIL 1, 2010

Revised Common (RCL)	Episcopal (BCP)	Roman Catholic (LFM)
Exod. 12:1-4 (5-10) 11-14	Exod. 12:1-14a	Exod. 12:1-8, 11-14
Ps. 116:1-2, 12-19	Ps. 78:14-20, 23-25	Ps. 116:12-13, 15-16bc, 17-18
1 Cor. 11:23-26	1 Cor. 11:23-26 (27-32)	1 Cor. 11:23-26
John 13:1-17, 31b-35	John 13:1-15 or Luke 22:14-30	John 13:1-15

FIRST READING

EXODUS 12:1-4 (5-10) 11-14 (RCL)
EXODUS 12:1-14A (BCP)
EXODUS 12:1-8, 11-14 (LFM)

Judaism and Christianity have in common this night of the shedding of blood. The Passover of the Lord, when the death angel slays the firstborn, is the instrument of God's deliverance. More than simply the last plague, the killing of the young Egyptians is decisive. As Martin Noth writes, ". . . Pharoah now at last declares himself ready to let Israel go . . . in the middle of the night, because the overwhelming power of Yahweh has been revealed to him in the slaughter of the first-born . . . ."[1]

It is likely that elements of Passover and the two feasts that accompany it—Unleavened Bread and the Dedication—were older socio-cultic observances adapted to the ritual needs of the Jewish rites. J. Coert Rylaarsdam explains, "But in Israel . . . they attain new meaning. . . . They attest that Israel belongs to Yahweh because of his redemptive action at the Exodus."[2]

Noth says that this account of the detailed instructions for the preparation and performance of what happened on that night of flight was written not only later but in a much more settled time: "The breadth and comprehensiveness of the instructions envisages the Passover sacrifice as later celebrated each year in peaceful times in a cultivated land . . . ."[3] The church, marking the night of Jesus' betrayal and death in its elaborate and beautiful rituals, would understand this.

RESPONSIVE READING

PSALM 116:1-2, 12-19 (RCL)
PSALM 116:12-13, 15-16BC, 17-18 (LFM)

The psalmist, having come through a desolate time, now raises a "thank offering." In retrospect, God was present and faithful through it all. The psalmist is grateful both for God's faithfulness and that he has not lost faith in the midst of suffering (vv. 8-10).

The psalm, then, is thanksgiving for personal victory. As Samuel Terrien writes, "Not unlike David on his day of military triumph, a man who is victorious against himself and has overcome tribulations of his soul is possessed by one paramount desire: to speak out the devotion which draws him toward his Saviour."[4] Delivered from the "snares of death," the psalmist no longer fears death (vv. 3, 15). His soul returns to its rest, to the quietness and confidence of those who have come through trouble and have found God to be faithful (v. 7).

PSALM 78:14-20, 23-25 (BCP)

Samuel Terrien has called this a psalm of "God's goodness and Israel's ingratitude."[5] The psalmist recalls "the glorious deeds of the Lord . . . the wonders that he has done" (v. 4): deliverance from Egypt; guidance by fire and cloud; water and food in the desert. "*Yet* they sinned . . ."; *Yet* from heaven "he rained flesh upon them like dust . . ."; "In spite of all this they still sinned . . ." (vv. 7, 27, 32). The pattern continues, their unfaithful complaining and wandering away, and the persistent provision of God. The psalm reaches its climax: "He chose his servant David . . . to be the shepherd of his people . . ." (vv. 70-71).

SECOND READING

1 CORINTHIANS 11:23-26 (RCL, LFM)
1 CORINTHIANS 11:23-26 (27-32) (BCP)

What is it that Paul has received and of which he now reminds the Corinthians? In Paul the Last Supper is not characterized as a Passover meal but a meal for the *anamnesis* of Jesus. The sacrificial motif is in the bread, "This is my body that is for you" (v. 24). Whether we are to think of this as an atoning or a vicarious sacrifice, it is in the breaking of bread that this is seen. In the cup is communicated the new covenant, what Hans Conzelmann calls the "cup of blessing."[6]

Some commentators see two types of common meals in the primitive church of Jerusalem: the frequent breaking of bread and the annual Passover meal. As E. Earle Ellis writes, "Only the latter was directly related to the Lord's Supper, and only in it was the *meal* a specific remembrance of Messiah's death." Christian worship outside Jerusalem merged the two meals (cf. 1 Cor. 11:20ff., 23ff.). Thus, in the Lord's Supper the joyful fellowship meal became the Love Feast, and the Passover meal became the Eucharist or Holy Communion.[7] It seems that in some cases the Eucharist—the bread and the cup—was bookends to the Agape Meal, as Conzelmann explains: "In Corinth . . . the whole Eucharist had been transposed to follow the meal."[8]

> Failure to live in a way that reflects the gospel is to receive the body and blood of the Lord unworthily.

Paul's recollection and reminder of the Lord's Supper is sandwiched between pastoral admonitions: against selfishness and factions on the one hand (vv. 20–22), and a lack of self-examination and discipline on the other (vv. 27–34). Failure to live in a way that reflects the gospel is to receive the body and blood of the Lord unworthily.

THE GOSPEL
JOHN 13:1-17, 31B-35 (RCL)
JOHN 13:1-15 (BCP, LFM)

The links of foot washing to Holy Baptism can be seen in Peter's embarrassment and Jesus' response to that, and in Peter's extravagance in asking to be washed all over. More profoundly, if we take the foot washing to be a prophetic action pointing to Jesus' passion and death, then the Lord's admonition to Peter that without this washing he has no part in him points to the coming salvific drama.

Raymond Brown entertains the possibility that the foot washing points to baptism, but he concludes that the primary reference is to Jesus' death.

> The simplest explanation of the footwashing, then, remains that Jesus performed this servile task to prophesy symbolically that he was about to be humiliated in death. Peter's questioning, provoked by the action, enabled Jesus to explain the salvific necessity of his death: it would bring men their heritage with him and it would cleanse them from their sin.[9]

If the foot washing is taken as an example of humble service—as it often is in our teaching and preaching—even there, Brown concludes, the essential thrust is toward Jesus' humiliating passion and redemptive sacrifice.[10] Peter's future, with Jesus and his community, depends upon entering into the passion and death of Jesus. And with the disciple, as with Jesus, this demands a measure of self-abasement. It should be remembered that even a Jewish slave could not be compelled to perform this act on his master's feet.[11]

LUKE 22:14-30 (BCP ALT.)

Luke's account of the Last Supper takes place in the context of a typical farewell speech. In Jewish and Christian communities such an occasion would include a hero figure who knows that he is about to die, a gathered primary group, a prediction regarding what was about to happen, and exhortation about what to do after his departure. As they sit at table, Jesus gives such a speech.

> Peter's future, with Jesus and his community, depends upon entering into the passion and death of Jesus.

The emphasis in Luke is on the community of the new covenant. First, echoing Jeremiah 31:31-34, Jesus promises the new covenant that will bind them to him and to each other. Second, this covenant will be sealed by his blood. Third, "given for you" suggests that his death is martyrdom for the sake of his people. Charles Talbert summarizes:

> Taken as a whole the words of Jesus over the bread and wine . . . speak of Jesus' death as a martyrdom which seals the new covenant charac-terized by life in the Spirit. Jesus asks that this death be memorialized in a repeated meal observed by his disciples. The foundational event in the community's life must not be forgotten.[12]

But it is possible to eat with Jesus and still betray him, just as it is possible to eat together in his name and yet fall into division and strife (vv. 21-23). The remedy for this is that the greatest among them will be servant of all, just as Jesus is among them as one who serves.

HOMILETICAL INTERPRETATION

Psalm 116. There is a moment in the eucharistic liturgy when the cel-ebrant lays open hands on the altar, and says: ". . . here we offer and present unto thee, O Lord, our selves, our souls and bodies, to be a reasonable, holy, and living sacrifice unto thee . . . ."[13] Being part of the assembly's liturgical action is a "thank offering" that extends outward to sacrificial living for the good of all. Hands laid upon the altar connect us to the sacrifice of Jesus and to self-giving in his name. We hear this in the offertory sentence: "Let us walk in love as Christ loved us and gave himself, an offering in sacrifice to God."

This thanksgiving in prayer and service is corporate, not just on our own. Samuel Terrien writes:

> The social concept is so powerfully ingrained within the religion of Israel that no joy can ever be expressed by an individual alone with his god, and the "church" is invited to share the feelings of any forgiven man. . . . "I will pay my vows now unto Yahweh in the presence of all his people" (Ps. 116:14-16).[14]

> **Being part of the assembly's liturgical action is a "thank offering" that extends outward to sacrificial living for the good of all.**

If spiritual salvation is the most important gift of all, then we can give thanks even for those hard times that have drawn us closer to God. The Swedish hymn "Thanks to God for My Redeemer" gives thanks for virtually everything. The popular image of the mysterious footprints in the sand—four prints become only two on a long stretch of the beach—tells of the presence of God who carries the believer through the hard times.

Psalm 78:14-20, 23-25. God's goodness does not depend upon the people's faithfulness. On the contrary, as they keep on complaining, God keeps on providing. Morris Niedenthal tells us that the gospel is in the indicative mode: God acts for our good even when we act unworthily. It is not a matter of "If you . . . , then God will . . . ," but "Because God has . . . , therefore you can . . . ."[15]

Exodus 12:1-14. Our Orthodox Jewish neighbors invited us to the Shabbat meal, up in the Pocono Mountains on a Friday evening at sundown. It was both surprising and familiar, as the candles were lit and the prayers that any Christian would recognize mingled with singing and laughter. The food had been prepared well ahead—there would be no work in this house, not even flipping a light switch, for the next twenty-four hours—and there was about our time there a wonderful stepping away from the busy world.

The exodus from Egypt was there too, the story of that bloody night and people fleeing in the darkness, threatened by armies and the towering sea. As the story got told around that happy table, it was like being at the Eucharist, remembering Jesus' dark night of suffering, the fear of his followers, and their being "brought over." The meal and all that accompanied it said loud and clear: God has brought us through! We are here, together and thankful! We have a future! It is that Sabbath meal that has bound together and encouraged Israel through many dark times, and one very like it that keeps the church of Christ in love and hope.

1 Corinthians 11:23-26 (27-32). Paul hands on what he has received—the story of Jesus at supper that night—to an imperfect community. The Corinthians are divided and undisciplined, some of them receiving the bread and cup unworthily. This is, of course, always the case, at all times and in all places where we presume to come to this table.

It was so noticeable, the fact that most Sundays she did not come forward to receive communion, this quiet woman who was there just about every Sunday. "I am not worthy," she said. "I just can't take the sacrament." She, Paul would no doubt agree, would probably be among those *most* worthy to receive, those who humbly open their hearts to God and one another as they put out their hands for the broken bread.

> Paul hands on what he has received—the story of Jesus at supper that night—to an imperfect community.

Do we receive what is given—from Jesus, from those who have come to this table before us, from the community in which we now live—because we are worthy, or even because every Sunday we feel like celebrating? In his novel *The Winter of Our Discontent,* John Steinbeck tells the story of Ethan Allen Hawley. So much is awry in Ethan's life, but most Sundays he sits in his New England family's pew and receives Holy Communion. He tells us that even when his soul is "as dry as a navy bean," for some reason he goes through this ritual.[16]

My grandmother always sat in the same pew in her Oklahoma church. Always after communion, when she had placed the little glass in the little rack with three holes, she would take hold of the back of the pew and put her head down to pray. One day, as a young boy, I noticed that the varnish was worn off the top of that pew. Looking back, that seems to me to be the day I discovered the communion of saints and caught a glimmer of what was being handed on to me.

John 13:1-17, 31b-35/13:1-15. If we take Raymond Brown's view, that the foot washing is a prophetic action pointing to Jesus' passion and death, and if we see our baptism—as Paul does—as dying with Christ, then this Maundy Thursday calls us simultaneously to thanksgiving and service. As Jesus bows and bends, he shows us the humility and love that led to his death, and its inextricable connection to the way we live together.

Visiting a seminary class, Hoyt Hickmon, a great Methodist church leader, was asked about his congregation in Nashville. He had told us about the church's multipurpose room—a place for the Eucharist on Sunday, tutoring local kids on weekday afternoons, and a dining hall for the homeless on Saturday. "Dr. Hickmon, which is more important, the Eucharist or all those other things you do in that room?" "Do you think," he answered, "that we would celebrate on Sunday the way we do if we didn't teach and feed people? And would we help teenagers with English and math, or cook for the homeless the way we do, if we didn't have communion together on Sunday?"

In the 1985 movie *Kiss of the Spider Woman*, two men share a Latin American prison cell. Valentino (Raul Julia) is in for giving his passport to a fugitive revolutionary, Molina (William Hurt) for molesting a youth. One macho, one gay, they are unlikely cellmates.

> As Jesus bows and bends, he shows us the humility and love that led to his death, and its inextricable connection to the way we live together.

Valentino gets dysentery, and in the resulting mess he is reduced to an embarrassed, needy child. Molina takes a towel, gets down on his knees, washes Valentino, and puts him to bed wrapped in a clean sheet. The sick man sleeps, and the cramped cell becomes, temporarily, an oasis of peace.

As Valentino is recovering, Molina, by trickery, comes back to the cell one day with amazing food: roast chicken, bread and cheese, canned peaches, chocolate, and tea. The two men—"revolutionary" and "faggot"—both of them soon to die for the labels pinned on them—lay out the food. Their little feast, spread on a cloth on the floor, takes over the whole cell, the heinous prison, and by the time they are stretched out full, the world itself has somehow, for a time, come right.

Such stories belong to this night when Jesus bends to wash their feet just as he will bow his meek head to suffering and death. On the night of the new commandment, to love one another as he has loved, we find the freedom of those who give up themselves to his sacrifice and their lives to humble service.

Luke 22:14-30. A farewell dinner would inevitably bring to mind one's legacy. If the departing leader has devoted his life to the people around the table, the shape of that community in the future would be uppermost in mind. As Jesus reminds the disciples that they live by a new covenant sealed by his blood he gives an example of how they are to be together: "I am among you as one who serves" (v. 27). As in John 13, Jesus himself—in his passion and in the foot washing that symbolizes that—becomes both the model and the means of grace for achieving his new community. The song puts it simply: "They will know we are Christians by our love." On this night when the narratives of the foot washing and the founding of the Last Supper come together in our liturgy, the source and shape of the church are before our eyes. As someone put it, the ground of all celebration is a circle of people who believe in each other and in something together. That was never more clear than on this night.

Notes

1. Martin Noth, *Exodus* (Philadelphia: Westminster, 1962), 88.

2. J. Coert Rylaarsdam, "Exegesis of Exodus," in *The Interpreter's Bible*, ed. George A. Buttrick (New York: Abingdon, 1952), 1:915–16.

3. Noth, *Exodus,* 94.

4. Samuel Terrien, *The Psalms and Their Meaning for Today* (New York: Bobbs-Merrill, 1952), 209.

5. Ibid., 191–92.

6. Hans Conzelmann, *1 Corinthians*, Hermeneia, trans. James W. Leitch (Philadelphia: Fortress Press, 1975), 197–201.

7. E. Earle Ellis, *The Gospel of Luke* (Grand Rapids: Eerdmans, 1966), 250.

8. Conzelmann, *1 Corinthians,* 199.

9. Raymond Brown, *The Gospel According to John I–XII*, Anchor Bible 29 (Garden City, N.Y.: Doubleday, 1955), 568.

10. Ibid., 569.

11. Ibid., 564.

12. Charles H. Talbert, *Reading Luke: A Literary and Theological Commentary on the Third Gospel* (New York: Crossroad, 1989), 209–10.

13. "Holy Eucharist I," in *The Book of Common Prayer* (New York: The Church Hymnal Corp., 1979), 336.

14. Terrien, *The Psalms,* 210.

15. Morris J. Niedenthal, "The Irony and Grammar of the Gospel," in *Preaching the Story*, ed. Edmund A. Steimle, Morris J. Niedenthal, and Charles L. Rice (Philadelphia: Fortress Press, 1980), 141–50.

16. John Steinbeck, *The Winter of Our Discontent* (New York: Viking, 1961), 112–15.

GOOD FRIDAY

APRIL 2, 2010

Revised Common (RCL)	Episcopal (BCP)	Roman Catholic (LFM)
Isa. 52:13—53:12	Isa. 52:13—53:12 or	Isa. 52:13—53:12
	Gen. 22:1-18 or	
	Wis. 2:1, 12-24	
Psalm 22	Ps. 22:1-21 or 22:1-11	Ps. 31:2, 6, 12-13, 15-16,
	or 40:1-14 or 69:1-23	17, 25
Heb. 10:16-25 or	Heb. 10:1-25	Heb. 4:14-16; 5:7-9
Heb. 4:14-16; 5:7-9		
John 18:1—19:42	John (18:1-40) 19:1-37	John 18:1—19:42

FIRST READING

ISAIAH 52:13—53:12 (RCL, BCP, LFM)

No one has captured better than James Muilenburg the compelling imagery and irony of the greatest of the Servant Songs. He writes:

> Note how the servant is introduced, how the speakers of 53:1-9 enter without any introduction, how the servant is intensely present but never named, how the lines succeed each other in short clauses, and how the whole poem is dominated by the contrast between humiliation and suffering on the one hand, and exaltation and triumph on the other.[1]

Muilenburg concludes that the "poem as a whole is one of triumph." From the poem's beginning, as on Good Friday, we move through the suffering and rejection of the servant, knowing that this darkness will be overcome at his exaltation.

In the servant's suffering the heinousness of sin is seen. His disfigurement—is it leprosy?—mirrors the distortion of God's creation, now being atoned and put right by the obedience of the servant. Despite his appearance and seeming helplessness, he will have "success," because of his wisdom, knowledge, and devotion to the right. The servant's success will be our salvation: all of us have gone astray, but God through this one puts things right. "Behind the story of the servant's tragic career—life, death, and burial—stands the purpose of God. . . . The servant lives in intimate fellowship and communion with God; his silence and patience and humility are the expression of his nearness to his covenant Lord."[2] It is this, his nearness to God, that sustains him in his suffering and fulfils the divine purpose.

GENESIS 22:1-18 (BCP ALT.)

Gerhard Von Rad calls this terrible narrative "the most perfectly formed and polished of all the patriarchal stories." He goes on to say that our exposition will be most accurate where it emphasizes the idea of radical obedience.[3] At least four perspectives should be kept in mind: Abraham's, God's, Israel's, and our modern view of things. Abraham is asked to sacrifice what God has given him and Sarah—that upon which their future hangs. God intends this as a test, revealed at the story's outset. Israel confronts the issue of human sacrifice—practiced by her neighbors—and what may have seemed a lesser offering, the sacrifice of animals. And we, of course, find no place for either, especially the sacrifice of one's child.

WISDOM 2:1, 12-24 (BCP ALT.)

We are reminded immediately of Ecclesiastes, its pessimistic view of the human experience and of the limits of life. One answer to this, presented here as a parody in verses 1-11, is a frank hedonism. Seeking all you can get, don't hesitate to take advantage of the weak and old, or to go after those who criticize your way of life (vv. 12-20). But this approach does not take into account "the secret purposes of God" (v. 22), that we are created for incorruption and in the image of God's eternity (v. 23).

RESPONSIVE READING
PSALM 31:2, 6, 12-13, 15-16, 17, 25 (LFM)

The nearness to God seen in Isaiah 52:13—53:12 sustains the psalmist as he prays for deliverance from impending trouble. The nature of the trial to come is not revealed, a "net that is hidden" (v. 4), an unseen trap that has been set. Against this unseen enemy, God is a rock and a fortress, a place to take refuge and to find an ultimate safety. We hear echoes of Psalm 23, also a song in the face of danger:

". . . for your name's sake lead me and guide me" (v. 3). Samuel Terrien describes the psalmists: "Faith alone kept them at the edge of the abyss. Faith, *emunah*—a word which is akin to amen—was for them a fence, a stay, the only protection against a fall into nothingness. They 'trusted' (*batach*) or 'relied' on a God whose will is love, and only then did they find 'security' (*betach*)."[4] (For more commentary, see the responsive reading for Palm Sunday/Passion Sunday.)

PSALM 22 (RCL)
PSALM 22:1-21 OR 22:1-11 (BCP)

For commentary on this text, please see the responsive reading (LFM) for Palm Sunday/Passion Sunday.

PSALM 40:1-14 (BCP ALT.)

For commentary on this text, please see the commentary on Psalm 70 (RCL), Wednesday in Holy Week.

PSALM 69:1-23 (BCP ALT.)

For commentary on this text, please see the responsive reading (BCP/LFM) for Wednesday in Holy Week.

SECOND READING
HEBREWS 4:14-16; 5:7-9 (RCL ALT.; LFM)

Here God's obedient servant is our ascended and sympathetic high priest. The Jewish high priest once a year made an act of atonement, for himself—he, too, was a sinful man—and for all the people. He, too, would have been sympathetic to the human condition, like Jesus who became one of us. But this great high priest goes farther. "Only one who himself knew all the temptations of human life and yet resisted them to the uttermost could not only sympathize but stretch out his hand to weaker brothers and lift them up."[5] The unique work of Jesus springs from his person, that he is fully God and fully human, as God acts through his obedient life and death to overcome our separation and to restore us fully to true humanity, to "At-one-ment" with God.[6]

William Neil titles his commentary on this text "Pilgrims' Progress." The aim of Christ's work is a restored humanity and healed relationships, with God and one another. "How can we become the kind of men and women God meant us to be, knowing, as we believe, that only in that way can we be said to be truly alive and to be experiencing all that life has to offer?"[7] Ironically, the life we seek is accomplished not by what we do, or what the Jewish high priest does, but by the surpris-ing work of God in the death of Christ. What the repeated work of priests, *standing* at their altars, could not accomplish, Jesus has brought about once and for all, and he is now *seated* at God's right hand.

> Ironically, the life we seek is accomplished not by what we do, or what the Jewish high priest does, but by the surprising work of God in the death of Christ.

The result of this is a community of faith, hope, and love (vv. 23-25). These are those who have been washed in baptism, come to prayer boldly, and even under threat of persecution meet together to celebrate and strengthen one another. The result of the work of our High Priest can actually be seen in the new covenant being lived out by men and women day by day, week by week.

THE GOSPEL
JOHN 18:1—19:42 (RCL, LFM)
JOHN (18:1-40) 19:1-37 (BCP)

Jesus' last words from the cross, and their juxtaposition, show us both John's understanding of that event and his dramatic manner of presenting its meaning. Jesus, the source of living water, dying in helpless humiliation: "I am thirsty" (19:28). Then, in the next breath, his last, he says: "It is finished" (19:30). The human agony of the cross is unavoidable as he cries out for water, but even there Jesus gives himself up to God's work of salvation.

> Jesus, the faithful Servant of the Lord, announces even as he dies his "success."

Raymond Brown writes: "In John's theology, now that Jesus has finished his work and is lifted up from the earth on the cross in death, he will draw all men to him (12:32). If 'It is finished' is a victory cry, the victory it heralds is that of obediently fulfilling the Father's will."[8] Jesus, the faithful Servant of the Lord, announces even as he dies his "success." Here now, in an unavoidable display of the results of human sin and the depths of human suffering, is the means of salvation for all who will look to him.

This will now become clear to those who along the way in John's telling of the story have missed it. Judas sits close to him at table but is far away. Later, he comes to the garden carrying a lantern. We last saw Judas leaving the table and going out into the night. Brown writes: "Perhaps this is why Judas and his companions come bearing lanterns and torches. They have not accepted the light of the world, and so they must have artificial light."[9] Peter, similarly, out in the yard while Jesus, on trial in Annas's court, is slapped in the face by a soldier, warms himself at the fire, rather than by staying close to Jesus. And even Pilate comes close, but fails to follow the truth that stands before him, the one whose true kingship he seems to sense, offering what he most deeply needs.

In that other word from the cross Jesus recognizes what will come of this, his being lifted up in pain and rejection. When he speaks to Mary and the beloved disciple, the new community of love comes into view, even in so unlikely a place. "Jesus' mother and the Beloved Disciple," Brown says, "are being established in a new relationship representative of that which will bind the Church and the Christian."[10] Brown also sees in the seamless tunic of Jesus a symbol of his royal priesthood: He dies on the cross both as the true King and the authentic Priest.[11] His kingdom that is not of this world will come to expression, however imperfectly, in the church as women and men are drawn to him and so to one another.

HOMILETICAL INTERPRETATION

Isaiah 52:13—53:12. Is the poem doleful or joyous? The prophet/poet calls us to behold God's servant, his terrible isolation and suffering. At the same time, his success is announced. He will accomplish the divine purpose and his reward will be great. In this context, the preacher could ask the familiar question: Why do we call this Friday *good*? The enigmatic power of the Crucified One appears and we are called to contemplation and silence in the presence of the mystery of our redemption.

> The enigmatic power of the Crucified One appears and we are called to contemplation and silence in the presence of the mystery of our redemption.

In the large narthex of The Church of the Servant in Oklahoma City, worshipers were greeted on Good Friday by a garbage can so battered that it would have been more at home on the streets of New York! "What is that doing in here?" "This must be some kind of joke!" But on Easter morning there it was, filled with the most beautiful and fragrant flowers imaginable.

"Behold, my servant . . . ." The one whose appearance is startling, whose disfigurement astonishes us, with "no form or majesty that we should look at him" (53:2), despised and rejected: He is the one. It is through him that "the will of the LORD shall prosper" (53:10). Some imaginative person fills a garbage can with extravagant flowers, we fill the dark church on Saturday night with candles and the ringing of bells, and Handel sings of this despised and rejected one: "The kingdoms of this world are become the Kingdom of our Lord and of his Christ . . ." (52:15).

Genesis 22:1-18. Most preachers will find this a difficult text, and some have refused to preach on it at all. Genesis makes the moral dilemma inescapable.[12] God's words to Abraham are themselves like a dagger being twisted in Abraham's heart: "Take your son, your only son, the one whom you love . . . ." What is asked of Abraham is completely incomprehensible: ". . . the child, given by God after long delay, the only link that can lead to the promised greatness of Abraham's seed . . . is to be given back to God in sacrifice."[13] Abraham obeys, and, after the test has passed, he names the place "the Lord will provide," a phrase that can be rendered "he shall be seen." Here lies the connection to Good Friday, the incomprehensible provision of God in the suffering Innocent on the cross. Today we try to *see*, somehow, in this terrible scene a gracious and saving gift.

Wisdom 2:1, 12-24. Anyone who has traveled in Europe will have seen those crucifixes by the roadside, with their pointed question: "Is it nothing to you, all ye that pass by?" There is something to be said for what has been called a seize-the-day way of life, to live life to the fullest. Good Friday, however, shows us self-giving love as the way to true and lasting life. It is for this reason that we can call this day *good*.

Psalm 31:2, 6, 12-13, 15-16, 17, 25. Most people would agree that what we cannot see is more frightening than what is there before our eyes. Monster movies are more impressive for their special effects than actually scary. It is the footfall on the step, what lurks silently behind the door, or who watches from the cliff along the terrifying river in James Dickey's *Deliverance*. It is the incomplete diagnosis, what the doctor does not say, even the envelope from the IRS or the bank that we leave unopened on the table. For the psalmist it is the "hidden net," the trap about to be sprung, that dismays.

Even that most beloved psalm tells of this anxiety: hunger and thirst are implied, the "darkest valley" looms, and the enemy is out there (Psalm 23). This enemy, though not named, is nonetheless threatening. As noted earlier, in the days of South Africa's apartheid, the toast at dinner was often "Confusion to the enemy!" and there was no question who the enemy was. Today we might ask, "What enemy?" and the answer might be "Whatever." The psalmist, fearful of what he cannot see or name, cries out to God, a rock of refuge, a place of safety whatever may be on the way.

Several hymns with homiletical possibilities come to mind when reading Psalm 31: "Rock of Ages," "The King of Love My Shepherd Is," "A Mighty Fortress Is Our God," and "Guide Me, O Thou Great Jehovah."

Hebrews 4:14-16; 5:7-9. One of the eucharistic prayers tells of Jesus' humanity and of his priestly work: ". . . in your infinite love you . . . sent Jesus Christ, your only and eternal Son, to share our human nature, to live and die as one of us, to reconcile us to you, the God and Father of all."[14] In his full humanity our great high priest has "passed through the heavens" (4:14). On the throne of his exaltation he remains sympathetic to those whose lot he knows so well.

In depictions of the ascension, the feet of Jesus often take a prominent place. As he "takes off," the tops of his feet, flattened out by the artist, are highlighted in the style of Rembrandt. Sometimes the scars of the spikes can be seen, even as there is about these ever-so-human feet a transcendent radiance: "How beautiful upon the mountain are the feet . . . ."

Hebrews 10:16-25/1-25. Gordon Lathrop tells us that we need at the center of our pastoral and liturgical life a "non-anxious presence."[15] This can be symbolized by a chair: the bishop's chair or simply the chair in which the presider sits. The calm demeanor of this person, Lathrop says, embodies the confidence of the congregation in the goodness of God and the presence of Christ with his people. It is this confidence that allows us to come with "boldness," to pray honestly, to be open to God and to one another.

The writer of Hebrews calls us to "approach with a true heart in full assurance of faith . . ." (v. 22). Because of the one who has taken on our flesh and is now ascended, we are able to live together as a community, "provoking" one another to love and good deeds (v. 24). It is Jesus, flesh of our flesh, now ascended and thus available to all, who is at the center, banishing anxiety and creating a community of faith, hope, and love (v. 25).

> Because of the one who has taken on our flesh and is now ascended, we are able to live together as a community, "provoking" one another to love and good deeds.

The collect for Good Friday suggests the nature of this community: "Almighty God, we pray you graciously to behold this your family . . . ."[16] *Family:* here is a picture of confident, purposeful people, gathered around one who knows them and has gone all the way for them.

John 18:1—19:42/(18:1-40) 19:1-37. Today the homiletical rule of thumb applies, perhaps more than on any other day: "The bigger the occasion, the smaller the sermon." The tradition of the "Seven Last Words" suggests that the preacher take small bites of this very large story. Who can preach on "The

Crucifixion"? Who would try on this Friday any kind of definitive sermon on "The Atonement" or "The Meaning of the Cross"? This is a day to add a modest word to the drama.

One possibility is to choose a character. Judas leaves the table and goes out into the night. We next see him in the garden, with a new and hostile group, carrying their flickering lamps as everything grows darker and darker. Peter, outside as Jesus begins his ordeal, trying to warm himself by the fire, fails a comparatively small test. Pilate seems to come close to acknowledging the kingship of Jesus, but gets no farther than temporizing and cowardly indecision. There is Annas, the old priest, who has the chance to question Jesus, to learn about him, who stands by as a policeman slaps Jesus in the face. The preacher could capture something of what this day means by focusing on any one of these players.

There is also Jesus' seamless tunic. The mother of Constantine, the story goes, found it in the Holy Land and brought it back to Trier, one of her son's provincial capitals. The great cathedral was built around the relic, and pilgrims still make the journey to see the holy garment in its splendid chapel just behind the high altar. Why did John include the tunic in his account? What could its meaning be? Raymond Brown provides a good start for the preacher, interpreting the meaning of the tunic in terms of the priesthood of Jesus.[17]

There are John's three words from the cross. Juxtaposing "I thirst" and "It is finished" contrasts the humanity and the majesty of the crucified Jesus, the agony and triumph of the cross. In not more than two gasping breaths, as John tells this story, Jesus is so terribly human in his suffering and so much God's own victorious Son. Also, as Brown has shown, the words to the beloved disciple and to Mary show the rudiments of the church: at the foot of the cross two people are called into a community empowered by the words of Jesus. Here is that "family, for whom our Lord Jesus Christ was willing to . . . suffer death upon the cross . . . ."[18] Legend has it that Mary and John went to live at Ephesus. It was to the church in that city that the most sublime of the epistles was written, calling the Ephesians "to live in love, as Christ loved us and gave himself up for us . . ." (Eph. 5:2).

> In not more than two gasping breaths, Jesus is so terribly human in his suffering and so much God's own victorious Son.

Notes

1. James Muilenburg, "Exegesis of Isaiah 40–66," in *The Interpreter's Bible*, ed. George A. Buttrick (New York: Abingdon, 1956), 4:615.

2. Ibid. 627, 629.

3. Gerhard Von Rad, *Genesis: A Commentary*, trans. John H. Marks (Philadelphia: Westminster, 1961), 233, 239.

4. Samuel Terrien, *The Psalms and Their Meaning for Today* (New York: Bobbs-Merrill, 1952), 273.

5. William Neil, *The Epistle to the Hebrews* (London: SCM, 1955), 53.

6. Ibid., 55.

7. Ibid., 109.

8. Raymond Brown, *The Gospel According to John I–XII*, Anchor Bible 29 (Garden City, N.Y.: Doubleday, 1955), 931.

9. Ibid., 817.

10. Ibid., 926.

11. Ibid., 920.

12. See *The New Interpreter's Study Bible* (Nashville: Abingdon, 2003), 42–43.

13. Ibid., 234.

14. "Holy Eucharist II," in *The Book of Common Prayer* (New York: The Church Hymnal Corp., 1979), 362.

15. Gordon W. Lathrop, *Holy Things: A Liturgical Theology* (Minneapolis: Fortress Press, 1993), 192–93.

16. "Good Friday," in *The Book of Common Prayer*, 276.

17. Brown, *The Gospel According to John I–XII*, 920.

18. "Good Friday," in *The Book of Common Prayer*, 276.

HOLY SATURDAY

APRIL 3, 2010

Revised Common (RCL)
Job 14:1-14 or Lam. 3:1-9, 19-24
Ps. 31:1-4
1 Peter 4:1-8
Matt. 27:57-66 or John 19:38-42

Episcopal (BCP)
Job 14:1-14
Psalm 130 or Ps. 21:1-5
1 Peter 4:1-8
Matt. 27:57-66 or John 19:38-42

FIRST READING

JOB 14:1-14 (RCL, BCP)

Job begins by a frank statement of the human lot: everyone born of woman has a few days that are full of trouble. The comparison to a flower is not to its beauty but its evanescence. So it is with people, who in Sheol—as close as Job and his friends would have come to any notion of afterlife, the realm of the shades—are much more dead than alive.[1] Even a tree has more hope of continuing life. It can put out shoots from a stump, even from old roots. As Job sees it, we are more like a lake that breaks its dam and dries up, or like a river that disappears in the sands of the desert: ". . . so mortals lie down and do not rise again" (v. 12).

From this Job makes an interesting request: Since the dead are unclean—that was the belief among the Jews—and since we are here for such a short time and soon gone, why bother with us so much? "Look away from them," Job asks, "that they may enjoy, like laborers, their days" (v. 6). Or perhaps, Job dares to hope, he might at death be hidden in Sheol, waiting for a better time. If mortals might live again, he says, he would be willing to wait a long time for that (vv. 13, 14).

LAMENTATIONS 3:1-9, 19-24 (RCL alt.)

This man feels targeted, especially in the verses omitted by the lectionary, 10-18: a bear lies in wait and an archer takes careful aim. He is the laughingstock of the people, he is being poisoned, and he is forced to break his teeth eating gravel. But even here, having forgotten what happiness is, he recalls some lines: "The steadfast love of the LORD never ceases" (v. 22). The mercies of God are fresh every morning, even when that is not as apparent as the rising sun.

RESPONSIVE READING

PSALM 130 (BCP)

As from the depths of the sea, the psalmist cries out for deliverance from the burden of guilt and shame. In darkness it is his soul, bruised and alienated by transgression, that looks for some light to break through, like a person alone in pain or fear, longing for the light, companionship, and relief that the morning can bring.

> As from the depths of the sea, the psalmist cries out for deliverance from the burden of guilt and shame.

Samuel Terrien emphasizes the psalmist's personal communion with God: "Hebrew worship was characterized from the earliest times by a naïve, unhampered, direct, and intimate dialogue between God and man. . . . [There is] a long habit of coming to God ashamed and yet unashamed, desperate and yet full of hope . . . ." Even more than God's holiness it is the attribute of mercy that inspires the psalmist's praise.[2]

PSALM 31:1-4 (RCL)

See commentary on the responsive reading for Palm Sunday/Passion Sunday and for Good Friday, above.

PSALM 21:1-5 (BCP ALT.)

This is one of nine royal psalms, and might well have been sung on the occasion of the king's triumphant return from battle, or on the occasion of his birthday. It assumes an intimate relationship between the king and God, a bond that makes his life good and long (v. 4). Whatever glory and majesty the king has comes as God's gift (v. 5), and in trusting God he find strength and serenity (v. 1). Samuel Terrien places this alongside the "supreme psalm of trust," Psalm 23, its "grace of serenity in joyful communion with a personally known God."[3]

SECOND READING
1 PETER 4:1-8 (RCL, BCP)

Since Christ has suffered and died in the flesh and so overcome the power of sin, we, too, are called to be done with the ways of the world. People around us who are still given to careless living will be surprised at us. A more sensible response to thinking about inevitable suffering and death would be to "live it up." But to hear the story of Jesus, and to enter into his suffering and death, is to be changed, to live the rest of one's life "no longer by human desires but by the will of God" (v. 2). This is hard to understand; it is like dying, some would say. Peter would agree, as would Paul (cf. Rom. 6:4), that participating in the death of Jesus leads us to righteous living and, even more importantly, to "constant love . . . [that] covers a multitude of sins" (v. 8).

THE GOSPEL
MATTHEW 27:57-66 (RCL, BCP)
JOHN 19:38-42 (RCL ALT., BCP ALT.)

Only Matthew includes the account of the guards at the tomb. Eduard Schweizer goes so far as to call Matthew's story "wrongheaded" in implying proof that Jesus' body was not stolen as adding evidence for the resurrection. It is true that there was considerable propaganda coming from Jewish missionaries that Jesus' body had been stolen. Matthew's community would have wanted to refute this; Schweizer believes that Matthew's story comes from that endeavor. But Schweizer goes on to say that "this story marks the first step along a road that runs counter to the witness of the Bible." In all the resurrection narratives, Jesus appears only to believers, and there is "a deliberate refusal to prove the resurrection in the face of unbelief."[4] Matthew, like Mark, tells us of the stone closing the door of the tomb: for Matthew it is a "great stone." An angel will roll the stone away, and will terrify the guards.

All of the Synoptics tell us of Joseph of Arimathea, and John's Gospel has Nicodemus coming with Joseph to the tomb. Joseph is rich, and as a well-placed man he has remained a secret disciple of Jesus. But now he is bold enough to approach Pilate to ask for Jesus' body. Nicodemus, who came at night to interview Jesus, now comes bearing a great quantity of burial spices. Here is one of the first examples of what was promised: "And I, when I am lifted up from the earth, will draw all people to myself" (John 12:32). Those words echo that first conversation with Nicodemus (John 3:14).

Raymond Brown suggests that two details of the burial of Jesus have theological significance. The first is a continuation of the theme that once Jesus has been lifted up, he draws all men to himself.[5] Nicodemus and Joseph, who have held back from public discipleship, now appear openly with their offerings. Second, the super-abundance of aloes and myrrh continue the theme prominent in John, and in Holy Week, of Jesus' kingship. Only royalty would have been buried with such extravagance. Burial in a garden also was reserved for kings. Brown writes: ". . . the theme that Jesus was buried as a king would fittingly conclude a Passion Narrative wherein Jesus is crowned and hailed as king during his trial and enthroned and publicly proclaimed as king on the cross."[6] The one who rides into the city on a donkey and is anointed in Bethany is now buried as a king.

> The one who rides into the city on a donkey and is anointed in Bethany is now buried as a king.

HOMILETICAL INTERPRETATION

Job 14:1-14. Job has no doubt that the dead are dead. At the very best they might drift in the realm of shades, Sheol. As Charles Dickens says of Marley in *A Christmas Carol,* he was "dead as a doornail." We have here no suggestion of our more common phrases: "passed away," "fallen asleep," or "departed." It is not as good for the dead even as for a tree: that might possibly bud at the "scent of water" (v. 9). The best that Job can imagine for the dead is that they might be "hidden," and eventually remembered by God (vv. 13-17).[7] But as Job compares the human lot to a dry lake or a disappearing river, he holds on to the possibility of being remembered and the image of the tree sprouting.

One Good Friday we ended the three-hour service with a special liturgy for children. Fishing around for some way to teach children about the day, I decided to give each child a beautiful, freshly cut flower. After leading them to say how beautiful the flowers were and what we might do with them—put them on the dinner table, give them to a friend, and so forth—I asked, "What will happen to these flowers?" We jumped straight to Easter when a child answered: "They will make seeds and that will make new flowers!" In the midst of death, we are in life!

> Reading Job on this Holy Saturday keeps us from forgetting that Jesus *died* on the cross, and that we really die, too.

Reading Job on this Holy Saturday keeps us from forgetting that Jesus *died* on the cross, and that we really die, too. That puts us in the proper place for receiving the good news of the resurrection, God's mighty act in bringing the *dead* to life.

Lamentations 3:1-9, 19-24. Two seemingly irreconcilable ideas converge in this lament. First, the writer thinks of himself as singled out for suffering, targeted:

". . . against me alone he turns his hand, again and again, all day long" (v. 3). "He has made my teeth grind on gravel . . ." (v. 16). Before our eyes is the brutal scene in Khaled Hosseini's *A Thousand Splendid Suns* when the cruel husband fills Mariam's mouth with stone and forces her to break her teeth chewing on them.[8] Job similarly sees himself the victim of deliberately inflicted suffering.

Then comes that amazing word: "*But* this I call to mind, and therefore I have hope: The steadfast love of the LORD never ceases, his mercies never come to an end" (vv. 21-22). This is the same conclusion to which Job will come: "Though he slay me, yet will I trust him" (Job 13:15).

How could those Jews in the midst of the Holocaust—driven from their homes, in hiding from a brutal regime, losing their families—say such a thing, keep on lighting the Sabbath candles and saying the prayers? No one has put this question more clearly than Elie Wiesel.[9]

The hymn "New Every Morning Is the Love" speaks to this point, as do two prayers, The Collect of Holy Saturday and the Collect for Quiet Confidence.[10]

Psalm 130. Anyone who has endured a night of sleepless pain, or who has sat through the darkness with a sufferer, knows the poignancy of these words: ". . . my soul waits for the LORD, more than those who watch for the morning" (v. 6). One of the collects for Evening Prayer includes this petition: "Tend the sick, Lord, Christ: give rest to the weary, bless the dying, soothe the suffering, pity the afflicted, shield the joyous; and all for your love's sake."[11] In the midst of suffering, people pray and hold on to the constancy of love.

> In the midst of suffering, people pray and hold on to the constancy of love.

Two famous sermons speak of the importance, the necessity, of learning to wait. Paul Tillich, in his sermon "Wait," says that waiting is inseparable from hope. We can only wait for that which we already—in some way, to some degree—have.[12] Edmund Steimle's sermon "Address Not Known," on the parable of the ten maidens, tells us that the capacity to wait in hope is the real gift of faith. Steimle says: ". . . God slams the door in the face of those not prepared to wait for him . . . ."[13] Today, of all days, as Jesus lies in the tomb, we are called to wait, however hard that may be.

Psalm 21:1-5. It might serve the preacher today to remember that the coronation ceremony for the British monarchs is a service of Holy Communion. The declining notion—not confined to the throne of England—that it is God who anoints kings, is clear in that liturgy. That God chooses and empowers the monarch is the assumption in Psalm 21. The question raised on Palm Sunday/Passion Sunday—"What kind of king is this?"—is in the air today. He is the one who knows and is known by God, who is his joy and his strength. His head marked with a crown of thorns will receive the diadem of gold (Ps. 21:3).

1 Peter 4:1-8. Oscar Wilde once said that "suffering is the most sensitive of all created things."[14] Going through suffering, and facing death, has a way of focusing the mind. That is the assumption of 1 Peter, an epistle concerned with holy living, that suffering "weans" us from the world and leads us to living and loving seriously. A good example would be the prodigal son—the "profligacy" and "excess of riot" that this text describes has the same root as the runaway boy's prodigality—who, hungry and lost among the pigs, "comes to himself."

The means and goal are the same: the aim is a love of true life and a living out of that. And it is love that "covers a multitude of sins." The suffering one endures can be a quick lesson in the truth of this. A good example out of my own pastoral ministry would be those veterans who have been through war, seen death up close, lost their buddies, and come home not willing to talk much about it but so obviously deepened down. These quiet and gentled men and women are given to serving others, to caring more tenderly for their wives and children, appreciative of being part of a community. We've all seen them.

> The means and goal are the same: the aim is a love of true life and a living out of that.

Matthew 27:57-66/John 19:38-42. Not many of us will preach on Holy Saturday. As close as I have come is morning or noonday prayers with the altar guild and other members of the congregation sprucing up and polishing. We could take a cue from that, and from Emily Dickinson's poem on the "solemnest of industries, putting love away that we shall not need again until eternity,"[15] and give a sermon on what we do on the day after a death. That could lead to reflection on not being clear about the next step, waiting, being content to be quiet and reflective, prepare where we can, and so on. In the Moravian cemetery—they call it "God's Acre"—in Winston-Salem, North Carolina, this Saturday is all scrub brushes and quiet talk as the people spend the day polishing the white marble stones and putting a bouquet of fresh flowers on each grave. When the sun comes up Easter morning everything gleams and the air is fragrant with love.

Nicodemus and Joseph come out on this day, finally ready to offer what they have: a tomb, the spices, and their witness, even on a day when so much remains uncertain and they are carrying the weight of having not been there fully for Jesus. But they are there now, caring for his body and waiting for what will come next. It is to such faith—however tentative and unsettled—that the living Christ will appear.

Notes

1. *The New Interpreter's Study Bible* (Nashville: Abingdon, 2003), 434–45.

2. Samuel Terrien, *The Psalms and Their Meaning for Today* (New York: Bobbs-Merrill, 1952), 31.

3. Ibid., 234.

4. Eduard Schweizer, *The Good News According to Mark* (Atlanta: John Knox, 1970), 52.

5. Raymond Brown, *The Gospel According to John I–XII*, Anchor Bible 29 (Garden City, N.Y.: Doubleday, 1955), 959.

6. Ibid., 960.

7. *The New Interpreter's Study Bible*, 434–35.

8. Khaled Hosseini, *A Thousand Splendid Suns* (New York: Penguin, 2007), 93–94.

9. Elie Wiesel, *Night* (New York: Bantam, 1986).

10. "Holy Saturday," in *The Book of Common Prayer* (New York: The Church Hymnal Corp., 1979), 283; "For Quiet Confidence," idem, 832.

11. Ibid. 124.

12. Paul Tillich, *The Shaking of the Foundations* (New York: Scribners, 1948), 149–52.

13. Edmund Steimle, *From Death to Birth* (Philadelphia: Fortress Press, 1973), 59–68.

14. Oscar Wilde, *De Profundis* (New York: Philosophical Library, 1951), 57.

15. Emily Dickinson, *The Complete Poems*, ed. Thomas H. Johnson (Boston: Little, Brown, 1890), 489.

THE GREAT VIGIL
OF EASTER

Revised Common (RCL)	Episcopal (BCP)	Roman Catholic (LFM)
Gen. 1:1—2:4a	Gen. 1:1—2:2	Gen. 1:1-2:2 or 1:1, 26-31a
Gen. 7:1-5, 11-18, 8:6-18, 9:8-13	Gen. 7:1-5, 11-18; 8:6-18; 9:8-13	
Gen. 22:1-18	Gen. 22:1-18	Gen. 22:1-18 or 22:1-2, 9a, 10-13, 15-18
Exod. 14:10-31; 15:20-21	Exod. 14:10—15:1	Exod. 14:15—15:1
Isa. 55:1-11	Isa. 4:2-6	Isa. 54:5-14
	Isa. 55:1-11	Isa. 55:1-11
Prov. 8:1-8, 19-21; 9:4b-6 or Bar. 3:9-15, 32—4:4		Bar. 3:9-15, 32—4:4
Ezek. 36:24-28	Ezek. 36:24-28	Ezek. 36:16-17a, 18-28
Ezek. 37:1-14	Ezek. 37:1-14	
Zeph. 3:14-20	Zeph. 3:12-20	

ELW adds:
Jonah 1:1—2:1
Isa. 61:1-4, 9-11
Dan. 3:1-29

Rom. 6:3-11	Rom. 6:3-11	Rom. 6:3-11
Psalm 114	Psalm 114	Ps. 118:1-2, 16-17, 22-23
Luke 24:1-12	Matt. 28:1-10	Luke 24:1-12
or John 20:1-18 (ELW)		

RESPONSIVE READING

PSALM 114 (RCL, BCP)

In this artistic little poem that is a model of concise and vivid description, the psalmist recalls Israel's deliverance from Egypt as he dances as lightly as gamboling lambs through God's mighty acts: water in the desert, the parting sea, the river diverted. Nature and history converge to praise the providence of God—in the most wonderful irony as the psalmist asks the river and the sea what is causing them to flee and the mountains what it is that disturbs them. Samuel Terrien writes:

> The divine maker of history is also the ruler of nature, and he summons the elements as witnesses and instruments of the people's destiny. The sea divides itself and transforms imminent death into life. The Jordan turns back and opens the gate to the promised country. The mountains shake and leap like animals of the spring flock, as God seals with his people the covenant which binds them to his design.[1]

It appears that the psalmist anticipates a journey, some transition. Dante used this psalm as a hymn for souls approaching purgatory. We can imagine that the psalmist faces the uncertainty and danger of the exodus, in his personal life or that of his people. In any case, looking back on saving history and turning his poetic eye toward the sea and the mountains, he finds comfort and confidence. What better psalm for this night of nights, when we celebrate the people of God being "brought over"?

> We can imagine that the psalmist faces the uncertainty and danger of the exodus, in his personal life or that of his people.

PSALM 118:1-2 16-17, 22-23 (LFM)

For comments on this text, please see the responsive reading for Palm Sunday/Passion Sunday.

SECOND READING
ROMANS 6:3-11 (RCL, BCP, LFM)

Having spent his first five chapters describing the human plight and making his case for justification by faith, Paul turns here to the implications of that idea for the common life of believers. The first question he addresses is obvious: If our salvation is all by grace, why not just go ahead living easily in sin? Paul's answer to this antinomian taunt is straightforward: "How can we who died to sin go on living in it?" (6:2).

Just as Jesus has settled the matter of our sins once and for all—echoes of Hebrews—we have not just given up our sins; we have *died* to them. What lies before is a new life, life *in Christ*.

Baptism shows this: we are buried with Christ in baptism and raised with him to an altogether different way of being in the world. The eucharistic prayer speaks of the gift through his body and blood of "new and unending life."[2] By participation in the death and resurrection of Jesus the believer is freed fully and ultimately from the power of sin and made a citizen of a new realm, God's reign in the human heart.

Paul would have had in mind baptism by immersion. In some churches that adhere to that practice, the initiate is plunged fully beneath the water to the accompanying words, "Buried with Christ in baptism," and comes up drenching wet—from a kind of drowning—to the announcement, "and raised with him to newness of life." In the early church, the new Christians were stripped naked, wearing not so much as a hairpin from the old life. The anointing, a clean white garment, and the procession to first communion all told of leaving behind what had been and becoming a new person in the body of Christ.

> Baptism shows this: we are buried with Christ in baptism and raised with him to an altogether different way of being in the world.

So, for Paul it is impossible to drag into this new life what has been decisively left behind. It is more than left behind: it is dead. He concludes: "So you must consider yourselves dead to sin and alive to God in Christ Jesus" (v. 11). What better piece of Paul's theology could there be for this night of nights, when we hear the stories of a people brought through the waters to a new and good land?

THE GOSPEL

LUKE 24:1-12 (RCL, LFM)

Like Paul, Luke does not focus his attention on the empty tomb. The women come to the tomb and find the stone rolled away and Jesus' body gone. This discovery leaves them in perplexity, as the two men ask why they would "look for the living among the dead" (v. 5). Even after the messengers rehearse Jesus' prediction of his crucifixion and resurrection, they remain noncommittal, and their report of the empty tomb leaves the Eleven similarly short of Easter faith.

It is only in the narrative that follows immediately upon the story of the empty tomb that Luke brings us to proclamation of the resurrection. "On that very day" the two travelers to Emmaus have heard reports of the empty tomb, "but their eyes were kept from recognizing," even as he opens to them the Scriptures. It is only after he breaks the bread before their eyes that they see, even in the dim light as they share that evening meal. As the light fades, they walk the seven miles back to Jerusalem to tell the others. What they have to say is now unambiguous, our words of greeting for Easter morning: "The Lord has risen indeed" (v. 34). For this night of nights, these two stories of Luke belong together, as Luke takes us from empty tomb to burning hearts.

MATTHEW 28:1-10 (BCP)
JOHN 20:1-18 (ELW)

Matthew and John have some striking similarities: neither tells of the anointing of Jesus' body; both tell of Mary coming to the tomb—Matthew has a second Mary—and both are sent by Jesus to tell "his brothers." But Matthew's account in comparison to John's story can only be called "spectacular." In Matthew there is a great earthquake, a mighty angel descending from heaven to roll away the stone, his garments dazzling like those of Jesus at the transfiguration, and the terrorized guards, trembling like dead men.[3]

By contrast, John tells of Mary Magdalene coming alone to the tomb, "while it was still dark" (v. 1). The stone is rolled away, and she immediately concludes that Jesus' body has been stolen. This is her report to Peter and the "other disciple": the body of Jesus is gone. The two disciples don't get much beyond that. They enter the tomb and see the grave cloths neatly laid aside; the second disciple makes something of this, "saw and believed" (v. 8). But then they simply go back to their homes.

Mary remains outside the tomb, still weeping for the loss of Jesus' body. She looks into the tomb to see two angels in white, sitting on the burial shelf where Jesus' body had lain. "Why are you weeping?" the angels ask. Mary has not budged: "Because they have taken my Lord . . . ." Then someone is behind her, asking the same question: "Woman"—he does not use her name—"why are you weeping?" Still she does not see. Then she hears "Mary," and knows that it is her "Teacher." She begins immediately to learn what it is to be a disciple—not to cling to him, but to be his witness. Now her witness has little to do with the empty tomb. It is unambiguous: "I have seen the Lord" (v. 8). On this night of nights, as we see with the eyes of faith, we raise our Easter acclamation.

> Mary begins immediately to learn what it is to be a disciple—not to cling to him, but to be his witness.

HOMILETICAL INTERPRETATION

Psalm 114. Iona, the small island off the west coast of Scotland where St. Columba landed in 565, is called "a thin place." Nature and grace converge in the varied landscapes—rocky seashore, sand beaches, hills and valleys, rapidly changing weather. Christians have been there for fifteen centuries, suffering bloody invasions and a demanding environment. Despite the isolation and comparative hardship, people through the centuries and today have been drawn to the island. Land and sea, variegated color and invigorating weather coalesce with the life of contemplative prayer and action for the gospel that has been Iona's history.

The poetic psalmist evokes this merging of nature and spiritual awareness as he calls river and sea, mountains and animals to praise God. The one who acts in history—leading, liberating, providing—is the creator of all things, and everything that lives and moves can join in praise to God. The line between cows dancing in springtime, joyous at their release into the open air, and the exultant human spirit—healed, forgiven, delivered—becomes thin.

The poet is friend of the prophet. As Walter Brueggemann has shown, the prophet is at heart a poet.[4] It is the poet's vision that empowers the prophetic voice: the prophet sees the world as it is, and imagines what it could be. The poet/prophet leads the young to see visions and the old to dream of a new and transformed world.

Tonight, as we read the stories of Israel's deliverance, celebrated in Psalm 114, this becomes a thin place too. In such earthy things—fire and water, darkness and light, bread and wine—God comes close. As we enter into the death of Christ and participate in his rising to life, absolutely anything can join into the celebration of that. On the days before Easter in Greece, the people open all the doors and windows of their houses (and of their churches), put the furniture and rugs outside, then sweep and polish and whitewash their houses. It is one more way of saying: Christ is risen indeed! Mountains and hills break forth into singing, the trees of the field clap their hands, and we make our homes and churches shine!

> It is the poet's vision that empowers the prophetic voice: the prophet sees the world as it is, and imagines what it could be.

In some of our churches this evening, people will bring bells from home and at the Easter Acclamation, as an extravagant number of candles are being lit around the altar, all sorts of bells will ring out: Christ is risen! Let everything that breathes praise the Lord! (Ps. 150:6).

Romans 6:3-11. Dying and rising with Christ may not be so obvious to congregations where infants are baptized before they know their names and the amount of water used could hardly effect a drowning, though the noise of a protesting baby could suggest a drowning! For Paul and those acquainted with Jewish baptismal practices, there would have been a more obvious link between immersion and burial.

Stanley Hauerwas and others have called for a more radical understanding of Christian initiation, and there is some movement toward restoring adult baptism by immersion.[5] What could symbolize a clean break with the old and a brand-new life in Christ? If on this night those coming for Holy Baptism were adults, stripped down and questioned by a bishop as to their belief and commitment, then plunged beneath the water, anointed with oil, and at last admitted to the Holy Mysteries, then we would have such a symbol: "Buried with Christ and raised with him to newness of life."

What we do have are Paul's powerful words. The preacher can describe the struggle: attachment to the old ways, the allure of secular values, the myriad means of becoming enthralled by money, drugs, unthinking habits—television, games, gambling, ideology, and the like. All of this can be described without carping: these things do happen to people, to all of us in some degree. There are also various forms of *antinomianism*, a five-dollar word for any number of unthinking attitudes: "Sure, I belong to the church, and I've had my kids done. But what does that have to do with anything?"; "Look, the world has too many do-gooders already"; "Come on, lighten up." And it can get more theological, as Paul knew: "Jesus has taken care of all that, so I can live free and easy." There is, of course, gospel truth in all of these attitudes.

But Paul is not willing to debate the issue. Life in Christ is something new, and what we are about is trying to actualize that in the way we live. For Paul it is not so much a matter of the will. He found himself constantly struggling between what he wanted to do but couldn't manage, and what he wanted to avoid but could not escape. No, Paul is a saint because he received this new life as a *gift*. This made sense for Paul. Despite the "thorn in the flesh," and the conflict between wanting and doing, what is most vivid for him is that one day he was one kind of man and the next he was quite another.

> Life in Christ is something new, and what we are about is trying to actualize that in the way we live.

The preacher could go into the idea of prevenient grace, God's free gift. When a child is presented for baptism and anointed, marked as Christ's own, there is a powerful symbol of something happening *to and for* a person. Also, this is a good time to ask people to "remember" their baptism, to imagine it and to think about its meaning. Having people stand up and repeat the Baptismal Covenant is a strong reminder of what it means to live *in Christ*.[6] Throwing water on the people with the words, "Remember your baptism," is not a bad idea either.

Paul's argument in chapter six for the radically new life in Christ begins with Romans 5:20: ". . . but where sin increased, grace abounded all the more." This could be a description of the central event of Holy Week, where sin does its worst and the outcome is good: sin is there in plenty, but grace overflows. Here the theology of Karl Barth is instructive. If Barth were preaching on this text, he would stand it on its head. Such a text, he once said, is like "a mountain from which we can only climb down."[7] Paul, like Barth, sees the possibility of a new life not in our ability but in God's incredible provision, in the revelation of the mercy of God seen in the passion, death, and resurrection of Jesus Christ. Quoting Paul in Romans 11:32—"For God has made all men prisoners, that he may have mercy upon all"—Barth says: "The apostle Paul . . . could not have started out with the affirmation that 'God has made all men prisoners' had he not first and foremost known and pondered the affirmation 'that he may have mercy upon all.'"[8] We can only understand the deprivation and sadness of sin when we have experienced the grace of God. Here lies the possibility for truly turning away from the old life, entering fully into life in Christ. The preacher will want to make vivid what it means to rise to new life through seeing in the events of this Holy Week the one who is lifted up and so lifts us up. Out of the shadows of this week and from the unfolding story of this ironic King comes the dawn of Easter morning.

> Out of the shadows of this week and from the unfolding story of this ironic King comes the dawn of Easter morning.

Luke 24:1-12. The preacher may want to take the congregation from this evening to the following one. Luke's story of the women and the empty tomb is completed in the story of the three travelers on the road to Emmaus.

The Eucharist combines two suppers: Jesus in the upper room on the night of his betrayal, and the supper at Emmaus at the close of the first Easter Day. At the first supper Jesus stoops to wash their feet; on the way to their house at Emmaus, he "bows and bends" once more, patiently teaching them. At both suppers he feeds them, and in the breaking of the bread they see him for who he is. Putting these two stories together shows Luke's understanding of the resurrection; it is much more than a declaration that the tomb is empty. This is also a good place, especially Emmaus, for speaking of *our* suppers with Jesus, in our homes and around the table of the Lord.

John 20:1-18/Matthew 28:1-10. Matthew, by comparison to the Fourth Gospel, is in the style of Cecil B. DeMille. The earth shakes and divine agents are on the scene to show the woman that his body is not there. On their way to tell his disciples, the women meet Jesus on the road. They take hold of his feet, most likely one more detail—in keeping with the empty-tomb tradition—to resist Gnostics who

> Mary Magdalene goes from weeping over his lost body, to recognizing him as her teacher, then letting him go, as she becomes his witness.

would spiritualize the risen Christ.[9] Jesus adds his own words to their message for the disciples: meet me in Galilee. He calls them back to the place where this story began, where he called them from their nets to follow him. Back there, he will send them out to tell the completed story to the whole world.

John's story also depends upon the women and their encounter with the risen Jesus, and the same word comes to them: "Go tell . . . ." Mary Magdalene goes from weeping over his lost body, to recognizing him as her teacher, then letting him go, as she becomes his witness. The motif of the ascension is here; she will not hold him back from going to the Father. Rather, she will go her own way, a witness of the resurrection and an empowered disciple. This discipleship and witness begins, in John's story, when Mary hears her name called. That is what convinces her and sends her on her way. The truth of the risen Christ—like the candle that each one of us holds on this night, the light of Christ in *my* hand—the Lord is risen indeed. Alleluia.

Notes

1. Samuel Terrien, *The Psalms and Their Meaning for Today* (New York: Bobbs-Merrill, 1952), 70.

2. "Holy Eucharist II," in *The Book of Common Prayer* (New York: The Church Hymnal Corp., 1979), 363.

3. Eduard Schweizer, *The Good News According to Mark* (Atlanta: John Knox, 1970), 523.

4. Walter Brueggemann, *The Prophetic Imagination,* 2nd ed. (Minneapolis: Fortress Press, 2001).

5. Stanley Hauerwas and William H. Willimon, *Resident Aliens: Life in the Christian Colony* (Nashville: Abingdon, 1989).

6. "Holy Baptism," in *The Book of Common Prayer*, 304–05.

7. Karl Barth, *Deliverance to the Captives* (New York: Harper, 1961), 86.

8. Ibid.

9. E. Earle Ellis, *The Gospel of Luke* (Grand Rapids: Eerdmans, 1966), 275–76.

NOVEMBER 2009

Sunday	Monday	Tuesday	Wednesday	Thursday	Friday	Saturday
1	2	3	4	5	6	7
8	9	10	11	12	13	14
15	16	17	18	19	20	21
22	23	24	25	26 Thanksgiving Day (USA)	27	28
29	30					

First Sunday of Advent

DECEMBER 2009

Sunday	Monday	Tuesday	Wednesday	Thursday	Friday	Saturday
		1	2	3	4	5
6 Second Sunday of Advent	7	8	9	10	11	12
13 Third Sunday of Advent	14	15	16	17	18	19
20 Fourth Sunday of Advent	21	22	23	24 Christmas Eve	25 Christmas Day	26
27 First Sunday of Christmas The Holy Family (LFM)	28	29	30	31		

JANUARY 2010

Sunday	Monday	Tuesday	Wednesday	Thursday	Friday	Saturday
					1 Holy Name of Jesus	2
3 Second Sunday of Christmas Epiphany Sunday	4	5	6 Ephiphany of the Lord	7	8	9
10 First Sunday after the Epiphany Baptism of the Lord	11	12	13	14	15	16
17	18	19	20	21	22	23
24 Second Sunday after the Epiphany	25	26	27	28	29	30
31 Third Sunday after the Epiphany Fourth Sunday after the Epiphany						

FEBRUARY 2010

Sunday	Monday	Tuesday	Wednesday	Thursday	Friday	Saturday
	1	2	3	4	5	6
7 Fifth Sunday after the Epiphany	8	9	10	11	12	13
14 Transfiguration of Our Lord Last Sunday after Epiphany	15	16	17	18	19	20
21 First Sunday in Lent	22	23	24 Ash Wednesday	25	26	27
28 Second Sunday in Lent						

MARCH 2010

Sunday	Monday	Tuesday	Wednesday	Thursday	Friday	Saturday
	1	2	3	4	5	6
7 Third Sunday in Lent	8	9	10	11	12	13
14 Fourth Sunday in Lent	15	16	17	18	19	20
21 Fifth Sunday in Lent	22	23	24	25	26	27
28 Sunday of the Passion Palm Sunday	29 Monday in Holy Week	30 Tuesday in Holy Week	31 Wednesday in Holy Week			

APRIL 2010

Sunday	Monday	Tuesday	Wednesday	Thursday	Friday	Saturday
				1 Maundy Thursday	2 Good Friday	3 Easter Vigil Holy Saturday
4 Easter Sunday	5	6	7	8	9	10
11	12	13	14	15	16	17
18	19	20	21	22	23	24
25	26	27	28	29	30	